MMUNITY COLLEGE LIBRARY
SKOCC JV6493
LIEN NATION 1ST ED. NEW YORK

Also by Peter Brimelow

The Wall Street Gurus:
How You Can Profit from Investment Newsletters

The Patriot Game:
Canada and the Canadian Question Revisited

Alien Nation

Alien Nation

Common Sense About America's Immigration Disaster

Peter Brimelow

RANDOM HOUSE
NEW YORK

Published in the United States by Random House, Inc., New York, and simultaneously in Canada by Random House of Canada Limited, Toronto.

Grateful acknowledgment is made to the following for permission to reprint previously published material:

RAOUL LOWERY CONTRERAS: Excerpt from "Racists Wish to Turn America as It Had Evolved in 1965," by Raoul Lowery Contreras, from the August 11, 1993, issue of *El Hispaño.* Copyright © 1993 by Raoul Lowery Contreras. Reprinted by permission.

HENRY HOLT & COMPANY, INC.: Two lines from "Epitaph on An Army of Mercenaries," from *The Collected Poems of A. E. Housman.* Copyright © 1950 by Barclays Bank Ltd. Copyright © 1962, 1965 by Henry Holt & Company, Inc. Reprinted by permission.

MACMILLAN CANADA AND HUGH MACLENNAN ESTATES: Excerpt from *Two Solitudes,* by Hugh MacLennan. Copyright © 1972. Rights throughout the United States are controlled by Hugh MacLennan Estates and administered by McGill–Queen's University Press, Montreal, Canada. Reprinted by permission.

NATIONAL REVIEW: Excerpt from "The Natives Are Restless," by Joseph Sobran, from the February 22, 1985, issue and from a letter from the August 3, 1992, issue. Copyright © 1985, 1992 by National Review, Inc. Reprinted by permission.

THE NEW REPUBLIC: Excerpt from an article by Michael Kinsley, from the December 28, 1992, issue. Copyright © 1992 by The New Republic, Inc. Reprinted by permission of *The New Republic.*

THE NEW YORK TIMES: Excerpt from "A Haitian Father," by A. M. Rosenthal, from the December 3, 1991, issue. Copyright © 1991 by The New York Times Company. Reprinted by permission

LIBRARY OF CONGRESS CATALOGING-IN-PUBLICATION DATA
Brimelow, Peter.
Alien nation: common sense about America's immigration disaster / Peter Brimelow.
p. cm.
Includes bibliographical references and index.
ISBN 0-679-43058-X
1. United States—Emigration and immigration—Government policy.
I. Title.
JV6493.B78 1995
304.8′73—dc20 94-12478

Designed by Beth Tondreau Design / Robin Bentz

Manufactured in the United States of America on acid-free paper

9 8 7 6 5 4 3 2
First Edition

For Alexander James Frank Brimelow
born New York Hospital, August 30, 1991

"This fair child of mine
Shall sum my count . . ."
—Shakespeare, Sonnet II

Contents

PART TWO: CONSEQUENCES

PART THREE: SHIPWRECK AND SALVAGE

Helpful Note from Author

There are lies, damned lies, and statistics. And, in the case of American immigration history, there are also myths. All very confusing. Herewith, a brief blazed trail:

1607 *First permanent English settlement at Jamestown, Virginia.*

1620 *Puritan settlement at Plymouth, Massachusetts.*
(The "Open Door Era"—Immigration actually regulated by colonies, later states, until 1875, with object of keeping out criminals, paupers and occasionally other groups considered undesirable, such as Irish servants.)

1776 *Declaration of Independence.*
(After Revolutionary War, immigration remains low until the late 1830s—the "First Great Lull.")

1790 *First federal naturalization law requires that applicants be "free white persons."*

1808 *Importation of slaves halted.*

1840s *Irish immigration, especially after potato crop fails in late 1840s, begins "Era of Mass Immigration," lasting until 1921 cutoff. Initially from northern and western Europe.*

1868 *Blacks finally guaranteed U.S. citizenship under Fourteenth Amendment.*

1875 *U.S. Supreme Court rules immigration federal, not state, responsibility.*

1882–1917 *Chinese, Japanese and other Asian immigration effectively stopped as it materializes; Asians substantially barred from U.S. citizenship.*

1890–1920 *"New Immigration" from southern, eastern Europe, builds up to "First Great Wave," peaking at 1.3 million in 1907.*

1921–24 *The "Great Restriction"—Quota Act of 1921, Immigration Act of 1924, sharply reduce immigration and, through a system of national-origins quotas, cause it to reflect the ethnic heritage of the existing American community, predominantly northern and western European.*

(The Great Restriction, combined with the Depression and World War II, results in forty years of very low immigration—the "Second Great Lull.")

1940s *Last restrictions on Asians acquiring U.S. citizenship dropped; limited immigration from Asia begins.*

1952 *The Immigration and Nationality Act—previous legislation consolidated, national-origins quota system extended.*

1954 *Rising illegal immigration effectively stopped by "Operation Wetback."*

1965 *The Immigration and Nationality Act Amendments—immigration increased; national-origins principle abolished; "family reunification" emphasized above skills needed by American economy. Not a move back*

toward free immigration—instead a complex, inflexible and perversely discriminatory system.
(1965 legislation inadvertently triggers renewed mass immigration, but heavily skewed toward a few Third World countries, thus shifting U.S. ethnic balance. Not an Open Door—rather, because of this skew, the "Era of Open Scuttles.")

1970s *Illegal immigration rising.*

1980 *Refugee Act. First explicit recognition of refugees as a permanent, distinct immigrant stream.*

1986 *Immigration Reform and Control Act. Amnesty for many illegal immigrants.*

1990 *Immigration Act. Further increases legal immigration, institutes small immigration lottery for countries squeezed out by workings of 1965 system.*

1990s *(Immigration policy brings about "Second Great Wave"—a record 1.8 million admitted in 1991; illegal immigration also running at 300,000 to 500,000 net each year.)*

Preface: Common Sense About Immigration

Sam Donaldson, ABC News: [Native-born Americans] don't have any more right to this country, in my view, than people who came here yesterday.

Cokie Roberts, National Public Radio: That's right.

This Week with David Brinkley, July 25, 1993

There is a sense in which current immigration policy is Adolf Hitler's posthumous revenge on America. The U.S. political elite emerged from the war passionately concerned to cleanse itself from all taints of racism or xenophobia. Eventually, it enacted the epochal Immigration Act (technically, the Immigration and Nationality Act Amendments) of 1965. And this, quite accidentally, triggered a renewed mass immigration, so huge and so systematically different from anything that had gone before as to transform—and ultimately, perhaps, even to destroy—the one unquestioned victor of World War II: the American nation, as it had evolved by the middle of the twentieth century.

Today, U.S. government policy is literally dissolving the people and electing a new one, in the words of the Bertolt Brecht poem that heads Chapter 3, where the process is described in detail.

You can be for this or you can be against it. But the fact is undeniable.

"Still," *Time* magazine wrote in its Fall 1993 "Special Issue on Multiculturalism," "for the first time in its history, the U.S. has an immigration policy that, for better or worse, is truly democratic."[1]

As an immigrant, albeit one who came here rather earlier than yesterday and is now an American citizen, I find myself asking with fascination: what can this possibly mean? American immigration policy has always been democratic, of course, in the sense that it has been made through democratic procedures. Right now, as a matter of fact, it's unusually *undemocratic,* in the sense that Americans have told pollsters long and loudly that they don't want any more immigration; but the politicians ignore them.

I suspect that *Time* magazine, like Sam Donaldson and Cokie Roberts in their conversation on ABC's *This Week with David Brinkley* that heads this chapter, must feel vaguely that "democracy" has something to do with everyone in the world being treated equally. (Which is not how current U.S. immigration policy actually treats them, but that's a detail.) Their notion of democracy, in other words, has degenerated to the point where it is assumed to require invalidating the right to an independent existence of the very *demos,* people, community, that is supposed to be taking decisions on its own behalf. Democracy becomes self-liquidating, like the famous bird allegedly discovered by World War II aviators that flew around in ever-decreasing circles until it finally, remarkably, disappeared.

Personally, I doubt it will prove possible to run the United States, or any other society, on this principle.

"Immigrants built America!" Americans are incessantly told. Again, as an immigrant, I don't agree. In this book, I discuss the surprising evidence that immigration is, and probably always has been, much less important to American economic growth than is conventionally assumed. America took off, economically and indeed morally, in the Colonial Era. That momentum continues, albeit now increasingly obscured.

But note that I am not saying that immigration, particularly selected immigration, is always without value—just that it is at most a luxury, rather than a necessity. For example, I am arguably displacing an American-born worker as a senior editor at *Forbes* magazine. I naturally like to think that my employers would miss my unique contribution. However, I am fairly sure that they would survive.

As a financial journalist, I am professionally inclined to find the economic argument about immigration compelling. But I know from experience that it is not. People habitually justify their immigration preferences in economic terms, but really they are motivated by a wide range of ethnic, moral and even psychological agendas. These agendas are not necessarily illegitimate (although I suspect most Americans would find some of them rather startling if they realized what they were). The point, however, is that they should be discussed.

"Immigrants do the dirty jobs no one else will touch," Americans are told, equally incessantly. I don't agree with this economic analysis either. But in this book, I act as if it were true. In discussing the many aspects of immigration policy, I inevitably touch on some issues of race and ethnicity that in American debate nowadays are usually taboo.

Taboos, however, are not just a matter of cowardice and mendacity. They also reflect a sincere human reluctance to give offense (which is why they tend to become rampant in diverse societies). Although it may sometimes appear otherwise, I am not abnormally anxious to give offense. I'm sorry that some readers may find parts of this book distressing, particularly when they are civilians, guiltless of the practice of journalism or politics.

The job, however, must be done. Race and ethnicity are destiny in American politics. The racial and ethnic balance of America is being radically altered through public policy. This can only have the most profound effects. *Is it what Americans want?*

And the taboo that prevents this simple reality from being debated also prevents discussion of the most obvious irrationalities in current immigration policy—such as its perverse de facto discrimination against skilled immigrants; and against those countries that, by accident, were not first through the door after 1965.

There is a fundamental distinction to be made between immigration in principle and immigration in practice. Obeisance to the former is preventing observation of the latter. Readers may well disagree with much in this book. But I believe that they will also be left disagreeing with at least some of the workings of the post-1965 immigration system. The point is this:

- **America's immigration system is broke and needs fixing. The only issue is: how much?**

And what do Americans want? I don't believe, after long and careful inspection, that they want anything very terrible for their fellow human beings. They seem to me as if they would accept any immigrant, of any complexion including plaid, given minimum goodwill and good intentions. (Which, however, I also suspect are now often lacking.) But there are limits. Enough, as Americans invariably say in private conversation, is enough.

This is not an unreasonable position. Unfortunately, and greatly to the discredit of the American political elite, there is no longer a respectable language in which to express it. I like to think of this book as a sort of toolkit of arguments for ordinary Americans. Some immigration enthusiasts will resent having their tranquillity disturbed. But their choice is to hear arguments for reform now, or for total restriction later.

Some readers of this book when it was still in manuscript have told me that my view of human nature is pessimistic. I am reluctant to accept this. I argue that the force that makes human differences an unavoidable, albeit not unmanageable, social reality is also precisely the force that makes individuals sacrifice their lives for their children. Whether this is nasty or profoundly noble is a matter of taste. Probably it is both. Either way, it exists.

I have also been told that I do not give sufficient credit to the idealistic, radical, even millenarian strain in the American political tradition. And this may well be true. My reading of the Founding Fathers, and their practical political tradition, is that they were in the main conservative realists. American political rhetoric, by contrast, certainly is often millenarian, right back to *Common Sense,* my fellow English immigrant Tom Paine's famous rationalization of the American Revolution. But that's not the same thing. (And it may be a warning against wordsmiths and rhetoricians like Paine misreading the American tradition—although, as we shall see, he was more realistic about immigration than is generally recognized.)

Nevertheless, when you debate immigration with its American enthusiasts, you reach the pained assertion *"But America's different!"* in just two or three exchanges. This is an alarming indication of how influential we wordsmiths and rhetoricians can be, even when wrong—and also of how desperately thin the substantive arguments for this immense historic gamble turn out to be, when given even the most casual prod.

You can hardly argue with this sort of faith. But you can doubt it. A generation ago, anti–Vietnam War demonstrators wittily retorted to the prospect of the military draft: *"Not with my life you don't!"* Now, we might reasonably say to advocates of this new adventure: *"Not with my child's future you don't!"*

I mean this quite literally. There is confusion nowadays about what it means to be a "nation," and a "nation-state." (I attempt to dispel it in Chapters 11 and 12.) But, essentially, a nation is a sort of extended family. It links individual and group, parent and child, past and future, in ways that reach beyond the rational to the most profound and elemental in the human experience.

The mass immigration so thoughtlessly triggered in 1965 risks making America an *alien nation*—not merely in the sense that the numbers of aliens in the nation are rising to levels last seen in the nineteenth century; not merely in the sense that America will become a freak among the world's nations because of the unprecedented demographic mutation it is inflicting on itself; not merely in the sense that Americans themselves will become alien to each other, requiring an increasingly strained government to arbitrate between them; but, ultimately, in the sense that Americans will no longer share in common what Abraham Lincoln called in his First Inaugural Address *"the mystic chords of memory, stretching from every battle field and patriot grave, to every living heart and hearth stone, all over this broad land . . ."*

And that when the time comes to strike those chords, no sweet sound will result.

Alien Nation

I

INTRODUCTION: HOW I CAME TO WRITE THIS BOOK

Essay Question 2

Global interdependence will be the norm by the year 2000. In this country English will be just one of the many languages commonly spoken and more than half the population will be people of color. Comment on the environment in which you grew up; has it prepared you for these changes? What knowledge and skills do you need for the twenty-first century?

Admissions Essay, Tufts University, 1993

From time to time while struggling with this book, and earlier, while writing the humongous "Time to Rethink Immigration?" *National Review* cover story that preceded it,[1] I've broken off to experience once again—it will be for such a short, short time—the inexpressible joy of changing my infant American son's dirty diaper.

Alexander James Frank Brimelow is an American although I was still a British subject, and his mother a Canadian, when he shot into the New York Hospital delivery room, yelling indignantly, one summer dawn in 1991. This is because of the Fourteenth Amendment to the U.S. Constitution. It states in part:

> All persons born or naturalized in the United States, and subject to the jurisdiction thereof, are citizens of the United States and of the State wherein they reside.

The Fourteenth Amendment was passed after the Civil War in an attempt to stop Southern states denying their newly freed slaves the full rights of citizens. But the wording is general. So it has been interpreted to mean that any child born in the United States is automatically a citizen. Even if its mother is a foreigner. Even if she's just passing through.

This "birthright citizenship" is by no means the rule among industrialized countries. Even if you are born in a manger, the Japanese, French and Germans say in effect, that still doesn't make you a bale of hay. The British used to have birthright citizenship, but in 1983 they restricted it—requiring for example that one parent be a legal resident—because of problems caused by immigration.

I am delighted that Alexander is an American. However, I do feel slightly, well, guilty that his fellow Americans had so little choice in the matter.

But at least Maggy and I had applied for and been granted legal permission to live in the United States. There are currently an estimated 3.5 to 4 million foreigners who have just arrived and settled here in defiance of American law.[2] When these illegal immigrants have children in the United States, why, those children are automatically American citizens too.

And right now, *two thirds* of the births in Los Angeles County hospitals are to illegal-immigrant mothers.[3]

In fact, a whole minor industry seems to have been created by those twenty-eight words added to the U.S. Constitution. One survey of new Hispanic mothers in California border hospitals found that 15 percent had crossed the border specifically to give birth, of whom a quarter said that their motive was to ensure U.S. citizenship for their child.[4]

All of which is just another example of one of this book's central themes:

- **The United States has lost control of its borders—in every sense.** A series of institutional accidents, of which birthright citizenship is just one, has essentially robbed Americans of the power to deter-mine who, and how many, can enter their national family, make claims on it . . . and exert power over it.

The heart of the problem: immigration.

THE IMMIGRATION INUNDATION

In 1991, the year of Alexander's birth, the Immigration and Naturalization Service reported a total of over 1.8 million legal immigrants. That was easily a record. It exceeded by almost a third the previous peak of almost 1.3 million, reached eighty-four years earlier at the height of the First Great Wave of Immigration, which peaked just after the turn of the century.

The United States has been engulfed by what seems likely to be the greatest wave of immigration it has ever faced. The INS estimates that 12 to 13 million legal and illegal immigrants will enter the United States during the decade of the 1990s. The Washington, D.C.–based Federation for American Immigration Reform (FAIR), among the most prominent of the groups critical of immigration policy, thinks the total will range between 10 and 15 million. An independent expert, Daniel James, author of *Illegal Immigration—An Unfolding Crisis,* has argued that it could be as high as 18 million.[5]

And the chaotic working of current U.S. immigration law has created a peculiar, but little-understood, reality. *The extraordinary truth is that, in almost all cases, Americans will have little more say over the arrival of these new claimants on their national community—and voters on their national future—than over the arrival of Alexander.*

This is because it's not just illegal immigration that is out of control. So is legal immigration. *U.S. law in effect treats immigration as a sort of imitation civil right, extended to an indefinite group of foreigners who have been selected arbitrarily and with no regard to American interests.*

Whether these foreigners deign to come and make their claim on America—and on the American taxpayer—is pretty much up to them.

AMERICA'S ONE-WAY IMMIGRATION DEBATE

Everyone knows that there are two sides to every question, except the typical American editor ordering up a story about immigration, for whom there is only one side: immigration good, concern about immigration bad.

This results in the anecdotal happy-talk good-news coverage of immigration that we all know and love:

> *XYZ was just Harvard's valedictorian—XYZ arrived in the U.S. speaking no English three months ago—XYZ PROVES THE AMERICAN DREAM IS STILL ALIVE!—despite those nasty nativists who want to keep all the XYZs out.*

Now, the achievement of immigrants to the United States (more accurately, of some immigrants to the United States) is indeed one of the most inspiring, and instructive, tales in human history. Nevertheless, there are still two sides to the question. Thus we might, equally reasonably, expect to see balancing anecdotal coverage like this:

> *In January 1993, a Pakistani applicant for political asylum (and, simultaneously, for amnesty as an illegal immigrant) opens fire on employees entering CIA headquarters, killing two and wounding three! In February 1993, a gang of Middle Easterners (most illegally overstaying after entering on non-immigrant visas—one banned as a terrorist but admitted on a tourist visa in error) blow up New York's World Trade Center, killing six and injuring more than 1,000!! In December 1993, a Jamaican immigrant (admitted as a student but stayed, illegal status automatically regularized after marriage to a U.S. citizen) opens fire on commuters on New York's Long Island Rail Road, killing six and wounding 19!!! WHAT'S GOING ON??!!?*

The case of Colin Ferguson, arrested in the Long Island Rail Road shootings, is particularly instructive. With a little help from President Clinton, talking the very next day at a lunch for journalists, it was rapidly converted into another argument for gun control.

Which missed the point completely. You can be for or against gun control. Arguably, the proposed federal legislation would not have helped here because Ferguson bought his gun legally, in California, which already requires proof of identity and a fifteen-day waiting period.

But Ferguson's own writings showed him to be motivated by hatred of whites. And this racial antagonism is a much deeper problem. In any rational mind, it must raise the question: *Is it really wise to allow the immigration of people who find it so difficult and painful to assimilate into the American majority?*

Because the fact cannot be denied: if Ferguson and the others had not immigrated, those fourteen Americans would not have been killed.

Although we might reasonably expect to see such balancing media coverage of immigration, don't hold your breath. There are powerful taboos preventing it. I discuss them in Chapter 6, on page 115. The result, however, is that the American immigration debate has been a one-way street. Criticism of immigration, and news that might support it, just tends not to get through.

This is no mere journalism-school game of balancing anecdotes. It involves the broadest social trends. For example, the United States is in the midst of a serious crime epidemic. Yet almost no Americans are aware that *aliens make up one quarter of the prisoners in federal penitentiaries*—almost three times their proportion in the population at large.[6]

Indeed, many problems that currently preoccupy Americans have an unspoken *immigration dimension.* Two further instances:

- *The health-care crisis.* Americans have been told repeatedly that some 30 to 40 million people in the country have no health insurance at any one point in time. Typically, nobody seems to know how many are immigrants. But immigrants certainly make up a disproportionate share—particularly of the real problem: the much smaller hard core, perhaps 6 million, that remains uninsured after two years.

We know that about 6 million of the 22 million U.S. Hispanics are uninsured at any one point. Since almost a third of U.S. Hispanics are foreign-born, it's obvious that immigrants and their children must be some and perhaps most of them. The hard core of uninsured, experts confirm, is substantially Hispanic. That probably includes many of the estimated nearly 2 million uninsured illegal immigrants permanently settled here, a heavily Hispanic group.[7]

- *The education crisis.* Americans are used to hearing that their schools don't seem to be providing the quality of education that foreigners get. Fewer of them know that the U.S. education system is also very expensive by international standards.[8] Virtually none of them know anything about the impact of immigration on that education system.

Yet the impact of immigration is clearly serious. For example, in 1990 almost one child in every twenty enrolled in American public schools either could not speak English or spoke it so poorly as to need language-assistance programs. This number is increasing with striking speed: only six years earlier, it had been one child in thirty-one.[9] Current law is generally interpreted as requiring schools to educate such children in their native language. To do so, according to one California estimate, requires spending some 65 percent more per child than on an English-speaking child.[10] And not merely money but, more importantly, teacher time and energy are inevitably being diverted from America's children.

(And it's not working anyway. The Bureau of the Census recently reported for the first time, because the phenomenon was previously unheard of, that 2.3 percent of native-born Americans now do not speak English "very well" and that 1.2 percent are "linguistically isolated"—living in households where no one aged fourteen or over speaks only English or speaks English "very well." Astonishingly, nearly a third of the immigrants who entered the country between 1980 and 1990 *and had become U.S. citizens* were "linguistically isolated"—although until 1990, English proficiency was usually a condition of naturalization.[11])

Immigration enthusiasts—a distinct American subspecies—like to say: *"We need immigrants to do the dirty work that Americans won't do."* I refute this argument in Chapters 7 and 8. But, as I have said, as an immigrant the dirty work I perform in this book is that which too many American pundits and politicians have declined to do. This involves not just forcing facts through against the traffic on that one-way street, but also getting the traffic moving in some spots where it has stopped completely to rubberneck at the wrong thing.

In this book, I show that the immigration resulting from current public policy

1. is dramatically larger, less skilled and more divergent from the American majority than anything that was anticipated or desired
2. is probably not beneficial economically—and is certainly not necessary
3. is attended by a wide and increasing range of negative consequences, from the physical environment to the political
4. is bringing about an ethnic and racial transformation in America without precedent in the history of the world—an astonishing social experiment launched with no particular reason to expect success

Contrary to the menacing assertion of the Tufts University admissions bureaucrats quoted at the head of this chapter, "people of color" will *not* be anything like half the American population in the year 2000. They will most likely be little more than a quarter. But the Tufts bureaucrats will get their wish, within the lifetime of my little son—*if, and only if,* current immigration policy continues.

RACISTS . . .

Some of my American readers will be stirring uneasily at this point. They have been trained to recoil from any explicit discussion of race. *And anyone who says anything critical of immigration is going to be accused of racism.* This is simply a law of modern American political life.

When you write a major article in a national magazine, you in effect enter into a conversation with Americans. And part of the conversation I got into by writing my *National Review* cover story illustrated this law. It was a muttering match with Virginia Postrel, editor of the libertarian *Reason* magazine.

Virginia flipped out at the word *experiment,* as used in point 4 above, and launched into a rendition of the pro-immigration moldy oldie "America Is an Experiment That Works." (This often happens.) I pointed out gently that the experiment in question was *not* America—but instead the 1965 Immigration Act and its imminent, unprecedented, ethnic and racial transformation of America. She replied angrily in print:

> . . . he [*me!*] thus defines authentic Americans not by their values or actions but by their blood. This is nonsense and, though I hate to use the term, profoundly un-American.[12]

Thus Virginia, like many modern American intellectuals, is just unable to handle a plain historical fact: that the American nation has always had a specific ethnic core. And that core has been white.

A nation, of course, is an interlacing of ethnicity and culture. Individuals of any ethnicity or race might be able to acculturate to a national community. And the American national community has certainly been unusually assimilative. But nevertheless, the massive ethnic and racial transformation that public policy is now inflicting on America is totally new—and in terms of how Americans have traditionally viewed themselves, quite revolutionary. Pointing out this reality may be embarrassing to starry-eyed immigration enthusiasts who know no history. But it cannot reasonably be shouted down as "racist." Or "un-American."

(I choose Virginia, of all the people who complained about my article, to show the fratricidal/sororicidal character of the emerging immigration debate. I regard her as a friend, and share her fascination with free markets—a professional hazard for me as a financial journalist, like overdeveloped biceps for an arm wrestler. This puts us together in a small, embattled minority. Another case is Robert L. Bartley, editor of *The Wall Street Journal.* He opened his attack in the *National Review* symposium on my cover story by noting acidly that he had personally helped me immigrate to the United States.[13] Quite right too, Bob—thanks again! But doesn't it show immigration can have unforeseen consequences?)

Because the term "racist" is now so debased, I usually shrug such smears off by pointing to its new definition: *anyone who is winning an argument with a liberal.* Or, too often, a libertarian. And, on the immigration issue, even some confused conservatives.

This may sound facetious. But the double standards are irritating. Anyone who has got into an immigration debate with, for example, Hispanic activists must be instantly aware that some of them really *are* consumed by the most intense racial animosity—directed against whites. How come what's sauce for the goose is not sauce for the *ganso*?

Still, for the record, I will give a more formal answer.

First, it is universally agreed that whatever impact immigration has must fall first on unskilled workers. *And in the United States, that means blacks.* Nor is this the first time that immigration has adversely affected these poorest of Americans. (For more on this, see Chapter 8, pages 173–75.)

"Immigrants are revitalizing American cities," say the immigration enthusiasts—genuinely unaware, it seems, that they are in effect expressing coded horror at the earlier effects of the great black migration from the rural South to the industrial urban North. Perhaps it is immigration enthusiasts, not immigration critics, who should be examining their motives.

Second, I have indeed duly examined my own motives. And I am happy to report that they are pure. I sincerely believe I am not prejudiced—in the sense of committing and stubbornly persisting in error about people, regardless of evidence—which appears to me to be the only rational definition of "racism." I am also, however, not blind.

Race and ethnicity are destiny in American politics. And, because of the rise of affirmative-action quotas, for American individuals too.

My son, Alexander, is a white male with blue eyes and blond hair. He has never discriminated against anyone in his little life (except possibly young women visitors whom he suspects of being babysitters). But public policy now discriminates against him. The sheer size of the so-called "protected classes" that are now politically favored, such as Hispanics, will be a matter of vital importance as long as he lives. And their size is basically determined by immigration.

. . . NATIVISTS . . .

"Nativist!" This magic word is another exorcist's spell always cast against anyone who dares question current immigration policy. Clearly, in the minds of many immigration enthusiasts, nativists are no different than the Black Hundreds—the anti-Semitic gangs implicated in the pogroms that accelerated immigration from Czarist Russia at the turn of the century.

Well, to adapt the song "The Farmer and the Cowman" from the musical *Oklahoma!:*

I'd like to say a word for the nativists.

In very significant ways, this common view of them is a myth.

The nativists were genuine American originals: members of the Order of the Star-Spangled Banner, a secret patriotic society about which its members were instructed to deny knowledge—supposedly the origin of their famous nickname, the Know Nothings. Organizing themselves as the American party in the mid-1850s, they scored stunning but short-lived successes on the eve of the Civil War.

But the Know Nothings were far from an ignorant mob, as immigration enthusiasts, probably misunderstanding that nickname, tend to assume. Recent research has shown that they were a cross section of solid middle- and upper-middle-class citizens. And the Know Nothings *never actually proposed restricting immigration*—just that, in the words of the Know Nothing governor of Massachusetts, Henry J. Gardner, Americans should take care to "nationalize before we naturalize" any new immigrants. Nor were the Know Nothings anti-Semitic.

The Know Nothings were, however, deeply suspicious of Roman Catholicism—at a time when enormous Irish Catholic immigration had begun, after the potato famine of 1845.

Anti-Catholicism is not a sentiment you often find in America today (although you can get a whiff of it talking to abortion-rights and gay-rights activists). And it needs to be set in the context of the time. No doubt bigotry played a part. But so did a quite rational concern that Roman Catholicism with its hierarchical structure, unlike Judaism with its self-governing congregations, was not a "republican" religion—one that would be compatible with democracy, free institutions, law, liberty.

After all, Pope Pius IX was now fervently denouncing "liberalism," by which he meant all free thought and free institutions, and supporting the despotisms that had crushed liberal revolutions all across Europe in 1848. Indeed, in 1853, enraged native-born Americans and immigrant "Exiles of '48" united to riot against the visit of papal nuncio Gaetano Bedini, called "the Butcher of Bologna" because of his role in suppressing the revolt against papal rule there.

Above all, *the Know Nothings were against slavery.* This stance was critical to their party's rise, when it provided a home for abolitionists disgusted with professional politicians' attempts to fudge the issue. And to its fall—forced to choose between abolition and nativism, the Know Nothings chose abolition. Most became Republicans. Several became famous in the Union army . . . notably its victorious general in chief, Ulysses S. Grant.[14]

The nativists were not Nazis: they were nationalists—culturally and politically. They saw their American national identity as inextricably involved with what President John F. Kennedy, assimilated descendant of that Irish influx, would later call "the survival and success of liberty." Their concerns about immigration and slavery were different sides of the same coin. They may well have been overzealous. But their descendants need not feel ashamed of them.

And, incidentally, the Know Nothings left one enduring legacy: America's system of secular public schools. It was created largely in response to their concern about "nationalizing" immigrants.

. . . AND IMMIGRATION ENTHUSIASTS

In some ways, the immigration debate reminds me of the debate about investing in gold, which was raging when I first entered financial journalism some twenty years ago. Everyone knew the pro-gold "gold bugs" were crazy. And they *were* crazy, some of them, or at least extremely odd. They wore funny suits and gave you business cards printed on gold stock. By contrast, the anti-gold people, who were respectfully unnicknamed, were the financial and academic elite. It was only after a while that you realized they were, however, just as fanatical.

I've said that anyone saying anything critical of immigration is going to be accused of sin. And perhaps rightly, in some cases. But I also think that Americans favoring immigration have their own moral problem. They are too frequently guilty of what theologians call "enthusiasm"—the tendency to stress the emotional experience of an issue over its rational aspect.

Immigration is indeed a very emotional issue for many Americans. Ellis Island is on the point of replacing the Winning of the West as the defining American experience. (Question: Why are there so many big-city cop shows and so few Westerns on television nowadays?)

But immigration enthusiasts should remember: the gold bugs were right. The price of an ounce of gold went from $42 to over $800, one of the most remarkable market moves in history.

MYTHS ABOUT IMMIGRATION

With the opposition intimidated, immigration enthusiasts have been able to get away with treating American immigration history as a sort of Rorschach blot, into which they can read their personal preoccupations.

My current favorite is a recent cover story in *American Heritage* magazine (published by my own employer, *Forbes.* Harrumph!). After subtly linking me and my *National Review* article with French crypto-fascists and German neo-Nazis, the writer went on to proclaim:

> what is at stake here is nothing less than the essential nature of the United States of America . . . only the United States takes special pride in describing American nationality as, by definition, independent of race and blood—as something that is acquired by residence and allegiance regardless of birthplace or ancestry.[15]

Of course this is absurd on its face: what about Australia and Canada today? But, as we shall see (see Chapters 3 and 11), it is also ludicrously false as a description of America's historic "essential nature." This was highly specific—racially, religiously, culturally—right up until modern times, reinforced when necessary by legislation. For example, the first naturalization law, in 1790, stipulated that an applicant must be a "free white person." Blacks became full citizens only after the Civil War. Restrictions on Asians becoming citizens were finally dropped only after World War II. How much more specific can you get?

Maybe America should not have been like this. *But it was.*

Myth-manufacturing of this type amounts to an intellectual shell game—Americans (including, no doubt, many immigration enthusiasts themselves) are being tricked out of their own identity.

And it infests U.S. immigration history. Thus the lines now commemorated on a (surprisingly inconspicuous) plaque beneath the base of the Statue of Liberty

> . . . Give me your tired, your poor,
> your huddled masses yearning to breathe free,
> The wretched refuse of your teeming shore . . .

are not part of the Declaration of Independence or some other pronouncement of the Founding Fathers. Instead, they are the reaction of a young Zionist, Emma Lazarus, to the Russian pogroms following the assassination of Czar Alexander II in 1881. They were added years after the dedication of the statue, which was a gift from France to commemorate the U.S. centennial, predated the Ellis Island era of mass immigration, and was originally supposed to symbolize not "the Mother of Immigrants," in Lazarus's phrase, but *Liberty Enlightening the World*—"liberty *under law,*" adds Federation for American Immigration Reform executive director Dan Stein, thinking grimly of recent amnesties for illegals.

And they aren't even true. American immigration has typically been quite selective, if only because the cost of passage was (until recently) an effective filter.[16] Early English settlers included Royalist gentry who went to Virginia, like George Washington's ancestors, and Puritan gentry who went to New England, as Oliver Cromwell and his family once planned to do.

And, whatever the Know Nothings may have thought, the Irish

immigrants swarming in after the 1845 potato famine were not the bottom of the barrel. Three quarters of them were literate; their fares were commonly paid by established extended families.[17]

There are many other immigration myths. For example, immigration into the United States was never really completely free. There were always some restrictions. Immigration from Asia was cut off in the nineteenth century almost as soon as it began. And even European immigration was carefully monitored, for example to screen out potential paupers and threats to public health. Arguably, this scrutiny was actually stricter when immigration policy was the responsibility of the individual states, as it was until 1875.[18]

And—this myth is really unkillable, no doubt because it so usefully frightens people from thinking about immigration policy—*the use of intelligence testing played no real role in the restrictive legislation passed in the 1920s.* Nor did intelligence testers ever allege that Jews and other immigrants of that period were disproportionately "feeble-minded." The claim that they did so is mainly based on what appears to be almost a wilful misreading of the work of the psychometric pioneer H. H. Goddard, which persists although it was exposed well over a decade ago.[19]

COMMON SENSE ABOUT IMMIGRATION

The antidote to myth is common sense. This book takes its subtitle from Thomas Paine's famous pamphlet *Common Sense,* the passionate argument for American independence from Britain that caused a sensation when it was published in early 1776.

There are some pleasing parallels here. Like me, Paine was an English immigrant—indeed, he had arrived in Philadelphia from England only just over a year before. But he still put on the American cause like a glove.

This is what it means to have a common political culture. In a real sense, the American Revolution was a civil war that split both peoples. Whole regiments of American Loyalists fought for the Crown; eight of the fifty-six signers of the Declaration of Independence were British-born. For Paine, the American Revolution was simply a transatlantic version of the radical cause in British politics.

Ironically in the context of my book, Paine himself is regularly cited by immigration enthusiasts because of his rhetorical conclusion that America should become "an asylum for mankind." Which just shows what happens when people don't read original sources. Earlier in *Common Sense,* Paine had made it clear that he was talking about asylum for *Europeans* ("we claim brotherhood with every European Christian"). And he explicitly grounded this claim on a common European culture distinct from that of the rest of the world. ("All Europeans meeting in America, or any other quarter of the globe, are *countrymen* . . ." [Paine's emphasis]).

Of course, I must modestly decline to make too much of the parallels between Paine and myself. Apart from anything else, he died a rather sad death, although not in poverty as is sometimes alleged, thanks to the generosity of the New York State government. (Another parallel I'm not holding my breath about.) And he was unmistakably a man of the Left, something I would hardly presume to claim.

As a radical, Paine had a political agenda—the break with Britain. And he read it into his account of the contemporary reality as gaily as any Tufts University Admissions bureaucrat. To minimize the link with Britain, he asserted that "Europe, and not England, is the parent country of America" and that "not one third of the inhabitants, even of this province, are of English descent."[20]

In fact, although Pennsylvania was perhaps the least English of the Thirteen Colonies, in 1790 white Americans as a whole were 60 percent English, almost 80 percent British, 98 percent Protestant. (And, of course, some 20 percent of the population were voiceless black slaves.[21])

Paine's move is a common one in the immigration shell game. Thus an exhibit at the Ellis Island Museum of Immigration has a notice reading: "BY 1789, WHEN GEORGE WASHINGTON WAS INAUGURATED PRESIDENT, WE WERE ALREADY A MULTI-ETHNIC AND MULTI-RACIAL SOCIETY."

This assertion is a lie. It may be a "Noble Lie," the kind that the classical Greek philosopher Plato thought rulers should tell in order to keep their subjects happy. But it is still flagrantly false.

America at the time of the Revolution was biracial, not multiracial, containing both whites and blacks. But the political nation—

the collectivity that took political decisions—was wholly white. And that white nation was multiethnic only in the sense that a stew can be described as half-rabbit, half-horse if it contains one rabbit and one horse. There were a few unusual fragments in the American stew of 1790. But, for better or worse, it tasted distinctly British.

WHAT ABOUT MY GRANDFATHER?

Many Americans have difficulty thinking about immigration restriction because of a lurking fear: *This would have kept my grandfather out.* In this book, I explore a rich variety of answers to this problem.

But it must also be stressed: *that was then; this is now.* There are important differences between the last Great Wave of Immigration and today's.

1. Then, there was an "Open Door" (essentially—and with the major exception of the restriction on Asians). Now, the 1965 reform has reopened the border in a perversely unequal way. Essentially, it has allowed immigrants from some countries to crowd out immigrants from others.

The 1965 Immigration Act did not open the immigration floodgates: it opened the immigration scuttles—the influx is very substantial, but it spurts lopsidedly from a remarkably small number of countries, just as when some of the scuttles are opened in one side of a ship. Which is why the United States is now developing an ethnic list—and may eventually capsize. *Your grandfather probably couldn't get in now anyway.*

And this brings us to another of this book's central themes:

- **The problem is not necessarily immigration in principle—it's immigration in practice. Specifically, it's the workings of the 1965 Immigration Act and its subsequent amendments.**

This cannot be stressed too much.

It's significant of the one-way American immigration debate that I have never met an immigration enthusiast who will defend the actual workings of the 1965 Act. When cornered. But they are not cornered very often.

And there are other differences between the First Great Wave ending in the 1920s and the Second Great Wave of the 1990s.

2. Then, immigrants came overwhelmingly from Europe, no matter how different they seemed at the time; now, immigrants are overwhelmingly visible minorities from the Third World. Not withstanding which—
3. Then, there was an aggressive public and private "Americanization" campaign (celebrated in Leo Rosten's 1937 comic classic *The Education of H*Y*M*A*N K*A*P*L*A*N*); now, there's "multiculturalism"—i.e., immigrants are officially not expected to assimilate.
4. Then, there was no welfare state and immigrants who failed often went home; now, there is a welfare state—and fewer immigrants leave.
5. Then, *immigration was stopped.* There was a pause for digestion—the Second Great Lull—that lasted some forty years. Now, there's no end in sight.

A LIBRA LAMENT

"What's your astrological sign?" the famous gold bug and investment-letter publisher Harry Schultz asked me in my early days as a financial journalist. (There's more interest in astrology on Wall Street than you might think—or fear.)

Libra, I told him.

"That's a problem for you," he said. "It means you see the other side too much—you have trouble making up your mind."

Maybe it's true. At least, I've never been tempted to offer investment advice. But the immigration debate is peculiarly Libra territory.

Immigration is not a subject like abortion, where both sides have been deeply entrenched for years. Instead, it cuts right across normal ideological lines, creating totally unexpected antagonisms and alliances. For example, I have found myself discussing my *National Review* cover story with a group of environmentalists . . . who voted for Patrick J. Buchanan in the 1992 presidential primaries because of their fear that immigration-driven population growth is ecologically insupportable. Probably both Buchanan and the professional environmentalist lobby in Washington would be equally astounded by news of this emerging electoral bloc.

At present, concern about immigration is regularly dismissed as racism. But historically, it has quite often been a progressive issue in America. Labor unions, fearing cheap labor, have been active restrictionists. The American Federation of Labor's Samuel Gompers, himself an immigrant from England, was particularly critical of the 1890–1920 Great Wave. In a powerful 1992 article from the liberal perspective in *Atlantic Monthly* magazine, arguing that immigration hurts blacks, the *Los Angeles Times*'s Jack Miles wrote, "My strong suspicion is that if FAIR succeeds in launching this debate, it will begin on the right [here he cited my *National Review* story] but quickly be seized by the left . . ."[22]

Chaos forces people to think anew. Writing about immigration forced me to rethink my own attitude toward environmentalism, which like other financial journalists I had tended to view as just another excuse for government regulation.

And, at least from the evidence of my conversation with Americans after my *National Review* article, immigration is one of those rare issues about which people are willing to change their minds. "I began thinking, as opposed to emoting, on this highly emotional subject when I read [my *National Review* piece]," syndicated columnist Don Feder, author of *A Jewish Conservative Looks at Pagan America,* was kind enough to write.[23]

In a debate as important as any that has ever taken place in America, that's one hopeful sign.

AMERICANS OUGHT TO BE ASKED

And why do I, an immigrant, care? For one reason, there is my American toddler, Alexander. He seems to like it here. A second reason: just as Thomas Jefferson said in the eighteenth century that every man has two countries, his own and France, so in this century no civilized person can be indifferent to the fate of America.

Anyway, for better or worse, immigrants have always worried

about immigration. At the 1787 Constitutional Convention, a former regular British army officer, Pierce Butler, was prominent among those delegates wanting a fourteen-year residency requirement for U.S. senators, although he himself had only arrived in 1773. A century later, an Irish immigrant, Dennis Kearney, was a leader of the agitation that halted Chinese immigration into California. (His—probably mythical—slogan: *"Americay for Americans, Begorrah!"*) The very term "melting pot" comes from a 1908 play about Great Wave immigration by an English-born Zionist, Israel Zangwill.

Beyond this—I have an infant memory of a time when I am not much older than Alexander. I am playing with my twin brother in the backyard of my aunt's home in a Lancashire cotton town. Suddenly, great whooping giants in U.S. Air Force uniforms (although with the crystal-clear recollection of childhood, I now realize that they had the lithe figures of very young men) leap out and grab us. We are terrified and struggle free.

Which always made me feel bad in subsequent years. They were far from home, lodging with my aunt. And they just wanted a souvenir photograph.

They were the Cold War tail of that vast host that had come to Britain during World War II, when the whole town had resounded night and day to the roar of B-17 engines on the test beds at the great Burtonwood air base, and everyone had been glad to hear them. They were, as Robert E. Lee once described his troops at a critical point in the Wilderness campaign, not professional soldiers but citizens who had taken up arms for their country. Nevertheless, Housman's "Epitaph on an Army of Mercenaries" applies to them:

> Their shoulders held the sky suspended;
> They stood, and earth's foundations stay.

I don't know what happened to them, although I remember one young wife showing us the first color slides we had ever seen, of Southern California, and explaining that they hoped to move to this breathtaking paradise—it was, remember, the early 1950s—when they got out of the service.

They will be old now, if they are still alive. I don't know what they or their children think of the unprecedented experiment being performed—apparently by accident and certainly with no apprehension of the possible consequences—upon the nation they so bravely represented.

I do know, however, that they ought to be asked.

PART ONE

Truth

2

THE VIEW FROM THE TENTH CIRCLE

These population dynamics will result in the "browning" of America, the Hispanization of America. It is already happening and it is inescapable.

—**HENRY CISNEROS,**
former mayor of San Antonio, Texas; Secretary of Housing and Urban Development in the Clinton administration

My grandparents came from Lebanon. I don't identify with the Pilgrims on a personal level.

—**DONNA SHALALA,**
Secretary of Health and Human Services in the Clinton administration

We are transforming ourselves . . .

—**DORIS MEISSNER,**
Commissioner, U.S. Immigration and Naturalization Service in the Clinton administration (who approves)

Dante, the great poet of medieval Italy, would have been delighted by the Immigration and Naturalization Service's waiting rooms. They would have provided him with a tenth Circle of Hell to add to the nine degrees of damnation he described in his most famous work, the *Inferno.*

There is something distinctly infernal about the INS spectacle. So many lost souls wait around so hopelessly, mutually incomprehensible in virtually every language under the sun, each clutching a number from one of those ticket-vending machines which may or may not be honored by the harassed INS clerks before the end of the civil service working day.

The danger of damnation is low—sort of. A Scottish friend

of mine did once find himself flung into the deportation holding tank because the INS misunderstood its own rules. And toward the end of my own ten-year trek through the system, I whiled away a lot of time watching confrontations between suspicious INSers and agitated Iranians, apparently hauled in because the Iran hostage crisis had inspired the Carter administration to ask just exactly how many of them there were enrolled as students in U.S. universities anyway.

(The INS was unable to provide an answer during the hostage crisis's 444 days. Or, as it turned out, at all.[1])

You can still get a pretty good blast of brimstone, however. Try suggesting that it might be another of those misunderstandings when, having finally reached the head of the line, you are ordered by the clerk to go away and come back another day with a previously unmentioned Form XYZ.

Your fellow huddled masses accept this treatment with a horrible passivity. Perhaps it is imbued in them by aeons of arbitrary government in their native lands. Only rarely is there a flurry of protest. At its center, almost invariably, is an indignant American spouse.

THE GREAT AMERICAN IMMIGRATION PARADOX

We are looking here at something crucially significant: *the Great American Immigration Paradox.* Just as New York City's government can't stop muggers but does a great job ticketing young women on Park Avenue for failing to scoop up after their lapdogs, U.S. immigration policy in effect enforces the law only against those who obey it.

Annual legal immigration of about 1 million—counting the 100,000 refugees and the 100,000 applying for political asylum—is overwhelmed by an estimated 2 to 3 million illegal entries into the country in every recent year.

Many of these illegal entrants go back home, of course. In fact, some commute across the border every day. But, year by year, the number of illegal immigrants who settle permanently in the United States grows. Here's how to think about it: if you balance the *gross illegal immigration* against *gross departures of illegals,* you find the *net increase in the illegal immigrant population.* A cautious INS estimate: this net illegal immigration has been running at about 300,000 to 500,000 annually.[2] No one, however, really knows.

The INS bureaucracy still grinds through its rituals. But the reality remains as President Ronald Reagan described it in 1983: *"This country has lost control of its borders."*

"And," Reagan added, *"no country can sustain that kind of position."*[3]

Indeed, the loss of control is even more complete than Reagan suggested. Much of the current legal immigration can't be kept out either. The majority of those lost souls in the INS waiting room will find salvation, in the form of U.S. residence, in the end.

This is because most legal immigrants—usually between a half and two thirds—are accepted more or less automatically under the various family-reunification provisions of current U.S. law.

Then there are *refugees,* who apply for admission while they are still abroad, and *political asylum seekers,* who apply once in the United States. And, similarly, the weird workings of the American legal system have made it virtually impossible to expel asylum seekers once they land on U.S. soil.

In fact in early 1993 another immigration scandal erupted: it emerged that foreigners were getting off planes at New York's John F. Kennedy Airport at an annualized rate rising rapidly through 15,000, applying for asylum and, because of lack of detention space, *being released into the United States on a promise to present themselves at a future hearing,* which not more than 5 percent ever did.[4] (Not that it matters if they do. An unofficial INS estimate is that eight out of every ten asylum applicants end up staying in the United States quite regardless of whether or not their applications are approved.[5])

This inability to expel asylum seekers once they set foot in the United States is why both the Bush and Clinton administrations were forced to order the interception of boats carrying would-be illegal immigrants from Haiti on the high seas. And it's why the Clinton administration had to beg humbly that the Mexican government halt and return home shiploads of smuggled Chinese.

As invariably happens with immigration policy, what was intended (or at least alleged) to be kind turns out to be cruel. We will be returning to this theme later.

Naturally, I take a deep personal interest in these immigration idiosyncrasies. After all, as it turned out I could have avoided my INS decade simply by ignoring the law and staying here after I graduated from Stanford University Graduate School of Business in 1972. That way, I would have been amnestied, along with what seems likely to be about 3 million other illegal immigrants, by the 1986 Immigration Reform and Control Act—known in the trade as "IRCA."

Hmmm.

Current immigration policy offers another parallel with New York. Just as when you leave Park Avenue and descend into the subway, when you enter the INS waiting rooms you find yourself in an underworld that is not just teeming but is also almost entirely colored.

In 1990, for example, only 8 percent of the 1.5 million legal immigrants, including amnestied illegals, came from Europe. (And a good few of those were individuals who were re-emigrating, having originally come from Asia or the Caribbean.)

You have to be totally incurious not to wonder: where do all these people get off and come to the surface?

That is: what impact will they all have on America?

It is a characteristic of the American immigration debate that even the simplest statement of fact meets with deep and persistent denial from immigration enthusiasts. Thus Professor Julian L. Simon of the University of Maryland is perhaps the most celebrated advocate of the economic advantages of immigration. In his famous 1989 pro-immigration polemic *The Economic Consequences of Immigration,* he states flatly: *"Contemporary immigration is not high by U.S. historical standards."*[6]

I saw this claim repeated by a Simon disciple, Steven Moore of the Cato Institute in Washington, D.C., in mid-1994. Quite obviously, a lot of people are deeply and emotionally attached to the comforting thought that this has all (yawn) happened before (ho-hum . . .).

Sometimes, but not always, the immigration enthusiasts attempt to defend the case for complacency by adding new statistical wrinkles. Occasionally, these are ingenious, and even relevant.

Well, in this section, we will iron out these wrinkles once and for all. We will pursue the issue of how immigration stands by comparison with U.S. historical standards to the bitter end.

But first, a caution:

- **How today's immigration compares with U.S. historical standards is ultimately irrelevant. The real question is: can today's immigration be absorbed?**

It hardly matters whether the floodwaters have reached the record level set in 1900—if, in the interim, a city has been built on the floodplain. In 1995, that city is arguably America's affirmative-action welfare state.

With that in mind, let's look at the facts about immigration (see Chart 1, pages 30–31).

Chart 1 does put the immigration enthusiasts' claim into something like perspective. Its message is simple and stark:

- **Immigration to the United States is indeed at historic highs. In the language of jet-plane test pilots, the United States now is pushing right to the outside edge of its performance "envelope."**

You can see at a glance that the recent immigration peak of 1990–91 towers far above the previous record set in 1907, during the First Great Wave at the turn of the century.

During the whole Great Wave decade, from 1901 to 1910, about 8.7 million immigrants arrived in the United States. In the decade of 1981 to 1990 just passed, legal immigration into the United States amounted to some 7.3 million. Which means that, counting illegal immigrants—who were not a factor in the earlier period, when the borders were more or less open—the 1981–90 numbers probably matched, and may well have exceeded, the earlier record.

Another glance reveals a further interesting phenomenon: the 1900–1914 Great Wave, which is the period that immigration enthusiasts always like to cite, was in itself quite exceptional. In fact, today's immigration is not just at record levels compared with

Chart 1

THE AMERICAN TRADITION: NOT IMMIGRATION—INTERMITTENT IMMIGRATION

Legal immigration to the United States 1820–2040

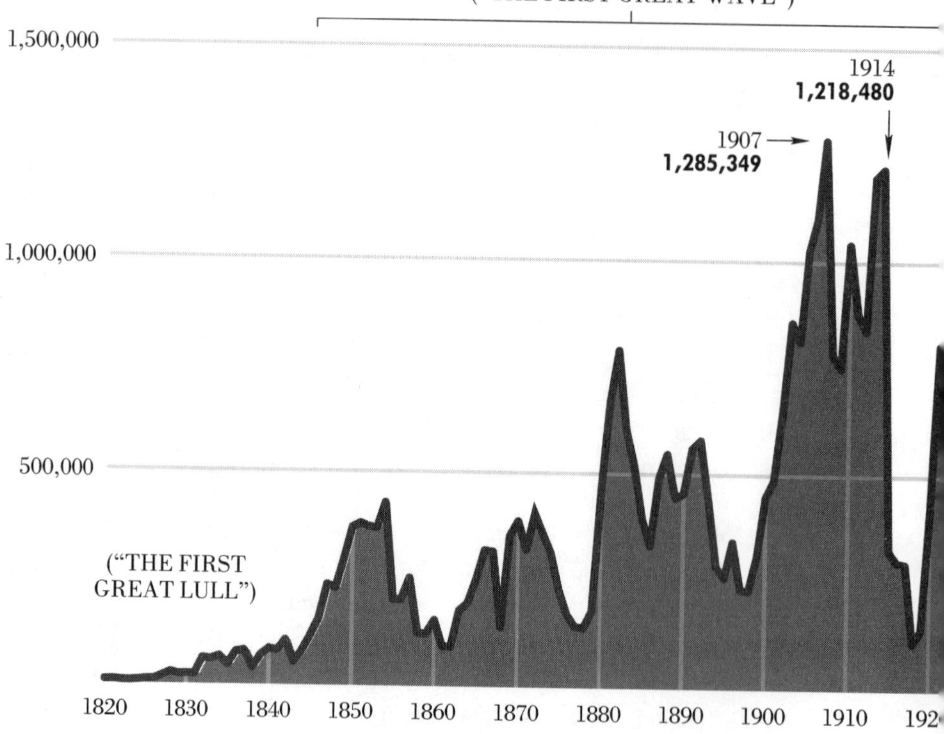

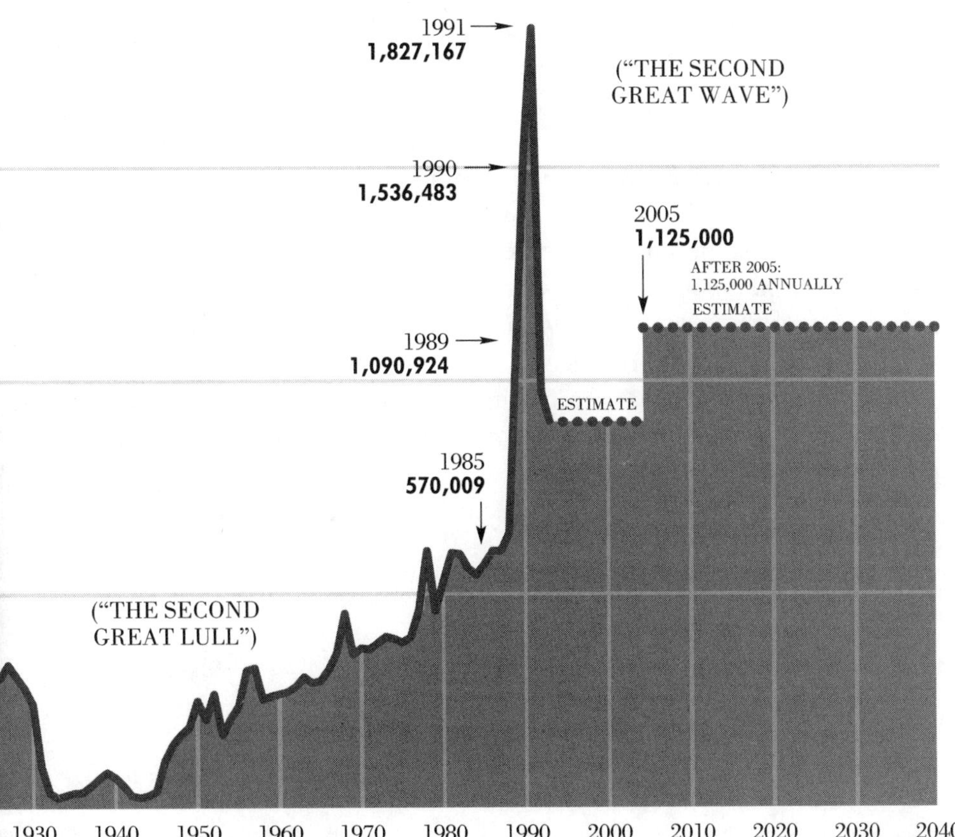
1991
1,827,167
("THE SECOND
GREAT WAVE")
1990
1,536,483
2005
1,125,000
AFTER 2005:
1,125,000 ANNUALLY
ESTIMATE
1989
1,090,924
ESTIMATE
1985
570,009
("THE SECOND
GREAT LULL")
1930
1940
1950
1960
1970
1980
1990
2000
2010
2020
2030
2040

1901–14: by comparison with overall U.S. historical standards, it is *extraordinarily* high.

Note also the rapid pickup after the 1965 reform. Immigration spiked up by 1968, as the legislation became fully effective. And it has never looked back.

A WRINKLE: ILLEGAL IMMIGRATION

But, but, BUT! some immigration enthusiasts protest. *It's unfair to include in recent annual figures the very large numbers of illegal immigrants amnestied each year by the 1986 IRCA legislation. That was an exceptional situation,* they say.

My attitude: the illegal immigrants came here, didn't they? After all, by including them in recent years, we are only compensating for not counting them in earlier years.

But I want to be fair (naturally). So let's adjust for IRCA. (See Chart 2, below.)

Chart 2

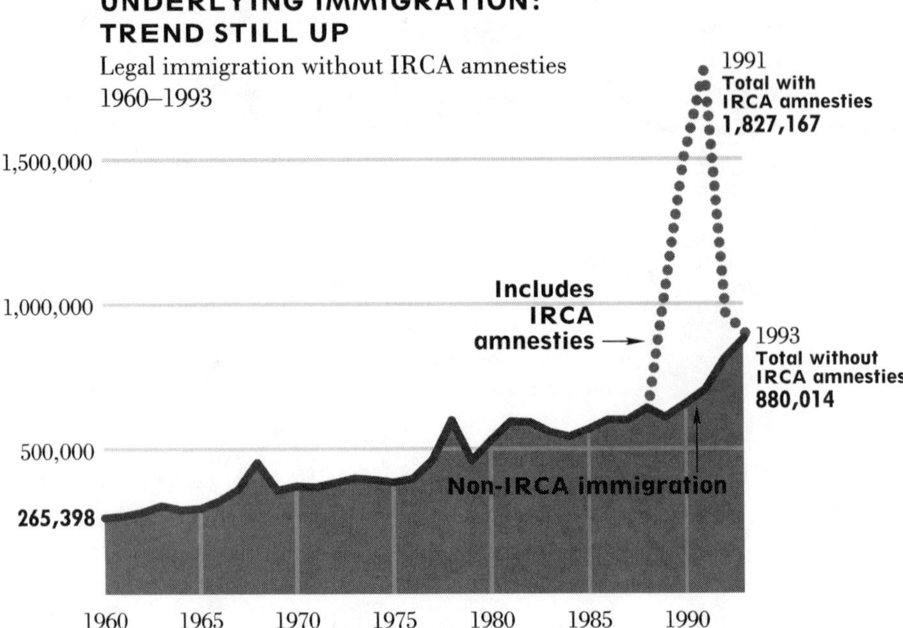

As it turns out, adjusting for IRCA reveals yet another interesting phenomenon. For most of American history, immigration has risen and fallen very sharply. On a chart, it looks like a saw-tooth mountain range. But after 1965, immigration has been building in a strikingly consistent way. It looks like a ramp . . . or a springboard.

Unlike previous waves, the post-1965 immigration does not seem to be affected very much by economic conditions in the United States—such as the 1990–91 recession that helped to turn President George Bush out of his job. In fact, the rising trend line over the entire period since the 1965 Act came into effect has been generally smooth—suspiciously smooth.

Why? There are two obvious reasons. Firstly, the emphasis placed by the 1965 Act on "family reunification" rather than the importation of workers to fill specific labor needs. Secondly, the magnet of the modern American welfare state.

Both have served to uncouple immigration from American economic conditions . . . and, not coincidentally, from American economic needs.

Let alone from political, cultural or national needs.

Which leads us to a central truth about the current influx:

- **The current immigration to the United States is not an economic phenomenon: it is a political phenomenon.**

We'll be returning to this truth later. Several times.

Now, let's not forget about those illegals. They are still coming. Indeed, after a short hesitation, they seem to be coming about as strong as ever.

Of course, illegal immigration is a difficult thing to measure. One way is to chart the Border Patrol's count of apprehensions at the border. The results are shown in Chart 3, page 34.

The Border Patrol estimates it catches about a third of all illegal immigrants as they attempt to cross the border. Since 1.3 million were apprehended in 1993, this suggests a remarkable *2 to 3 million* illegal immigrants may have succeeded in entering the country in 1993.

And, as a result, the permanent illegal-immigrant presence in the United States is beginning to build up again. As we saw, the INS

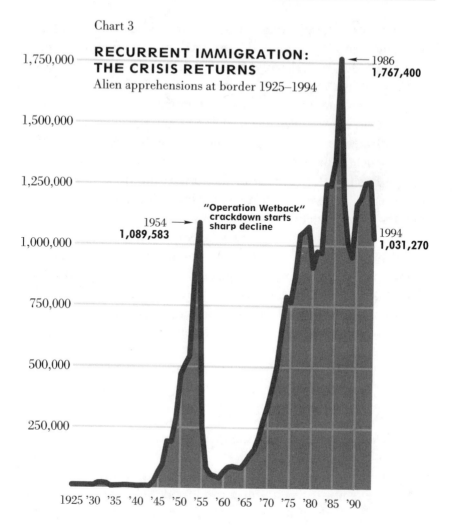

estimate is that the net increase is a flow of 300,000 to 500,000 each year, and that there is a stock of some 4 million illegals now in the United States. Suppose the net increase has been 500,000 annually. That would once again mean that by subtracting IRCA legalizations but adding new net illegal immigration, 1990 and 1991 were unarguably the record years in U.S. immigration history (for what the record's worth).

Could be. Who knows? Enormous numbers of illegal aliens are crossing the U.S. border constantly, in both directions.

"They're just commuters," immigration enthusiasts like to sniff. But in fact the gross number of illegals is important. It is a measure of the impact on the border region. It is a measure of the public health problem—infection can be spread by even brief contacts. Also, it's a measure of the precarious future.

Because the situation is highly leveraged. Suppose even a small additional proportion of those 3 million illegal entrants each year decide to stay for good—say one in ten, or 300,000. Then the rate of increase of the illegal population permanently in the United States would have suddenly nearly doubled, at least, from between 300,000–500,000 to 600,000–800,000 annually.

And it would be quite some time before anyone found out for sure.

Except, of course, the long-suffering residents of San Diego and other border counties. And no one in the national media pays attention to them anyway.

In effect, by allowing its borders to vanish under this vast whirling mass of illegal immigrants, the United States is running on the edge of a demographic buzz saw. One day, it could suddenly look down to find California or Texas cut off.

Whatever else the IRCA legislation was supposed to do, it has quite clearly failed to control illegal immigration. Politicians of all parties are now making noises about addressing the problem.

This has happened before. Look at the surge of illegal entries in the early 1950s. President Eisenhower brought it under control in 1954 with "Operation Wetback," a coordinated attack on illegal immigration both at the border and within the United States. So it can be done.

Still . . . what's the betting on another amnesty?

ANOTHER WRINKLE: RELATIVE IMMIGRATION

"But, but, BUT, BUT!!" immigration enthusiasts protest again. *"You can't just look at absolute numbers of immigrants. You have to look at immigration relative to the American population. And looked at like that, it's not historically high at all."*

Well, at first sight, this does seem like a reasonable wrinkle, doesn't it? How easily a given wave of immigration can be handled does seem related to the size of the host population.

Thus, for example, during the previous Great Wave in the first years of the twentieth century, the total U.S. population was in the process of rising through the level of only a third of what it is today. The Bureau of the Census recorded just over 90 million Americans in 1910, when just over 1 million immigrants arrived. But there were just over 250 million Americans in 1993, when about 1 million legal immigrants were reported.

So in 1910, immigration amounted to just over 1 percent of the American population. But in 1990, immigration amounted to only 0.4 percent—or say 0.6 percent, adjusted for illegals.

Don't get carried away by all this reasonableness, however. Absolute numbers matter—absolutely. In at least two ways.

Firstly:

- *Absolute numbers matter because concentrations can cause trouble.* Immigrants do not spread all across the United States in a thin, tactful layer just six one-hundredths of a native-born American thick. Or even four one-hundredths thick. They invariably accumulate in specific localities.

For example, the INS reports that more than three quarters of all legal immigration goes to just six states: California, Texas, Illinois, Florida, New York and New Jersey. And most to just six metropolitan areas: Los Angeles, Anaheim, Chicago, Miami, New York and Washington, D.C.[7]

When the immigrants' absolute numbers in these localities pass a certain point, their communities achieve a critical mass. Their alien languages and cultures become, at least for a while, self-sustaining. And the natives start asking themselves: "Are we still living in America?"

For example, the Cubanization of the Miami area has become legendary. But Cuban immigration since 1960 has been only about 650,000—a fraction of the 19 million legal immigrants who have come to the United States since 1960. The Cuban community in

Florida, with its American-born offspring, is probably about 500,000. It has been, however, enough to transform the area.

"For the better!" immigrant enthusiasts say. Maybe—although it would be interesting to know what the Americans living in southern Florida would have said in 1960 . . . had they been asked.

Whether the transformation was for better or worse, however, is irrelevant. The point is this: quite small absolute numbers of Cuban immigrants were sufficient to create this enclave. And the post-1965 immigrant influx has been quite large enough to create many such enclaves—turning America into a sort of Swiss cheese.

There is an American tradition of worrying about these immigrant enclaves that goes back at least to George Washington. In 1785, he objected to the organized importation of English immigrants to form buffer settlements on the frontier, arguing that their foreign allegiance might survive precisely because they were "detached and unmixed with citizens of different sentiments . . ."[8] Almost a century later, in 1874, a proposal to reserve western land for communities of German-speaking Mennonites was rejected by Congress on similar grounds.[9] Today, of course, such enclaves are viewed as delightful examples of diversity.

Secondly:

- *Absolute numbers matter because comparisons can be deceptive.* It may seem reasonable to insist on expressing immigration relative to host population size. But it does cause something of a statistical mirage.

A moment's simple arithmetic shows you why: it is mathematically impossible to maintain any very high proportion of immigrants, relative to a country's host population, as the host population grows. After all, immigration has never been *relatively* higher than when the second Pilgrim Father came down the gangplank. That increased the Plymouth Colony's population by 100 percent in just a few seconds. It went from one Pilgrim to two Pilgrims. No recent period can match that relative immigration rate. But immigration can still be at crisis levels.

Today, the United States is the third most populous country on earth, after China and India. Regardless of whether the current level of immigration relative to U.S. population is historically high, it is still high enough to mean that in recent years, the United States has been taking almost half of all the legal immigrants going to the developed world.

In other words, half of all the legal immigrants in the developed world are zeroing in on a country with 7 percent of the world's land surface and less than 5 percent of its population. No wonder the boat is starting to rock.

Still, just to be fair (again), let's look at immigration relative to U.S. population (see Chart 4, pages 40–41).

Points positively leap out:

- *The Era of Mass Immigration is only an episode in American history.* Visible on Chart 4: the Second Great Lull of 1920–1965—and the lesser known, earlier Great Lull prior to the 1840s. Although numbers weren't kept before 1820, immigration from Europe was virtually halted by the Napoleonic Wars from 1792 to 1815.[10]
- *Current immigration is significant—even allowing for the statistical mirage caused by today's much larger U.S. population.* Note that expected immigration levels above 1 million a year through the 1990s will work out at above five per thousand, well above Immigration Era lows. Adding 3 million annual gross illegal immigrants—almost twelve per thousand—would take the total to Immigration Era peaks.
- *Even during the Immigration Era, there were dramatic ups and downs.* These pauses constitute a hidden dimension of American immigration history. They have vitally assisted the process of assimilation.

  By contrast, the current underlying legal immigration is building steadily but relentlessly.

YET ANOTHER WRINKLE: NET IMMIGRATION

Not just illegal immigrants go back home. Legal immigrants also decide to leave the United States. Sometimes in very large numbers.

Although you don't hear as much about it, as many as a third of the 1880–1925 Great Wave seem eventually to have gone back home, over 3 million in each of the first two decades of this century. By some accounts, net immigration was actually negative in some years in the 1930s, during the 1925–1965 Second Great Lull. More people were leaving the United States than were entering it.

So just as *gross* illegal entries have to be set against *gross* illegal exits to get *net illegal immigration,* so *gross* legal immigration should really be set against *gross* emigration of legal immigrants. That gives us *net legal immigration.*

Net immigration is very difficult to measure. As a free country, the United States has traditionally made little effort to keep track of people wishing to leave. But the evidence suggests that this phenomenon of net immigration amounts to another hidden dimension of American immigration history, to match the pattern of pauses. And funny things are happening in this dimension too.

One estimate of net immigration, both legal and illegal, has been made by the demographers Jeffrey S. Passel and Barry Edmonston of the (generally pro-immigrant) Urban Institute of Washington, D.C. (see Chart 5, page 42).

Passell and Edmonston adjusted INS data for illegal immigrants, refugees and various other special categories, which have become very large since the 1965 Immigration Act. And they made their own estimate of departures. Their conclusion:

> Net immigration in the 1900–1910 decade was 4.9 million—well below the 8.2 million *net* figure we estimate for the 1980s. In fact, our estimates suggest that the 1970s (not the 1980s) were most comparable in terms of net immigration to the 1900–1910 decade, with the 1980s *clearly* exceeding all other decades.[11]

Note the funny thing that is happening in the net immigration dimension: *significantly more of the post-1965 Second Great Wave immigrants seem to be staying in the United States—in contrast to the pre-1920 First Great Wave immigrants.*

Why? Passel and Edmonston don't say. But there is one obvious difference between early-twentieth-century America and late-twentieth-century America: the welfare state.

And in fact, there is new and disturbing evidence that the post-

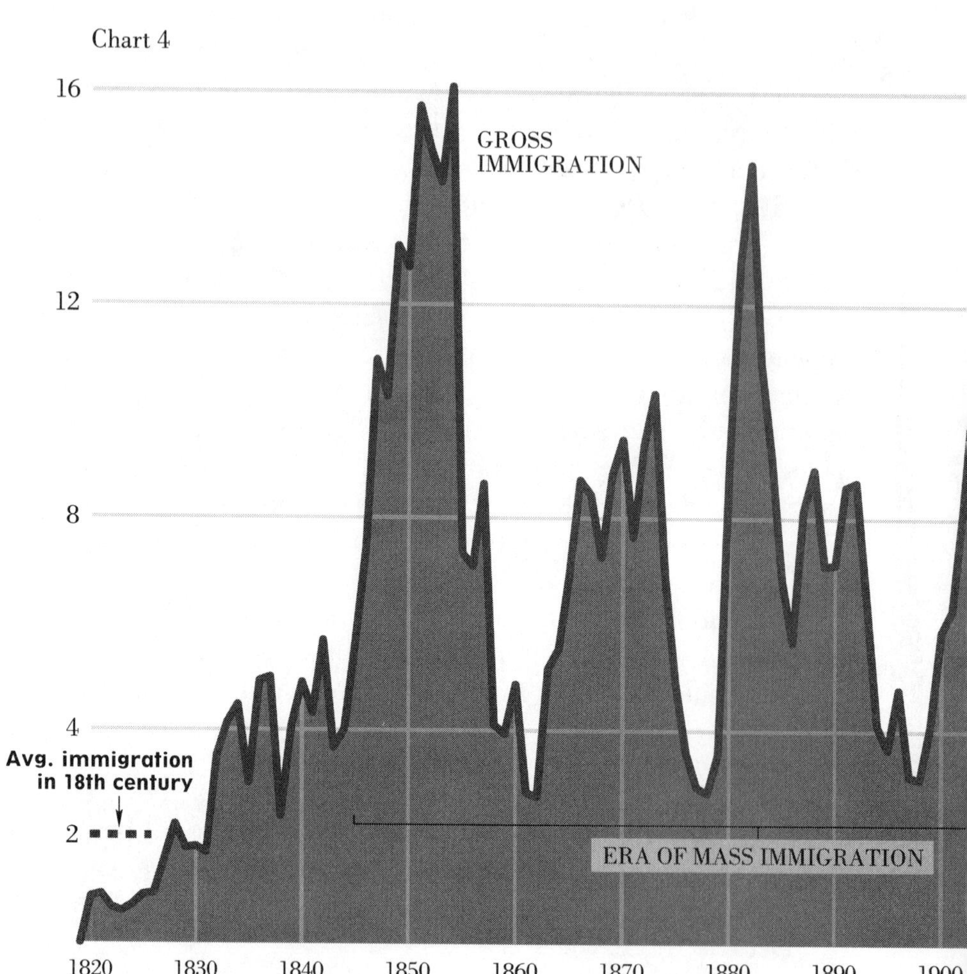
Chart 4
16
12
8
4
2
GROSS
IMMIGRATION
Avg. immigration
in 18th century
ERA OF MASS IMMIGRATION
1820
1830
1840
1850
1860
1870
1880
1890
1900

IMMIGRATION COMPARED TO U.S. POPULATION: A STATISTICAL MIRAGE?

Annual rate of gross legal immigration per thousand of U.S. population 1820–1992

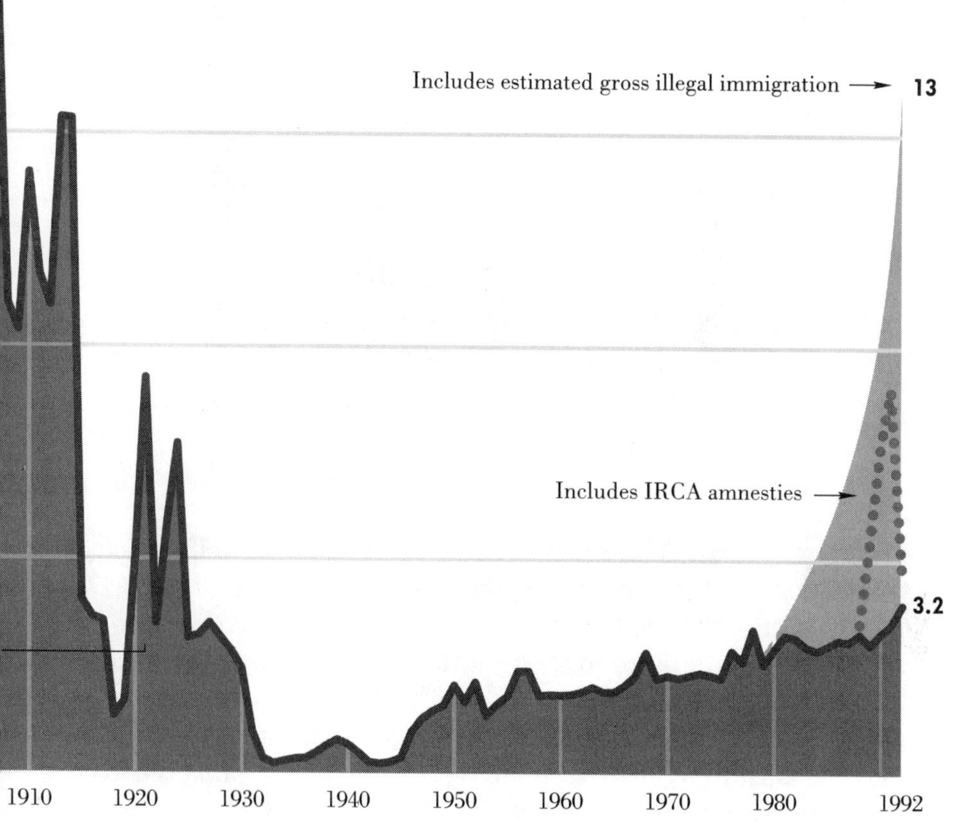

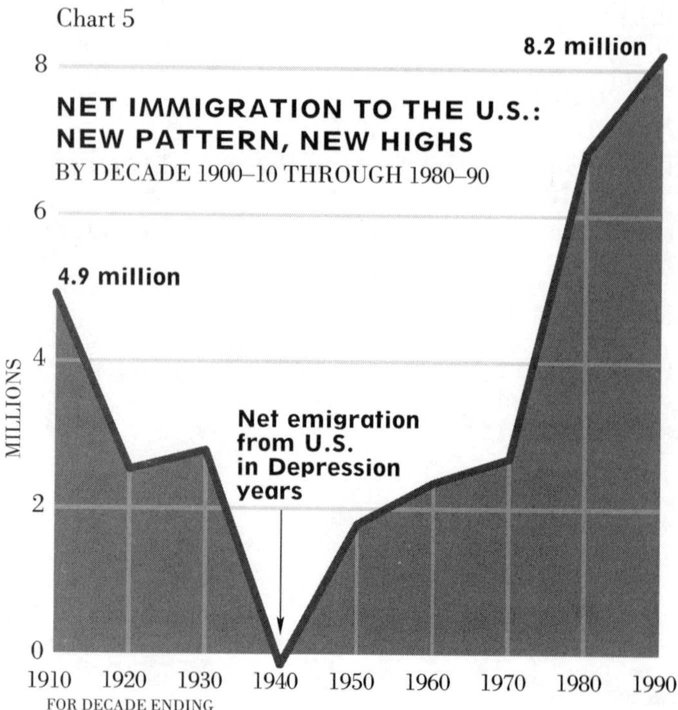

1965 Second Great Wave immigrants are going on welfare in sharply higher proportions than in the past. (See Chapter 7.)

To put it brutally: the failures are no longer winnowed out. Instead, they are encouraged to stay—at the expense of the American taxpayer.

This greater net immigration may well be yet another symptom of the central truth we discovered above: *current immigration is not an economic phenomenon; it is a policy phenomenon.* The policy in this case is transfer payments, from the American taxpayer to (in some degree) immigrants.

Thus as we iron out the wrinkles, the immigration enthusiasts' case for complacency gets steadily weaker.

WRINKLING BACK: IMMIGRATION RELATIVE TO BIRTHRATE

So much for the immigration enthusiasts' wrinkles. Now let's introduce one of our own. It is a crucial point invariably omitted in pro-immigration polemics:

- *At the beginning of this century, the U.S. birthrate was much higher, as much as twice what it is now.* Now American Anglos are reproducing below replacement levels—generally defined as 2.1 children per woman. *So post-1965 Second Great Wave immigrants are having a proportionately much higher demographic impact on America than the pre-1925 First Great Wave.*

Hence the steadily shifting ethnic balance.

Demographers like to measure this effect by expressing immigration as a proportion of *population change.* Population change, of course, is the birthrate (which is down in this case), less the death rate (which is also down), plus net immigration (up). According to the Urban Institute's Jeffrey Passell and Barry Edmonston, the result looks like what you see in Chart 6, below.

Chart 6

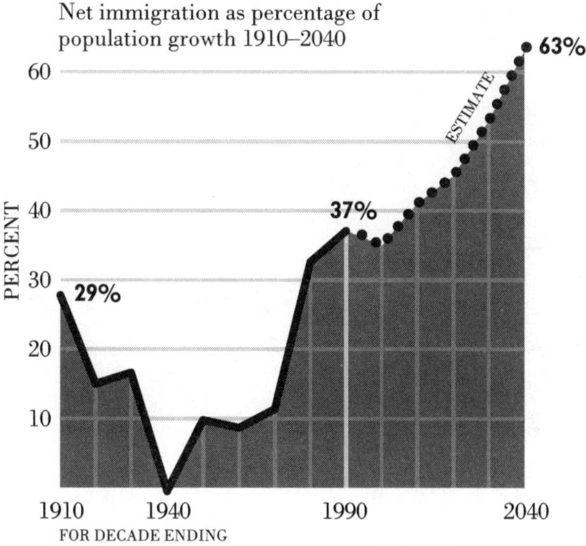

Now we are really getting somewhere. These calculations by Passel and Edmonston clearly show that the post-1965 Second Great Wave of Immigration has driven the United States way outside its historical envelope. Immigration in the 1980s was contributing a significantly higher proportion of population growth (37.1 percent) than it was in the legendary 1900–1910 decade (27.8 percent). In fact, *immigration had already contributed a higher share of population growth in the 1970s (32.6 percent).*

But the band played on—notwithstanding these numbers, there was all that persistent happy talk from immigration enthusiasts about immigration being really still quite low.

Looking at immigration's contribution to population growth, however, still does not finish the story. As we noted above, after immigrants arrive in the United States, they have children too. In fact, in some cases they seem to have children at a faster pace than the native-born Americans. So the true impact of immigration is the proportion of immigrants *and their descendants* in the American population. (See Chart 7, below.)

Chart 7 provides Passel and Edmonston's estimate of this impact. The lower line tracks the proportion of the U.S. population that is foreign-born—in other words, the immigrants. This remained high through the nineteenth century, as high immigration

Chart 7

THE FOREIGN PRESENCE: STARTING BACK UP...

Foreign-born and foreign-stock (immigrants plus U.S.-born children) as a percentage of U.S. population 1870–2040

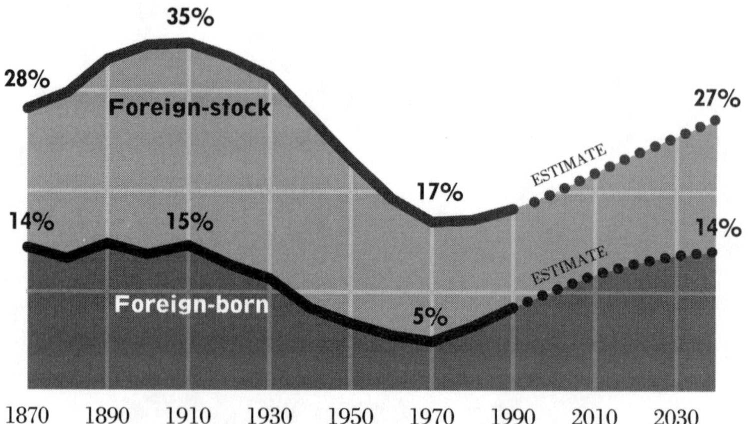

was matched by rapid natural growth. Then it fell sharply during the 1925–1965 Second Great Lull. But it rebounded after the 1965 Immigration Act. By 1990, the foreign-born proportion had more than doubled. Passel and Edmonston project that in the foreseeable future it will rise to the high levels last seen in the nineteenth century.

The upper line tracks the proportion of "foreign stock"—which Passel and Edmonston define as immigrants and their children (but not grandchildren and subsequent generations). And this is also on the move. It is projected to reach some 27 percent in 2040. This is about where it was in 1870, after the great Irish and German immigrant wave of mid-century.

Make no mistake: what we are looking at here is a demographic event of seismic proportions. Don't be deceived by another of those statistical mirages. In 1870, the Bureau of the Census reported a total U.S. population of barely more than 38.5 million. By contrast, U.S. population in 2040 is projected to be over seven times as large. In order to produce a "foreign stock" proportion of similar magnitude, the absolute size of the projected immigrant movement into the United States in the twenty-first century must be enormous—and the natural increase of the native-born Americans virtually stalled.

And this is exactly what seems to be happening.

THE ULTIMATE WRINKLE: THE WEDGE

One leading authority on immigration is the demographer Leon Bouvier, former vice president of the Population Reference Bureau, adjunct professor of geography at Tulane University School of Public Health, and most recently, author with Lindsey Grant of *How Many Americans? Population, Immigration and the Environment* (Sierra Club, 1994). Recently, using slightly different assumptions than his Urban Institute peers, Bouvier asked the question: *what would have happened if there had been no immigration at all after 1970?* (The 1970 Census, of course, was closest to the point at which the 1965 Immigration Act became effective.)

And, Bouvier added, what will happen next?

In other words, Bouvier allowed not only for post-1970 immigrants and their children—the group that Passell and Edmonston defined as "foreign stock"—but also for their children's children . . . and all of their descendants.

He got this startling answer. I call it the Wedge Chart (see page 47).

The two decades from 1970 to 1990 were always bound to be interesting, demographically speaking. It was the period during which the post–World War II Baby Boom generation would start to have their own children.

As it turned out, however, this Baby Boom echo was quite muted. Boomer women averaged less than two children apiece. So, somewhat unexpectedly, population growth would have been quite moderate—just an additional 23 million Americans by 1990.

Except for the 1965 Immigration Act. That policy switch allowed a flood of immigrants who, with their descendants, more than doubled population growth—to over 46 million.

And the answer to Bouvier's question is going to get even more startling. He projects that immigrants and their descendants will make up about two thirds of U.S. population growth during the 1990s. Thereafter, they will supply *virtually all* population growth.

By 2050, the Census Bureau estimates U.S. population will have reached 391 million. By Bouvier's count, at that point *more than a third (36 percent) of the U.S. population will be post-1970 immigrants and their descendants*—a staggering 139 million people.

On Chart 8, this immigration component looks like a wedge, because the native-born Americans are expected to have stabilized and even slightly reduced their numbers in the next century. Environmentalists praise this restraint—they think it is the ecologically responsible thing to do. And maybe it is. But this restraint by native-born Americans is wasted anyway. The resulting gap is much more than filled by immigration policy.

And here, finally, after ironing out all immigration's statistical wrinkles, we reach the bitter end.

- **Immigration policy is quite literally driving a wedge between the American nation, as it had evolved by 1965, and its future.**

Chart 8

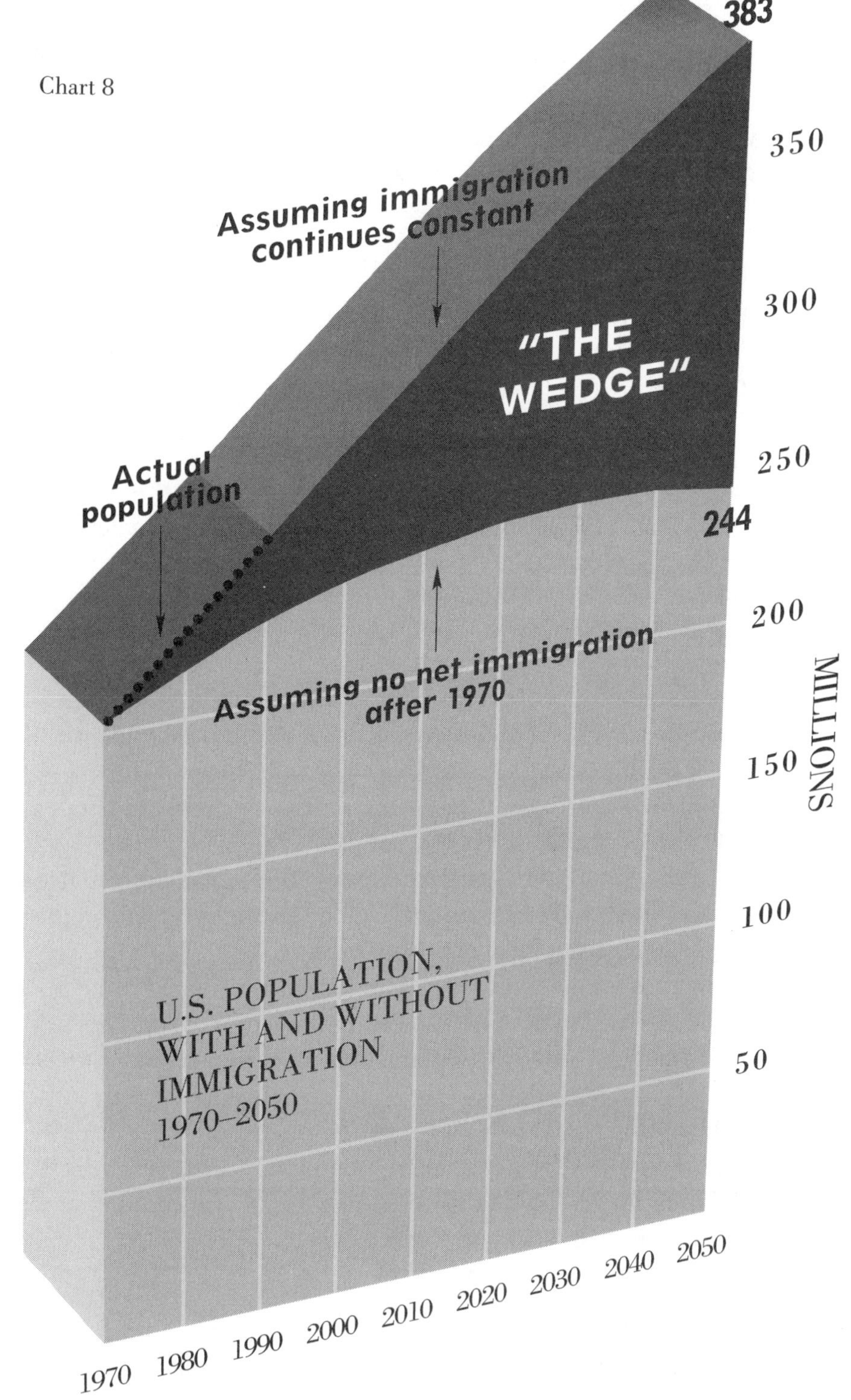
383
350
Assuming immigration continues constant
300
"THE WEDGE"
250
Actual population
244
200
Assuming no net immigration after 1970
MILLIONS
150
100
U.S. POPULATION, WITH AND WITHOUT IMMIGRATION 1970–2050
50
1970
1980
1990
2000
2010
2020
2030
2040
2050

Sounds too harsh? Well, this much is undeniable: the American nation of 1965 is going to have to share its future, and its land, with a very large number of people who, as of that year, were complete strangers. Foreigners. Aliens.

"Oh, but they'll assimilate," insist the immigration enthusiasts. *"They always have."*

To which the only possible answer is: *they'd better.*

Because America has never faced a greater challenge. This projected new population growth is quite comparable to—could even exceed—anything experienced in the great Immigration Era of the nineteenth century.

To put it in perspective, consider this arresting fact:

- If there had been *no immigration at all* into the United States after 1790, the American population in 1990 would still have been an estimated 122 million—just less than half (49 percent) of the actual 249 million.[12]

That is, the United States in 1990 would still have been much bigger than the reunited Germany (80 million) and virtually identical to Japan (123 million).

Surprised? It's just the natural result of very high early birthrates and the length of time that has elapsed. For example, almost all (92 percent) of the 31 million American blacks are descended from just 427,000 slaves who were brought to the United States, mostly in the strikingly short period between 1740 and 1810.[13] Even more remarkable, more than 16 million Americans are estimated to be descended from the 21,000 English Puritans who took part in the "Great Migration" to New England that occurred between 1629 and 1640.[14]

To put it another way: two centuries of immigration were responsible for about half the actual 1990 population. But just ninety years of immigration look likely to be responsible for more than a third of the projected 2050 population.

Or consider this further fact:

- The proportion of the American population that was of southern and eastern European origin, essentially all stemming from post-

> 1870 immigration and provoking the intense controversy that culminated in the Great Restriction, is estimated to have been only about 13 percent of the total U.S. population in 1930.[15]

The proportion of the total U.S. population stemming from post-1970 immigration was already over half that (8 percent) in 1990—and rising.[16]

Everyone agrees that America's assimilation of its nineteenth-century immigration was exceptional in world history. But contemplating what the United States has done, and is now being required to do again, reminds me of the sign American garage mechanics like to have up on their wall:

> MIRACLES ARE ACCOMPLISHED BEFORE BREAKFAST
> THE IMPOSSIBLE TAKES LONGER

In the 1890–1920 period, the relative size of the Colonial-stock population served as a powerful stabilizer. And, although the First Great Wave of Immigration crested very high, it also broke and was ended very quickly. The numbers are quite different today.

Even apart from the really crucial questions:

- **Are these immigrants as assimilable as those in the previous waves?**
- **Is the United States still as capable of assimilating them as it was in 1900?**

We will consider *those* questions on pages 216–19.

IS THIS REALLY GOING TO HAPPEN?

All of these demographic projections, of course, must make some fairly daring assumptions about things to come. In particular, the Wedge scenario assumes the continuation of current low fertility rates among the native-born Americans. And it also assumes that immigration continues at the present level. Either could prove untrue, or both. For example, immigration could be lower. Or it could be higher.

But one projection can be made with a pretty fair degree of certainty: *no real immigration pause is going to happen spontaneously.* Unlike other immigration waves in American history, this latest wave shows absolutely no sign of receding anytime in the foreseeable future.

Nor is there any particular reason to suppose that it will.

Everyone has heard a lot about the world's "population explosion." It's a cliché. But guess what? It's really happening. Indeed, the explosion is so dramatic that the demographer Michael S. Teitelbaum of New York's Alfred P. Sloan Foundation has written that it *"can be described without exaggeration as revolutionary, a virtual discontinuity with all human history."*[17]

Most of this growth is in the Third World. Since the 1965 Immigration Act, immigration to the United States has been predominantly from the Third World—over 90 percent in the early 1990s. But there's plenty more where that came from (see Chart 9, page 51).

Note that Chart 9 assumes the United States will grow rapidly, because of continued heavy immigration. But nevertheless, it is still totally dwarfed by the Third World demographic overhang. And that overhang hangs over more and more as the twenty-first century wears on.

Let's suppose the United States will grow at the very fastest rate the Bureau of the Census considers possible. Then it would have about 500 million people in 2050. That's twice as many as today—something to think about if you ride the New York City subway or drive on Southern California's roads. But even that entire, unimaginably swollen, American population would still be only about *half a decade's projected growth* for the Third World.

Which leads us to an important conclusion:

- *Third World population problems cannot be solved by immigration to the United States. The numbers simply do not compute.*

The United States is not a safety valve: it is a pint pot, into which a quart (or in this case several gallons) just won't go.

But current immigration policy is to try anyway.

Chart 9

THE THIRD WORLD OVERHANG

Population in the U.S., assuming continued immigration, and in the developing world 1990–2050

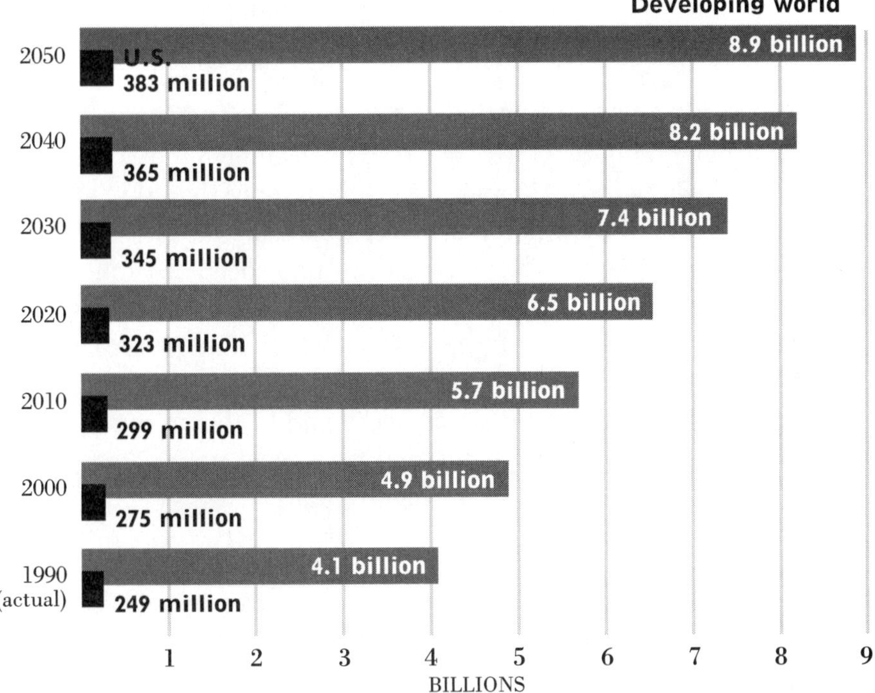

Of course, not all those people are ready to come. But many are. David A. Coleman, Lecturer in Demography at Oxford University's Department of Applied Social Studies and Social Research, has estimated current demand to emigrate from the Third World to the West at 60 million persons.[18]

And the Third World demographic overhang may be even more ominous than it looks at first sight. For three reasons:

Firstly:

- Most Third World populations are much younger than that of the United States. For example, well over 45 percent of Africans are younger than fifteen, whereas just over 20 percent of Americans are.[19]

This means that a much higher proportion of Chart 9's Third World population blocks is about to move into the twenty–forty age range—the group most likely to emigrate.

Secondly:

- Within the Third World, an immense migration to the cities is underway. And that's usually the first step that leads to emigration.

The United Nations Population Fund estimates that the Third World urban populations will increase, in absolute numbers, about sixteen times between 1950 and 2025. That's more than three times the growth rate of the First World's cities during industrialization in the nineteenth century.[20] It means profound social disruption.

Demographers have a rather insensitive name for the great sprawling megalopolises of the Third World like Mexico City, Cairo or Calcutta: they call them *"primate cities."* But that does give a good impression of their savagery and of their King Kong–like domination of their respective countries. And ever more people are taking that first step of migrating to them.

Thirdly:

- Third World population growth is particularly vulnerable to environmental disaster. And this will create "environmental refugees."

Poor, ignorant, desperate people are quite naturally more likely to deforest, overgraze and overcultivate all the land they can get their hands on. Thus the UN estimates that 450 million people today live in areas subject to soil erosion, floods and other environmental hazards. And the UN has also calculated that if "global warming" becomes a reality, some 16 percent of the population of Egypt and 10 percent of the population of Bangladesh, for example, could become "environmental refugees."[21] That's over 20 million people just from those two countries alone.

Scared by that world population overhang? Or contemptuous of such a cliché? (Even though clichés can be true, they get boring.) Both reactions are common. So: a final word about population growth.

People who think about population growth tend to divide into two contending camps. Those in the first camp really are seriously scared—one celebrated case is Stanford University's Paul Ehrlich, author of the 1968 bestseller *The Population Bomb.* They think that world population will soar right past the capacity of the planet to sustain it, leading to environmental catastrophe, mass starvation and an eventual collapse right down to (and even below) sustainable levels. This pattern of boom and bust happens regularly in nature. It is quite typical for insects. Perhaps not coincidentally, Ehrlich is by profession an entomologist—a zoologist who studies insects. His specialty: butterflies.

The second camp of population-growth watchers are contemptuous because they are optimists. One prominent optimist: the University of Maryland's Julian Simon. Optimists argue, essentially, that human beings are not butterflies. Human beings, they say, have the intelligence to adapt to conditions. Thus the population of the world has increased more than six times since 1800. But output increased even faster, because of the inventions that revolutionized industry and—less often recognized—agriculture. Despite all that population growth, living standards everywhere are far higher now than they were then.

Moreover (the optimists add) as societies become richer, birthrates tend to fall. This is what happened in the developed Western World. There's even a name for the phenomenon: "The Demographic Transition."

My Libra-like reaction: both sides make important points.

On the one hand, there have indeed been cases of human population catastrophes. The population of Ireland grew rapidly after the introduction of the potato, from 1.25 million in 1600 to 8.5 million in 1840. Then it collapsed, after disease repeatedly destroyed the potato crop. Eventually, it declined to a low of 4.5 million in 1900.

For that matter, the population of Europe fell by more than a quarter in the final years of the Roman Empire. It did not recover until A.D. 1000.

On the other hand, the optimists are quite right about the Industrial Revolution. And world population growth is indeed starting to slow. The UN projects that it will probably stabilize (at a mere 11.5 billion—almost twice today's level!) in about two hundred years.

For the purposes of immigration policy, however, the point to grasp is this:

- If the population optimists are right, they are right *in general.* There is plenty of room for unpleasantness *in detail.*

In the context of the grand upsweep of world population over the next century, something that appears now perfectly predictable, one of those unpleasant details could easily be the snuffing out of the American nation—like a candle in a gale.

ODD COUNTRY OUT

Immigration is responsible for a virtually unique American peculiarity: the U.S. population is (as we have seen) projected to go on growing into the next century. By contrast, almost all the other countries in the industrialized First World are expected to stabilize (see Chart 10, below).

Chart 10

THE DEVELOPED WORLD: POPULATIONS STABILIZING—EXCEPT FOR U.S. (AND CANADA)

Projected increase in developed world's populations 1993–2025, 1993–2050

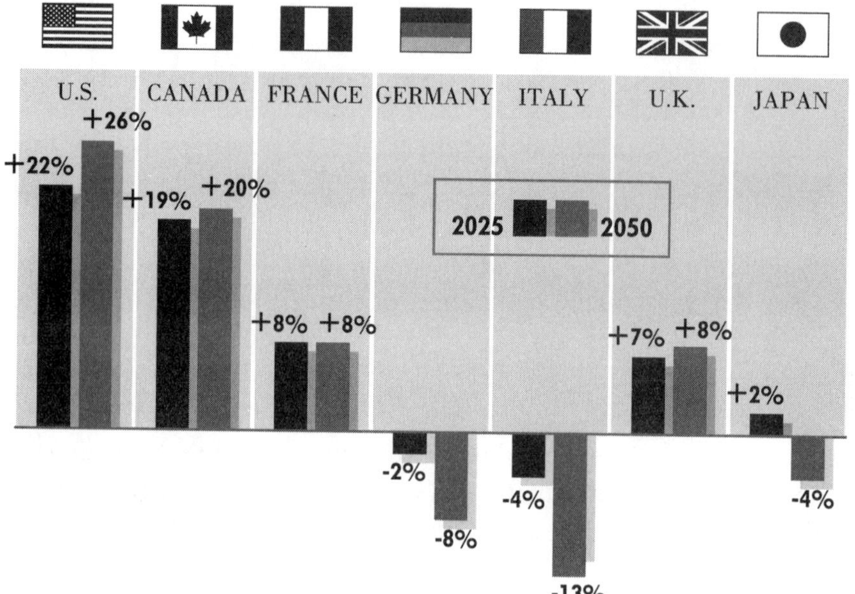

Environmentalists worry about this American oddity. They are concerned that the U.S. population will exceed the country's "carrying capacity"—the number of people that its natural resources, combined with current technology, can support on a sustainable basis.

But immigration enthusiasts, and some others, welcome continued U.S. population growth. "Other industrial nations must cope with static or declining labor forces," crowed *Business Week* recently (August 9, 1993). "The U.S. ratio [of workers to aged dependents] will still be higher than that of most other advanced nations . . ."

Maybe. Except that raw labor input is probably not very important to economic growth. (See Chapter 8, page 166.) But, meanwhile, when contemplating the glories of an ever-expanding U.S. population, remember this point:

- The post-1965 immigration is not only much bigger than expected; it is also less skilled. And it is becoming even less so.

There should be no surprise about this. It is a direct consequence of the 1965 Immigration Act's stress on "family reunification." The act skewed immigration selection away from those who wanted to come here because they had marketable skills—and even away from those whom American employers had found and wanted to bring here.

Even worse, the evidence is that *relative lack of skills among the post-1965 immigrants seems likely to be repeated among their children.*

This contradicts another of those Statue of Liberty myths: peddlers' sons are supposed to become rocket scientists. Some do. But most don't. They never did. Recent research has found that disparities in economic performance between some of the 1890–1920 immigrant groups have persisted for as much as four generations.[22] It is not a problem that can be solved by the American education system.

The conclusion is clear, if unwelcome:

- *By importing so much unskilled labor, the United States is, as a practical matter, permanently degrading the quality of its workforce.*

So that growing U.S. population, compared to the other industrialized countries, could be a boost. But it could also be a burden. (For more on this, see Chapter 7.)*

THE ULTIMATE QUESTION

But there is a question that is ultimately far more important than economics:

- **Regardless of whether the immigrant wedge being driven into the United States will be a boost or a burden—*will it be American?***

This question greatly concerned Americans during the 1890–1920 period that culminated in the First Great Wave. They instituted a systematic campaign of "Americanization." And, in the end, they shut immigration off almost completely.

But the issue is much more acute today. For the first time, virtually all immigrants are racially distinct "visible minorities." They come not from Europe, previously the common homeland even for the 1890–1920 immigrants about which Americans were so nervous. Instead, these new immigrants are from completely different, and arguably incompatible, cultural traditions. And, as we have seen, they are coming in such numbers that their impact on America is enormous—inevitably within the foreseeable future, they will transform it.

---

*As this book was in galleys, the greatest intellectual uproar for many years was caused by the publication of Richard J. Herrnstein and Charles Murray's *The Bell Curve: Intelligence and Class Structure in American Life* (Free Press), which argued that scientific evidence shows human intelligence exists in a measurable way, is profoundly important in society, is largely hereditary, and differs, on average, between races. In a little-noticed passage, Herrnstein and Murray blamed the 1965 Immigration Act for a sharp deterioration in immigrant quality. They estimated that the current influx has an average IQ of 95, at least 5 points below the white American mean. If they are right, of course, this suggests the consequences of current policy are far more disastrous than anything argued in this book. However, I figure I've taken enough risks already and merely report their view for what it is worth. There are quite enough reasons to worry about immigration without using Herrnstein and Murray's work. Would-be demagogues should note that I do not so use it here.

This is an absolutely extraordinary situation. To grasp just how extraordinary, consider this:

- **There is no precedent for a sovereign country undergoing such a rapid and radical transformation of its ethnic character in the entire history of the world.**

We will examine this extraordinary situation in the next chapter.

3

THE PINCERS

Wouldn't it
Be simpler in that case if the Government
Dissolved the people and
Elected another?

—**BERTOLT BRECHT,**
"The Solution"

As a journalist, I adore angry letters from readers. They give you that warm, comforting feeling that somebody, somewhere, cares. The letter below, however, was particularly stimulating. It's one of the responses that *National Review* ran after my immigration cover story.

> [To the question of who should immigrate] Brimelow . . . provides the same tired answer given by every ethnic group: "More people who look like me." . . . He implicitly suggests that the *real* reason for curbing immigration is to maintain the racial hegemony of white Americans.[1]

Needless to say, on reading this complaint, I was immediately stricken by guilt. You always are. Even though what I had actually suggested was a moratorium—no immigration at all.

But then it occurred to me: Suppose I had proposed more immigrants who look like me. So what? As late as 1950, somewhere up to nine out of ten Americans looked like me. That is, they were of European stock.

And in those days, they had another name for this thing dismissed so contemptuously as "the racial hegemony of white Americans."

They called it "America."

Significantly, the writer of the letter, Patrick Burns of Arlington, Virginia, noted that he was himself a demographer. Yet the mere mention of America's changing ethnic patterns provoked him to this angry reaction—in a demographer, the equivalent of a doctor fainting at the sight of blood.

Which is just another reminder of the intense, if unacknowledged, emotion that drives so many of the American immigration enthusiasts.

CONSTRUCTING THE PINCERS

The reality, of course, is that ethnic ebb and flow is central to the history of American immigration. Chart 11 (page 60) captures both its proportions and its absolute size.

Chart 11 makes two points immediately obvious.

- *Point 1:* the historic role of immigration from northern and western Europe—Britain, Ireland, Germany, Scandinavia.

Even in the fabled Ellis Island of 1901–10, this inflow was still very strong. In fact, in those years immigration from northern and western Europe was quietly about as high as it has ever been.

So Chart 11 has revealed another significant difference between the 1890–1920 Great Wave and the post-1965 Second Great Wave. In the earlier period, the continued immigration from the traditional northern and western European sources meant that not all immigrants were alien to American eyes. And it also meant that the native-born Americans were receiving continuous ethnic reinforcement. Neither of these conditions is true today.

Chart 11

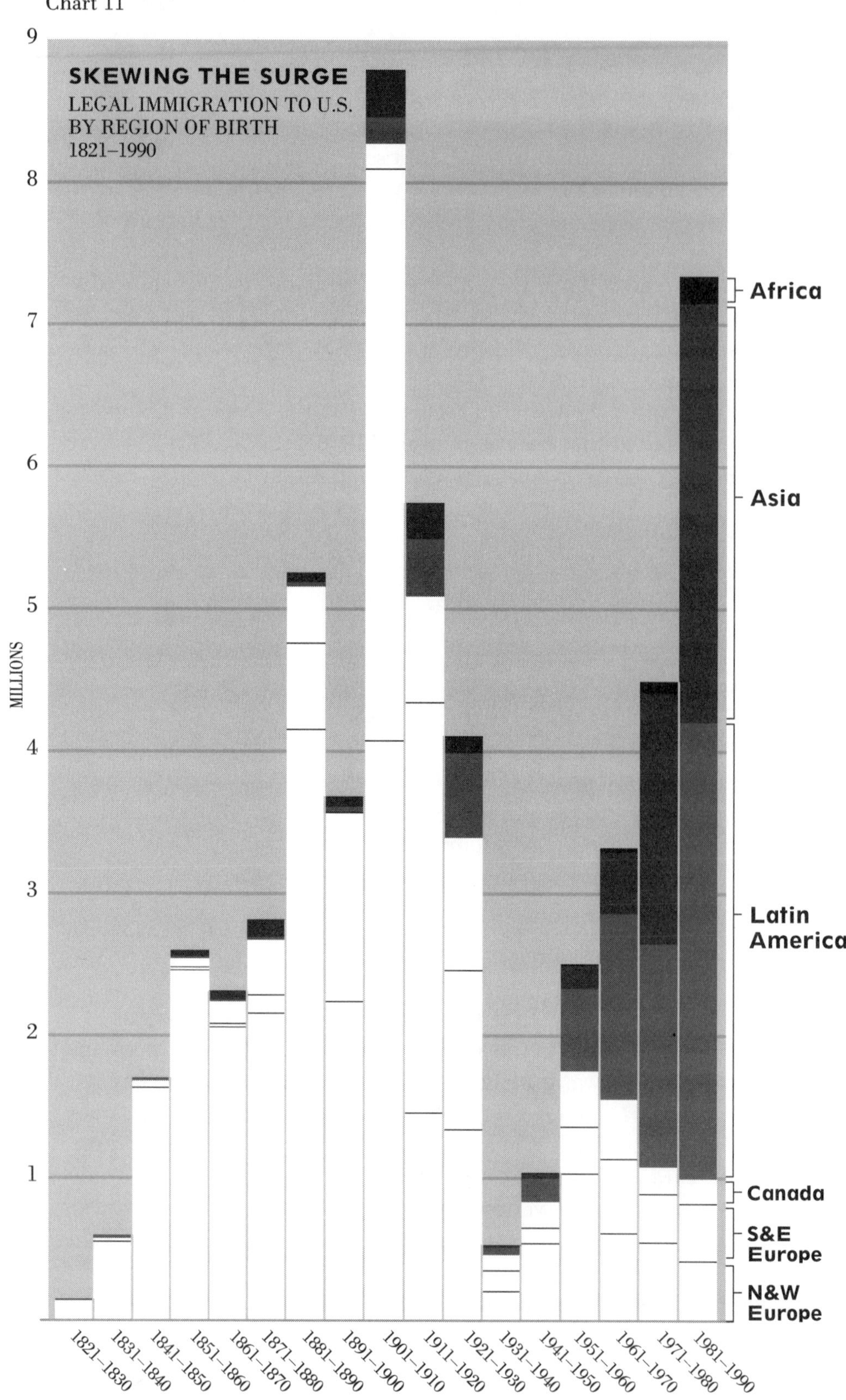

SKEWING THE SURGE
LEGAL IMMIGRATION TO U.S.
BY REGION OF BIRTH
1821–1990
MILLIONS
9
8
7
6
5
4
3
2
1
1821–1830
1831–1840
1841–1850
1851–1860
1861–1870
1871–1880
1881–1890
1891–1900
1901–1910
1911–1920
1921–1930
1931–1940
1941–1950
1951–1960
1961–1970
1971–1980
1981–1990
Africa
Asia
Latin America
Canada
S&E Europe
N&W Europe

And yet nevertheless, despite this lubricating flow of familiar immigrants from traditional sources, Americans *still* decided on immigration restriction in 1921. . . .

- *Point 2:* the revolutionary effect of the 1965 Immigration Act. The effect of the 1965 Act was not merely the absolute size of the influx it triggered (see Chart 1, pages 30–31). Even more important, it *dramatically skewed the sources of that influx.*

Immigration from northern and western Europe was immediately choked off. It had been rising as people reconstructed their lives after the chaos of World War II.

But look at the effect on immigration from eastern and southern Europe: it appears to have been almost as restrictive. This was not at all expected.

The result: by the late 1980s, immigration from all of Europe was dipping below a tenth of the total inflow.

(And this tenth, incidentally, no longer means "white." European immigration now includes a fraction of immigrants into Europe from Asia, the Caribbean and Africa who have decided to move on.)

Equally visible on the chart, and in dramatic contrast: surging Hispanic immigration. Throughout the 1980s, it was generally a third or more of total legal immigration. In 1991, the peak year of the IRCA amnesty for illegal immigrants, it surged to nearly 65 percent. If you count the post-IRCA illegal immigration, which is overwhelmingly Hispanic, the Hispanic inflow is probably never below half of the current immigration to the United States, which is of course at record levels.

And, also dramatically clear on the chart: the 1965 Act's reinvention of Asian immigration. Virtually halted by restrictions imposed in the nineteenth century, this had already begun to rise after these restrictions were lifted during World War II. By the 1980s, it was exploding. In some years, Asian immigrants outnumbered Hispanic (legal) immigrants—a considerable feat.

Finally, the 1965 Act can be seen to have invented one quite new type of immigration: a black inflow, both from Africa itself and from the Caribbean.

In the decades after the end of the slave trade in 1808, practically no Africans volunteered to come to the United States. But after the 1965 Immigration Act, a significant and rising African inflow began. By the 1980s, African legal immigration is a noticeable 2 to 3 percent of the total inflow—see Chart 11. Thus in 1991, there were more legal immigrants from Nigeria (2,794) than from Italy (2,336). IRCA amnesties brought the Nigerian total up to 7,912 while barely budging the Italian total: to 2,619.

But up to half of these "African" immigrants seem to be whites. The U.S. government's contradictory hang-ups about race make more precise information unobtainable.

Non-Spanish Caribbean immigration, by contrast, apart from some Asians, is almost entirely black. Small waves, chiefly from the British West Indies, arrived at various points in this century, mostly before the 1921–24 restrictions. Then came the 1965 Immigration Act. Caribbean immigration shot up. By the 1980s it was reaching astonishing proportions, given the very small size of the parent populations. It regularly matched, and in some years actually exceeded, immigration from all of Europe.

In 1988, for example, the Caribbean (population about 13 million) provided over 12 percent (78,000) of that year's 650,000 legal immigrants to the United States. Europe (population 680 million) provided just 10 percent (65,000).

In 1991, there were nearly three times the legal immigrants from Jamaica alone (18,025) than from the newly reunited Germany (6,272). Again, IRCA amnesties brought the Jamaican total up to 23,828 but barely budged the German total: to 6,509.

CLOSING THE PINCERS

So what impact will all of this have on America? In one word: profound. As reported and projected by the Bureau of the Census, it can be seen on Chart 12 (page 63).

I call this "The Pincer Chart." For obvious reasons.

The Pincer Chart's powerful message:

- **The U.S. government officially projects an ethnic revolution in America. Specifically, it expects that American whites will be on the point (53 percent) of becoming a minority by 2050.**

Chart 12

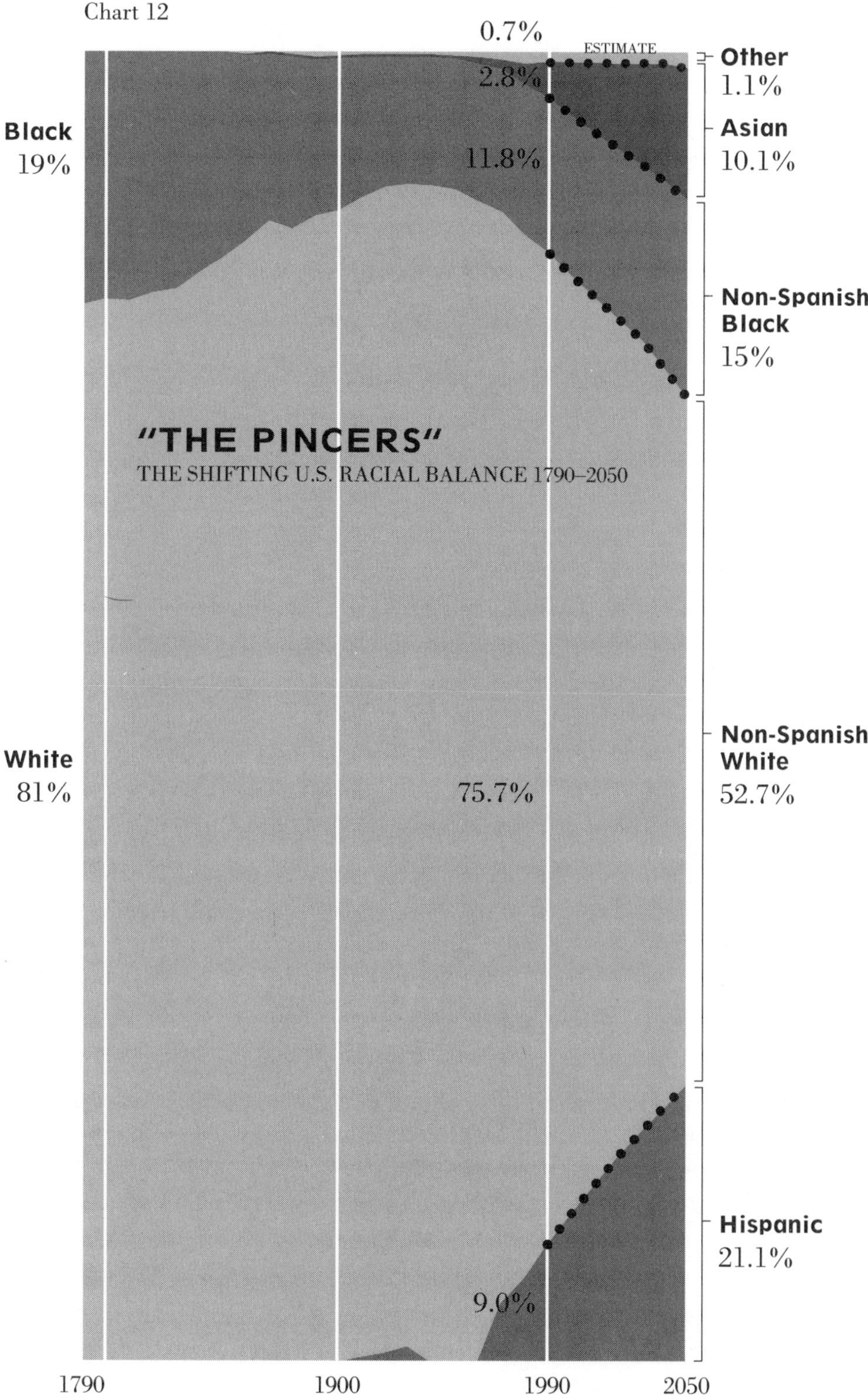

"THE PINCERS"
THE SHIFTING U.S. RACIAL BALANCE 1790–2050
ESTIMATE
0.7%
2.8%
11.8%
75.7%
9.0%
Black
19%
White
81%
Other
1.1%
Asian
10.1%
Non-Spanish Black
15%
Non-Spanish White
52.7%
Hispanic
21.1%
1790
1900
1990
2050

My little son Alexander will be fifty-nine.

I won't be here, of course. And (I'm sorry to say) neither will most of you reading of this page. Still, we probably stand a chance of making it to 2020. In that year, the Census Bureau projects that just less than 64 percent of Americans will be white. And among children under fifteen, whites will be on the point of becoming a minority.

(The Bureau of the Census is apparently afraid to estimate the fateful day when American whites actually cease to be a majority. Leon Bouvier thinks it will have occurred by 2060. Alexander will be sixty-nine.)

Let's pause now for a word from the Senate sponsor of the 1965 immigration bill, Philip Hart (D.-Michigan), speaking in that year to denounce critics of his legislation:

> [T]he notion was created that 190 million [the population of the American nation of 1965] is going to be swallowed up. None of us would want that, the bill does not seek to do it and the bill would not do it.[2]

Ah yes. And, lest we forget, the president of the United States, Lyndon B. Johnson, signing the bill into law in a ceremony at the foot of the Statue of Liberty on October 3, 1965:

> This is not a revolutionary bill. It does not affect the lives of millions. It will not reshape the structure of our daily lives or add importantly to our wealth and power.[3]

(He was right about the wealth and power at least. See Chapters 7 and 8!)

A white minority is not the only aspect of the ethnic revolution visible in the Pincer Chart. The chart also shows that, just recently, the United States suddenly ceased to be what it had been throughout its history: a biracial society.

Blacks are now outnumbered by the other minorities in total for the first time ever—the 1990 census reported . . . to almost total media silence. The Census Bureau now projects that *blacks will be displaced by Hispanics as the largest single minority sometime in the second decade of the next century.*

Black political leaders, such as the Reverend Jesse Jackson, seem to think that all minorities are allies and potential recruits to the "Rainbow Coalition." But, as usual with immigration, ordinary blacks take a much dimmer view. Enormous majorities of blacks tell pollsters that immigration is a problem and that Border Patrol funding should be increased.[4] They quite reasonably worry that the new minorities are rivals out-competing them and muscling in on programs, such as affirmative action, that were originally designed to help blacks alone.

Either view may be right. Or, possibly, both.

But blacks' loss of majority-minority status will be critical. Throughout their history, Americans have worried about the long-established, complex and difficult relationship between whites and blacks. It has been the focus of enormous national concern. But now, suddenly, there are new minorities, each with their own grievances and attitudes—*quite possibly including a lack of guilt about, and even hostility toward, blacks.*

Political life is much more demanding. Americans have so much more to worry about.

And that means that the black-white relationship is inevitably going to lose its exclusive claim on national attention.

DEEP-DENYING THE PINCERS

If you mention this impending ethnic revolution to some Americans, you can get really hostile reactions. Quite common are:

- *"I don't believe it."* Well, go argue with the Bureau of the Census.

Of course, it is true that the Census Bureau has had to make some fairly daring assumptions in developing its projections. Indeed, following standard operating procedure for demographers, the Bureau has issued a "Lowest Series" of projections using lower assumptions. In that scenario, American whites will be 57 percent of the population in 2050. Big deal. And the Bureau also has a "Highest Series," using higher assumptions. That has American whites at 51 percent in 2050. The Bureau thinks the "Middle Series" projections used in the Pincer Chart are the most likely. In the recent past, the Bureau has proved too cautious.

- *"I think that really oversimplifies things."* Maybe. Maybe not. And, after all, the Pincer Chart is extraordinarily dramatic—it could oversimplify a great deal and still leave a pretty shocking underlying reality.

But see my effort at good liberal self-doubt in Chapter 15, below.

- *"I think it's all happened before. Look at us and the Indians!"* Many Americans have only a hazy notion even of immigration mythology. They often assume that America's historic immigration has been larger, more diverse and, above all, much less interspersed with pauses for digestion than it actually was. And, surprisingly often, they start telling you about the Indians.

They're wrong, of course. The whites tended to try acquiring land by treaty with the Indian tribes, rather than just infiltrating. Remember Manhattan Island, bought by the Dutch for sixty guilders (twenty-four dollars) in 1626—a sum that, if the Manhattan tribe had invested it at a 7 percent interest rate, would have by now compounded to over $1.5 trillion, over a quarter of total American output.

But suppose these Americans were right about the Indians. Well, go ahead—just look at what happened to them.

- *"So what? Why do you care so much about race?"* Ah yes. Ahem. The most common, and the most dangerous, reaction. You have to be careful with this one.

I've already given one reason. Because of affirmative action quotas, it absolutely matters to me as the father of a white male how large the "protected classes" are going to be. And that is basically determined by immigration. But there are other reasons. See Chapter 6, below.

Now let's examine the Census Bureau's projections, as expressed in the Pincer Chart, more closely.

To get a sense of perspective, we have to go back to the beginning. And in the beginning, the American nation was white.

That sounds shocking because blacks were almost a fifth (19.3 percent) of the total population within the borders of the original Thirteen Colonies. But almost all these blacks were slaves. They had no say in public affairs. They were excluded from what I have called *the political nation*—aka "the racial hegemony of white Americans" . . . aka "America." And the first federal naturalization law in 1790 was absolutely explicit about this: applicants for citizenship had to be "free white persons."

After 1790, both black and white racial groups grew rapidly through natural increase. But the whites were also reinforced by immigration. By the early twentieth century, the white proportion of the U.S. population had reached almost nine tenths of the total. And it stayed that way for nearly fifty years. The 1940 Census reported the record: 89.8 percent of America was white. The 1950 Census found almost exactly the same: 89.5 percent.

The blacks were now beginning to be integrated into the political nation. But now they were a rather smaller factor. Fundamentally, America remained a white society, which was slowly, painfully, trying to come to terms with a black minority.

This stability was shattered by the 1965 Immigration Act. And the gradual trend of the previous century was abruptly reversed. Indeed, much more than reversed.

In the Census year of 1960, the U.S. population was 88.6 percent white. In 1990, it was only 75.6 percent white. Thus in 1960, 170 years after the first Census, the white proportion of the population had risen 8 percentage points. Now, in just thirty years, it had fallen 13 percentage points. And it was still falling—fast.

(Actually, the American official hang-up about race questions is making the "white" category increasingly problematic. Thus the proportion of "European Americans" in 1990 was arguably already a couple of percentage points lower than the Census figure because the Census Bureau counts all Middle Easterners and North Africans as "white." On the other hand, some in the "Hispanic" category are clearly of European stock—for example most, but not all, of the Cubans. In 1990, just less than half of all Hispanics told the trusting Census Bureau that they were white. Since four fifths originate in Mexico or Central America, where the populations are overwhelmingly mestizo, this seems exaggerated.)

The upper arm of the pincer in Chart 12 is partly made up of blacks. The black population of the United States is growing faster than the white population partly because its birthrate is higher. But not that much higher. Over the age of twenty-four or twenty-five, the birthrate for blacks and for whites is the same. Blacks with higher levels of education actually have fewer children than comparable whites.

In addition, however, for the first time since the slave trade ended, the black population is now being noticeably reinforced by immigration. One estimate is that about 5 percent of the black population in 1990 was contributed by immigrants and their American-born offspring since 1970. (For comparison, immigration since 1970 contributed only about 2.1 percent of the white population.)[5]

Another part of the pincer's upper arm is Asian. And this is almost entirely caused by recent immigration. One estimate: almost 70 percent of the Asian population in 1990 was contributed by immigrants since 1970 and their American-born offspring.[6]

The lower arm of the pincer is Hispanic. And again, this is largely the creation of immigration. One estimate: about 43 percent of the 1990 Hispanic population was contributed by immigrants since 1970 and their American-born children.[7]

White Americans, alone of all U.S. racial groups, are not expected to expand much. Their natural increase is below replacement. Their reinforcement by immigration is paltry. The Census Bureau expects the white population to stabilize at 210 million in about 2030.

THE FLINCH FROM THE PINCH

White Americans may be stabilizing their numbers, but not their neighborhoods. Nor is anyone else.

The 1990 Census made it clear that the pincer's tightening grip is already beginning to pinch. And Americans are flinching—they are polarizing geographically. "We are now seeing white flight from whole states and regions," says William H. Frey, a demographer and research scientist at the University of Michigan's Population Studies Center. He calls it "the flight from diversity."

The most dramatic case: California—which is being abandoned by lower-income whites in particular, exactly the group that would appear to be most vulnerable to competition from unskilled immigrants. Much of this white flight is flocking to the intermountain West, which seems likely to emerge as part of America's white heartland.

Less noticed, minorities are polarizing too. Asians move to California's Bay Area—they now make up 29.1 percent of San Francisco County—and to the Los Angeles megalopolis, even if they originally settled in other parts of the United States. Blacks are concentrating in big cities, like Washington, Atlanta and Dallas, where strong black middle classes have established themselves, often reversing the historic black migration from the South to the North and West. Hispanics occupy a great arc from California's Central Valley to Texas. All races are moving to Florida—but within that huge state, they settle quite different areas: Hispanics in the southeast; whites in the southwest and north; blacks in the urban areas.

Complicating this pattern, highly-educated whites continue to migrate into rapidly changing areas like Southern California. Here, ominously, a dual economy seems to be emerging, with a white and Asian upper class and a black and brown proletariat.[8] It may be convenient in the short run. But in the long run, it may well prove a sociological San Andreas Fault.

This is an astonishing contrast to the United States at the time of the Civil War. Then, most Northerners simply never saw a black. Naturally, they could not understand the fierce politics of the few states where blacks were present in large numbers—let alone an extreme example like South Carolina, where blacks were actually in the majority, albeit slaves. (Other minorities, of course, did not exist.)

Even when the American population was more homogeneous, Americans had difficulty understanding one another. "Sectionalism" has always been a factor in politics, with for example the Midwest and the Eastern Seaboard disagreeing about isolationism in the 1930s.

But it's going to get harder. The experience of an Anglo-Cuban society like Greater Miami is going to have little in common with an Anglo-black society like Atlanta or even with an Anglo-Mexican society like San Antonio. These will be communities as different

ALIEN NATION

America is polarizing—because of immigrant clustering and assortative migration of the native-born. If trends continue, areas with above-average minority populations will become much more so. Note that Asians are also above their national average (2.9%) in much of California, the New York area and elsewhere. Blacks in northern cities are often too concentrated to show well here. Whites overwhelmingly dominate the heartland—the "Wobegon Nation"? (Apologies to Garrison Keillor.)

U.S. IN 1900

Blacks sole minority before migration to cities of North and West

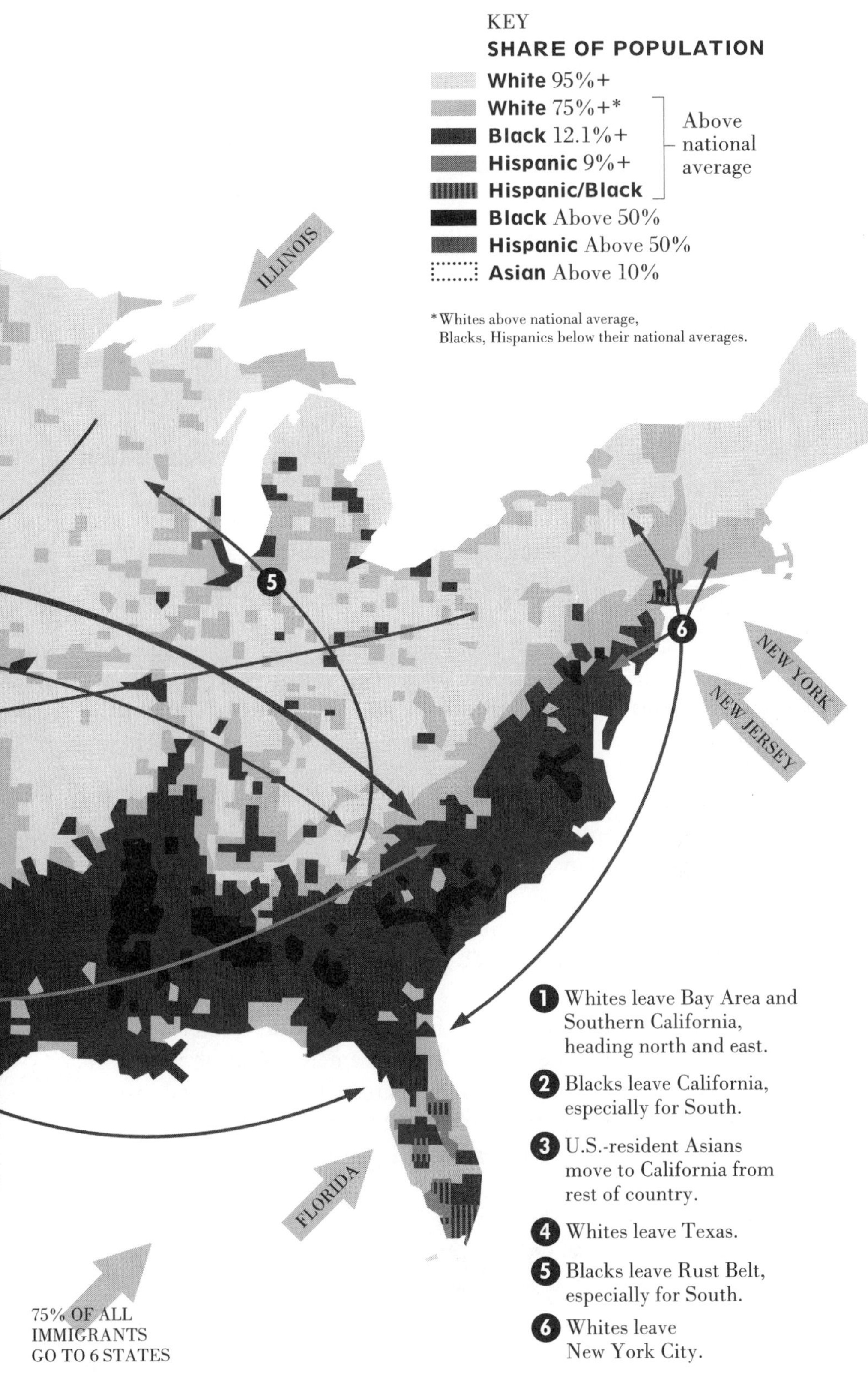
KEY
SHARE OF POPULATION
White 95%+
White 75%+*
Black 12.1%+
Hispanic 9%+
Hispanic/Black
Above national average
Black Above 50%
Hispanic Above 50%
Asian Above 10%
*Whites above national average, Blacks, Hispanics below their national averages.
ILLINOIS
NEW YORK
NEW JERSEY
FLORIDA
75% OF ALL IMMIGRANTS GO TO 6 STATES
1 Whites leave Bay Area and Southern California, heading north and east.
2 Blacks leave California, especially for South.
3 U.S.-resident Asians move to California from rest of country.
4 Whites leave Texas.
5 Blacks leave Rust Belt, especially for South.
6 Whites leave New York City.

from one another as any in the civilized world. They will verge on being separate nations.

And the existence of these different communities will raise the classic problem of federalism: why should any one of them submit in a larger political unit to the majority when it shares nothing with that majority? Particularly if the community is being visibly taxed for others' benefit.

All large political units will have difficulty containing these contradictions. This will begin locally (Staten Island trying to leave New York City), proceed to the state level (the northern counties trying to leave California) . . . and eventually could appear nationally (the Pacific Northwest going off with an independent British Columbia and Alberta?).

The demographer and economist B. Meredith Burke reports asking an official in the State Department's Bureau of Refugee Affairs what size of population he considered too much for California.

> "Oh, 100 million or so," he replied airily. "Look," he instructed me, "eventually it will get unpleasant enough so that everyone will move out and the situation will resolve itself. That's the free market solution."[9]

Maybe this is a free market solution. *But it's not a free market problem*—any more than it would be if the government decided to stop enforcing the law . . . or allow an invasion.

WHY THE PINCERS, ANYWAY?

In 1953, there were riots in East Berlin against the Soviet-imposed Communist regime. These riots were extremely embarrassing to the East German Communists. They claimed their dictatorship was justified in the name of the working class. Now that same working class was taking to the barricades, in classic revolutionary style, to oppose them.

According to left-wing playwright Bertolt Brecht, then recently returned to Berlin, the secretary of the Authors Union actually had leaflets distributed that said the people had forfeited the government's confidence and could win it back only by working harder. This struck even Brecht as a little much. Hence the bitterness of his famous joke in the poem cited at the head of this chapter—why didn't the government just dissolve the people and elect another one?

For good or ill, the U.S. political elite seems to be taking Brecht's suggestion seriously. As we have seen, the United States is now in the grip of an ethnic revolution. That grip is strengthening inexorably because of immigration. That immigration was caused by the 1965 Immigration Act. And that 1965 Immigration Act was the creation of politicians—some of whom are still in office.

Just as Brecht suggested, the American nation as it had evolved by 1965 is being dissolved by public policy—by the U.S. government.

In the next chapter, we will see how the pincers of this ethnic revolution got their grip.

4

HOW DID IT HAPPEN?

What all the wise men promised has not happened, and what all the damned fools said would happen has come to pass.

—**LORD MELBOURNE,**

the great liberal aristocrat, Whig party leader and reforming prime minister of Britain in the 1830s, commenting on the results of one such reform

How did it happen?

Even now, many Americans still simply do not realize what is causing this ethnic revolution that is transforming their country. They tend to assume that some kind of natural phenomenon is at work—that Hispanics, for example, went from 2.6 percent[1] of the U.S. population in 1950 to 9 percent in 1990 because they somehow started sprouting out of the earth like spring corn.

Americans tend to assume this partly because they are, in fact, regularly told that a natural phenomenon is indeed at work. The standard American media treatment of demographic and multicultural issues simply slides right over the role of immigration.

Thus *Time* magazine proclaimed happily in its April 9, 1990, cover story (*"What Will the U.S. Be Like When Whites Are No Longer the Majority?"*) that

> the "browning of America" will alter everything in society, from politics and education to industry, values and culture . . .

and that, of course, "it is *irreversibly* the America to come" (my emphasis).

Buried in eight pages of text was this one weasel phrase: *"If current trends in immigration and birthrates persist . . ."* Even here, the reference to birthrates is misleading, because it includes births to recent immigrants. Six sevenths of the Hispanic population, and five sixths of the Asian population, is due to immigration since 1900, most of it since 1970.[2]

No natural phenomenon is at work. And the point cannot be emphasized too strongly:

- **The current wave of immigration—and therefore America's shifting ethnic balance—is wholly and entirely the result of government policy.** Specifically, it is the result of the Immigration Act of 1965, and the further legislation of 1986 and 1990.

  The three fundamental questions of immigration policy are how many get admitted? who? and how is this enforced? All are uniquely within the power of American government officials. Even if they prefer to let these questions be decided, as often at present, by default.
- **Put it this way: American immigration policy may be made by commission. Or it may be made by omission. But it is still made in America, by American politicians.**
- **In other words: it's their fault.**

It was a change in public policy that opened U.S. scuttles to the Third World inflow after 1965. A further change in public policy could shut them. Public policy could even—we're talking *strictly* theoretically, of course—reopen the scuttles on the European side and start to shift the ethnic balance back.

Or public policy could go in some quite new direction. It is quite common to hear conservatives (who have a romantic streak) say: *"Asian immigration will be the salvation of America."* Maybe. But, in that case, why not have more Asians and fewer Hispanics?

THE DECEPTIVE REVOLUTION OF 1965

U.S. immigration policy was not transformed in 1965 without debate. There was a debate. It just bore no relationship to what subsequently happened.

Staunch defenders of the national-origins quota system, such as the American Legion and the American Coalition of Patriotic Societies, allowed themselves to be persuaded by advocates of the new legislation that it really enacted a sort of worldwide quota. This was because the 1965 Act was to include for the first time a "ceiling" of 120,000 on immigration from the Western Hemisphere—including all of Latin America. (The 1921–24 restrictionist legislation had placed no specific ceiling on immigrants from the Western Hemisphere. But as a practical matter the other requirements, usually including a job offer, had held down their numbers.)

This new worldwide quota, its advocates maintained, would no longer be skewed toward northern and western Europe. In the era of Civil Rights legislation, that policy was too embarrassingly easy to caricature as "racist." But the new policy would still restrict overall immigration to around (or *slightly* above) the then current level, which was averaging 250,000 to 300,000 a year.

A detailed account of Congress's deluded intent and the dramatic consequences appears in Lawrence Auster's devastating *The Path to National Suicide: An Essay on Immigration and Multiculturalism,*[3] perhaps the most remarkable literary product of the Restrictionist underground, a work which I think will one day be seen as a political pamphlet to rank with Tom Paine's *Common Sense.*

Today, it is astonishing to read in Auster's account the categorical assurances given by the 1965 Immigration Act's supporters. "*What the bill will not do,*" summarized its floor manager, Immigration Subcommittee chairman Senator Edward Kennedy (D.-Massachusetts):

> First, our cities will not be flooded with a million immigrants annually. *Under the proposed bill, the present level of immigration remains substantially the same. . . . Secondly, the ethnic mix of this country will not be upset. . . .* Contrary to the charges in some quarters, [the bill] will not inundate America with immigrants from any one country or

> area, or the most populated and deprived nations of Africa and Asia. . . . In the final analysis, *the ethnic pattern of immigration under the proposed measure is not expected to change as sharply as the critics seem to think.* [Emphases, needless to say, added by me.]

Kennedy also went on to denounce those "critics" of his bill in the terms that all students of the American immigration debate have come to know and love:

> The charges I have mentioned are highly emotional, irrational and with little foundation in fact. They are out of line with the obligations of responsible citizenship. They breed hate of our heritage . . .

Every one of Senator Kennedy's assurances has proven false. Immigration levels *did* surge upward. They *are* now running at around a million a year, not counting illegals. Immigrants *do* come predominantly from one area—some 85 percent of the 16.7 million legal immigrants arriving in the United States between 1968 and 1993 came from the Third World: 47 percent from Latin America and the Caribbean; 34 percent from Asia. (What's more, nearly half of all the 1968–93 immigration came from Spanish-speaking countries, dramatically contrasting with the First, polyglot Great Wave and enough to establish for the first time the possibility of permanent "bilingual"—more accurately, Spanish-language—enclaves in the United States.) Also, immigrants *did* come disproportionately from one country—20 percent from Mexico. (Indeed, 74 percent of the legal immigrants came from just 15 of the 191 sovereign countries in the world, and not even the largest of them. See Appendix 2, page 285.) And as we have seen, immigration from Africa (about 2 percent of the post-1968 total) has reappeared for the first time since the abolition of the Slave Trade.

Finally, and above all, the ethnic pattern of immigration to the United States *did* change sharply. In fact, it could hardly have changed more sharply. And the ethnic mix of the country *has,* of course, been upset.

Emotional, huh? Irrational? Little foundation in fact?

It would be wrong to blame Edward Kennedy . . . exclusively. Others of the bill's major supporters gave even more sweeping promises about how it would work.

Indeed, my own personal favorite fact-founded piece of unemotional rationality came from the senator from Massachusetts's brother, the senator from New York. Robert Kennedy, who until the previous year had been attorney general with the full resources of the U.S. government behind him, gave this confident assessment of future Asian immigration under the proposed act:

> It would be approximately 5,000, Mr. Chairman, after which immigration from that source would virtually disappear; 5,000 would come in the first year, but we do not expect that there would be any great influx after that.

Total Asian immigration between 1968, when the legislation went into effect, and 1993: 5,648,420.

Tragically, Robert Kennedy himself was to be assassinated by an immigrant counted by the INS as "Asian": Sirhan Sirhan, born in Jerusalem, who entered the United States from Jordan under a special program for Palestinian refugees in 1956.[4]

Why were the 1965 Act's supporters all so wrong? The kindest answer must be staggering technical incompetence. They simply did not think through just how the immigration system that they had put together would really work.

HOW THE IMMIGRATION SYSTEM WORKS

Properly speaking, the United States does not have an immigration system. It has an immigration shambles.

This, of course, is an occupational hazard with democratic government. It's just the sort of thing that makes democracy so entertaining.

But the result in the case of American immigration policy is peculiarly complex, capricious, paradoxical and (yes!) irrational. In my experience, everyone exposed to the system loathes it, including those overwhelmed INS clerks and even the immigration lawyers who directly profit from its complexity.

Despite some subsequent tinkering, the basic elements of the system remain those of the 1965 Act.

They are (*with my running commentary*):

- *An overall ceiling, or worldwide quota, for immigration to the United States.* In the 1990 Immigration Act, this was set at around 700,000. *(But actually this ceiling, or quota, is illusory—legal immigration was running around 880,000, not even counting 150,000 new asylum applications, IRCA amnesties and so forth, as will be discussed below.)*
- *Every country treated equally.* All are entitled to contribute a maximum number of immigrants (recently 25,620) to the United States. *(Regardless of size—compare India with Monaco! Regardless of historic contribution to the American population—compare Britain, Ireland and Germany with Mexico, the Philippines or Dominica! Regardless of whether the country splits up, like Pakistan and Bangladesh, which promptly doubled their entitlement—again, putting U.S. immigration policy in foreign hands!)*

So this was the 1965 Act's first major change: abolition of the principle of preference for northern and western Europeans.

But remember that there are 191 independent countries in the world, up from some 120 in 1965. And 191 into 700,000 goes 3,664.9 times—far less than the 25,620 to which each country is supposedly entitled. If one country fills its quota, others can't.

Immigration, however, is something that builds momentum. Successful immigrants send word home that, hey, the water's fine, come on in. And their friends and neighbors do start to come—something demographers call an "immigration chain." So the first countries to get through the door after the 1965 Act have been able to keep filling their quotas. And, by filling the worldwide quota, they have been in effect able to shoulder the latecomers aside.

Which is what has happened to Europe. At first sight, the 1965 Immigration Act treated all countries equally. But its workings as they developed, choked off, as a practical matter, immigration from the historic homeland of America. De jure discrimination *in favor of* Europe (some southern and eastern Europeans were always able to come here, unlike Asians) had been replaced by de facto *discrimination against* Europe.

- *Within each country quota, the highest priority given to "family reunification."* The details get complicated, but U.S. citizens and Resident Aliens are variously allowed to import spouses, adult

> children with spouses and children, brothers and sisters with spouses and children . . . All get preference over immigrants with skills but no relatives. *(So there's a tendency over time for "family reunification" to crowd out skilled would-be immigrants from the same country, with the result that skill levels in each country's immigrant flow start to decline. And skilled workers from other countries, which might be already getting crowded out from the worldwide quota, have even more difficulty getting in to start their own "immigration chain" at all.)*

So this was the 1965 Act's second major reversal of the American policy established since the 1920s: downgrading of skill requirements in favor of "family reunification."

I put "family reunification" in inverted commas because, after all, the immigrant would achieve the truest reunification with all of his family if he returned home. Indeed, "family reunification" permits immigrants, after their arrival, to acquire and import foreign spouses, forming new families that never existed to be "disunited" in the first place.

For that matter, immigrant families are little more disunited geographically than many American families, with their adult children scattered from sea to shining sea . . . and even further. As an immigrant, I am endlessly fascinated by this phenomenon, and make a hobby of collecting spectacular examples. But these American families reunite electronically, and through vacation trips. They don't seem to feel the need to live in the same location.

The effect of the new "family reunification" policy was much more radical than appears at first sight. It does specify fairly close relatives (although not as close as other immigrant-receiving countries require). But after arriving, these close relatives can turn around and sponsor *their* close relatives. A "chain letter" effect begins, ultimately ramifying far beyond the original immigrant. And the close-knit "extended families" typical of the premodern societies of the Third World made this development even more certain.

Of course, if a country's quota has been filled, these family members do have to wait in line for slots to open up. In 1993, family-preference applicants made up 95 percent of the *3.4 million* individuals in line for U.S. immigration visas. Some country queues are astonishingly long. Applicants now receiving permission to enter the United States have waited in some cases for as long as sixteen years.[5]

Obviously, from these countries, no skilled would-be immigrant without family connections need apply.

But even immigrants who do apply with family connections have trouble, because of those country queues. Talking about immigration on David Newman's KXYT Detroit-area radio show, I once had the heart-rending experience of a call from an elderly European widow in great distress because she couldn't bring her sister, also widowed and her only family in the world, to America to live with her. How could this possibly be, when the borders plainly were out of control?

Ever since, I have regretted that I flinched from saying on air what I believe immigration lawyers say in private: *bring her in as a tourist and overstay, no one will do anything.* It's the Great American Immigration Paradox again—the law is enforced against those who obey the law.

- *No limits on immediate family of American citizens.* Outside each country quota, spouses, parents and minor children of *U.S. citizens* (as opposed to resident aliens) are admitted *without numerical restrictions.* And, of course, without any concern for their skills. *(Thus completely end-running any "worldwide quota.")*

This provision, in combination with the "family-reunification" provision within the quota, has proved devastating to the predictions of the 1965 Act's supporters. Not only do resident aliens receive extensive "family reunification" rights—remember how easy it is to get U.S. citizenship. After only five years, a resident alien can acquire all the additional rights of the native-born, including importing spouses, etc. Under its current immigration law, the United States is compelled to accept all of them.

- *No limits on "refugees" and "asylees."* Also outside any country quotas, refugees and asylum-seekers have been admitted in numbers determined each year in consultation between the president and Congress. Recently these numbers have been rising under various political pressures. In 1993, 119,482 refugees were approved for admission to the United States, and there were 150,386 applications for asylum from people already in the country. The backlog of asylum applications is mounting quickly: at the end of 1993, some 333,000 were pending *(which also completely end-runs any worldwide quota).*[6]

The truth is that the "refugee" and "asylee" categories have become just a special sort of expedited immigration program. *Thus more than 80 percent of refugees admitted have relatives already here*[7]—something that would hardly happen if they were selected at random from the dispossessed of the world.

Virtually all pretense that "refugees" are fleeing war or persecution was abandoned in 1989, when Senator Frank Lautenberg (D.-New Jersey) succeeded in passing legislation requiring that all Jews from the territory of the Soviet Union, plus members of two small Christian minorities, Ukrainian Catholics and Evangelical Protestants, should be presumed to be "refugees" for the purpose of admittance to the United States.

Remember, this was during *glasnost.* Moreover, the policy has continued *after* the collapse of Communism. But the Jews at least, whether persecuted or not, certainly had a place to go: Israel. Still, nearly 50,000 "refugees" from the former Soviet Union arrived in the United States in 1993, of whom 80 percent are thought to be Jewish. In 1994, when the Lautenberg Amendment was quietly extended for the third time, for another two years, some 55,000 ex-Soviet "refugees" were expected, probably almost half the "refugee" total.[8]

(Which is still not quite as good a deal as the Cuban lobby has engineered: the 1966 Cuban Adjustment Act, which effectively guarantees that *any* Cuban reaching the United States can obtain legal immigrant status within a year.)

Refugees and asylees are not merely *expedited* immigrants: they are also *subsidized* immigrants. Unlike ordinary immigrants, they are eligible for extensive federal aid as soon as they arrive.

- *Plus . . .* Then there's the IRCA amnesty of an estimated 3 million illegal immigrants who arrived prior to 1982 *(the ultimate end run of any worldwide quota).*

- *Plus, plus . . .* Then there's continued illegal immigration—adding up to perhaps another 4 million illegal immigrants settled in the country since IRCA's 1982 cutoff. *(Why not bet on another amnesty end run?)*

A final immigration end run, opened in the 1990 Act, illustrates how corrupt the debate has become:

- *The "diversity lottery."* An additional 40,000 to 50,000 visas were set aside for a group of countries deemed to have been underrepresented—squeezed out—of the 1965–90 stampede. The visas were to be allocated by *lottery—! (Thus totally passing up any chance to ensure that these immigrants met American needs.)*

By "diversity," of course, the politicians meant the exact opposite. In fact, they were trying to restore some European immigration, above all for relatives of Senator Kennedy's Massachusetts constituents. But, of course, they didn't want to admit this. However, several African countries are among those eligible for the lottery. Which has enabled Jerry Tinker, Senator Kennedy's veteran immigration aide, to justify the provision as follows: "Now an unemployed Nigerian can immigrate to the U.S. for work."

Sure. But it does help if the unemployed Nigerian is an Irish citizen. Some 40 percent of the lottery slots were reserved exclusively for them.

I had asked Tinker if Kennedy could reply in writing to questions about how he reconciled his stated goals in 1965 with the situation today. Tinker had agreed, but now reported that "Senator Kennedy has no time for a written response." Still, Tinker was kind enough to provide an answer to my curiosity as to whether the senator still thought immigration should conform to the demographic goals he had so stoutly endorsed in 1965:

"No. Many things have changed since then."

Sure.

"No one could have foreseen the consequences of the 1965 Act," Tinker argued. He claimed these consequences occurred because of a drop in immigration demand from Europe and an explosion of pent-up demand in Asia—largely due, he repeatedly insisted, to an *unexpected number of Korean GI brides and their relatives.*[9]

(Immigration experts laugh out loud when they hear this: even in 1990, Koreans made up only a tiny fraction—0.3 percent—of the U.S. population.[10] But Tinker's guileless answer is an interesting sign of just how unaccustomed the top immigration enthusiasts are to any critical questioning.)

THE VINDICATED CRITICS OF 1965

In fact, of course, people did foresee the consequences of the 1965 Immigration Act. And they pointed them out at the time—to Senator Kennedy, among others.

For example, the Senate's hearings on the 1965 legislation produced one unsung heroine: Myra C. Hacker of Upper Montclair, New Jersey, who testified as an opposition witness with what must now be seen as remarkable prescience. She represented the New Jersey Coalition, part of the American Coalition of Patriotic Societies that had been formed by John B. Trevor and others in support of restrictive legislation in the 1920s.

Mrs. Hacker attacked the bill's supporters for misleadingly focusing only on the slight increase in the overall quota. The truth, she said, was that the bill was certain to increase immigration substantially. This was because unused northern and western European quota slots were to be given to countries who would use them. She specifically drew attention to the nonquota provisions that would enable any worldwide quota to be end run. And she forecast that the bill would result in annual immigration of "a half million or more."

This number was half as much again as any supporter would admit to. But, as it turned out, she was wildly restrained.

"At the very least," Mrs. Hacker said, *"the hidden mathematics of the bill should be made clear."*[11]

DO EUROPEANS WANT TO EMIGRATE?

Jerry Tinker was probably just as wrong to claim that Europeans did not—and, he added, do not—want any longer to emigrate. This is a common allegation, and naturally there are fluctuations. But in fact the 1965 Immigration Act cut back a continuing flow from Europe.

The number of British immigrants, for example, had been running at 20,000 to 30,000 a year. It was immediately reduced by more than half and has never recovered. In 1991, it was about 13,000. (The damage done to the number of Canadian immigrants was even more dramatic. It had been running close to 40,000 a year; it fell to below a quarter of that number. In 1991, it was still only just over 10,000.)

The British reaction is instructive. Always exceptionally inclined to emigrate, they did not stop when their access to the United States was curtailed. They continued to leave Britain at a rate of 100,000 to 200,000 a year. What seems to have happened is that they, along with other Europeans, were simply diverted elsewhere—for example, between 1965 and 1991, some 540,000 British emigrated to Canada; a substantially larger number emigrated to Australia. All told, there are now estimated to be some 3 million British citizens living overseas.

Which illustrates an observation by University of California at San Diego economist George J. Borjas, in his 1990 study of immigration, *Friends or Strangers: The Impact of Immigrants on the U.S. Economy,* which in many ways is the recommended antidote to Julian Simon's *Economic Consequences of Immigration.* Borjas, himself a Cuban immigrant, made this point:

- **U.S. immigration policy does not exist in a vacuum. There is a worldwide market for immigrants—especially skilled immigrants.**[12]

For example, in recent years Canada and Australia together have been taking a total of about 400,000 a year—almost half as many as the United States. (Australia has recently cut back sharply; Canada is struggling to prevent its family-reunification flow from crowding out its preference for skilled immigrants.)

With its 1965 reform, the United States in effect reduced its competitive "offer" to European emigrants. Indeed, in many cases, it ceased to make an offer at all. So they went elsewhere. And they took their skills—which, as we shall see in Chapter 7, tend to be higher than those of Third World immigrants—with them.

"Borjas concludes we're losing the competitive race for skilled immigrants," Robert B. Reich, then with Harvard's John F. Kennedy School of Government and now President Clinton's Secretary of Labor, wrote in reviewing Borjas's book in *Washington Monthly* magazine.[13]

Moreover, all dogmatic assertions about future immigration patterns are dangerous. Witness the sudden influx of more than 100,000 illegal Irish immigrants in the late 1980s. This produced the political pressure which necessitated Kennedy's (and Tinker's) unprincipled lottery deal in the 1990 legislation.

In addition, there was the wholly unexpected unfreezing of a sea of potential immigrants in Eastern Europe in the early 1990s, as the long Communist winter came to an end.

Not that those Eastern Europeans can get into the United States even if they want to.

And this is a profound tragedy. For there is no more important foreign policy problem facing the United States than the stabilization of the lands comprising the former Soviet bloc, to ensure that no further dragons arise there to trouble the final years of this most troubled of centuries. And there could be no surer way of binding that region into the civilized world than allowing, for a period at least, the immigration to the United States of hundreds of thousands of its tormented (although, incidentally, highly skilled) populace.

They would be rescued from Eastern Europe's economic collapse. They would remit monies to their families back home, a form of foreign aid far more efficiently targeted than any government-to-government grant. They would provide some personal inoculation against the anti-American demagoguery into which the politics of these newly liberated societies might easily degenerate. And many of them would eventually return home—as large proportions of immigrant waves always do—with capital, skills and the vital experience of functioning in a free, capitalist society.

But today the United States simply does not have the flexibility to accept large numbers of Eastern Europeans. Such a change in policy would require legislation, which would never pass a Congress where immigration is entirely held hostage by ethnic and other lobbies. (After the passage of the 1990 Act, a particularly sordid spectacle, INS officials made a trivia game of marking sections of the legislation that had been designed for special interests. Result—"Top to bottom. Almost every single section," according to one INSer quoted in an eye-opening account by Knight Ridder Newspapers' Pete Carey and Steve Johnson.[14])

And anyway, the result of the post-1965 immigration binge is that ordinary Americans are heartily sick of immigration and want no more.

One of the great strengths of the United States has been carelessly, culpably, dissipated.

The moral of this story is one to which we will return time and again:

- **If the United States had a rational immigration policy, it could afford to make exceptions. Because it has an irrational immigration policy, it is forced into inflexibility.**

NON-DEFENDING THE UNDEFENDABLE

On close examination, many immigration enthusiasts turn out to be perfectly well aware that current policy is deeply flawed.

One interesting case is the prominent pundit Ben J. Wattenberg, a senior fellow at the American Enterprise Institute for Public Policy Research in Washington, D.C., and coauthor of the bestseller *The Real Majority.* Many people will know him for his nationally syndicated newspaper column and his PBS television series.

Wattenberg has the knack of thinking in resounding phrases. (Which is not always very helpful when you're dealing with a complex subject like immigration, as a matter of fact. But, being a journalist, I like it anyway.) Thus he has popularized the idea that the United States, drawing its population from every corner of the globe, can become what he calls "the first Universal Nation."

A former speechwriter for President Lyndon B. Johnson, Wattenberg is one of those lifelong moderate Democrats who became discontented with the liberal domination of their party in the 1970s and drifted into alliance with the Republicans. In the Reagan years this group began to be described as "neoconservatives." And Wattenberg's romantic vision of America's future has entranced quite a few of his newfound conservative friends.

But no one, liberal or conservative, seems to have noticed that in Wattenberg's book *The First Universal Nation,* he actually advocated an approach he christened "designer immigration." He wanted a policy radically reoriented toward skills rather than family reunification. He also wanted to keep out illegals more effectively and to end what he described as the "odd situation" whereby Europeans are effectively discriminated against.

Of course, he hastened to add, this would not cut back on Third World immigrants as such. Instead, the overall numbers of immigrants would be increased.[15]

(Partly this is because Wattenberg worries about the U.S. population. He thinks that it absolutely must keep growing if America is to remain the greatest world power. He's even written an evangelical book about it, called, resoundingly, *The Birth Dearth.* But I don't agree. I think quality is more important than quantity—a stable population would be just fine, so long as its skills keep improving.)

I contacted Wattenberg while writing my *National Review* cover story. He sent word he thought that the 1990 Act, which did increase immigration and add more skills slots but did nothing about the family-reunification flaw, was merely "a good solid half-step forward." And he added that he "still advocates designer immigration."

After my article was published, Wattenberg was nice enough to contribute to a symposium of responses that appeared in the *National Review* of February 1, 1993. And he made a further proposal that, in the prevailing political climate, was distinctly courageous.

The United States should reassert control over the immigration influx, Wattenberg told *National Review*'s readers, and allow in some more Europeans. Via more "designer immigration"—300,000 "Liberty Visas" for post-Communist Eastern Europe. In addition, however, Wattenberg quietly slipped in another general "designer immigration" requirement. On top of skills and education, he wrote, *"We would do well to add English-language proficiency."*

Wow! That would make a *big* difference (seriously). The Census Bureau reports that a remarkable 47 percent of the U.S. foreign-born population do not speak English "very well" or "at all." So emphasizing English proficiency would inevitably cut down immigration a lot. Particularly of Hispanics. Some 71 percent of foreign-born Mexicans report not speaking English "very well." Essentially all of them—96 percent—speak Spanish at home.[16] In addition, an English-language requirement would probably increase immigration from the developed countries of Europe (and possibly from former British colonies in Asia and Africa).

CONCLUSION: ARE WE BETTER OFF?

Part of the cultural diversity I bring to the United States from Britain is a certain (ahem) contempt for American debating technique. I can't help it. It's inbred.

American competitive debaters are given their topics in advance and earnestly learn all the arguments by heart. But British competitive debaters are told their topics, and which side they must take, only at the last moment. They are expected to succeed by quickness of wit and whatever facts they can dredge (or make) up.

As a result, British debaters attack each other's arguments—and each other—directly, in part because they have nothing much else to do. American debaters, however, tend to blunder up and down the stage, ignoring opposing arguments, brandishing their carefully crafted wooden swords at the audience like bad actors in quite different plays.

Needless to say, presidential debates are particularly painful for me. In 1980, I winced when Ronald Reagan flourished this pre-cut cardboard cutlass at the audience to remind them of the foreign and domestic record of President Jimmy Carter:

> Are you better off than you were four years ago? Is it easier for you to go and buy things in the stores than it was four years ago? Is there more or less unemployment in the country than there was four years ago? Is America as respected throughout the world as it was? Do you think that our security is as safe, that we're as strong as we were four years ago? . . . If you don't think that this course that we've been on for the last four years is what you would like to see us follow for the next four, then I could suggest another choice that you have.[17]

But it worked. Or something worked. (I find American methods generally do. My objections are purely to style, not substance.)

It helps to think about the 1965 Immigration Act and the resulting system in this context. Consider these two points:

- What if the 1965 Immigration Act had done what its supporters said it would do?

Immigration would have been held to (say) 350,000 a year. The U.S. population in 1990 would have been 239 million instead of 250 million. And according to the 1965 bill's advocates, the U.S. ethnic balance would not have been altered at all. That means the American population would still be where it was in 1960: almost 89 percent white (including most Hispanics, whom the 1960 Census did not break out separately but probably comprised less than 3 percent in total); almost 11 percent black; less than 1 percent Asian.

But then, you have to wonder if the 1965 bill's advocates could count.

- What if there had been *no immigration at all* after 1970?

According to the Urban Institute's Jeffrey Passel and Barry Edmonston, the American population in 1990 would have been an estimated 230 million—about 20 million lower than it actually was. Blacks and Hispanics, with birthrates higher than whites although converging, would have been 12 percent and 5 percent, respectively; Asians would have been 1 percent. And non-Hispanic whites would have been about 82 percent.[18] (The Urban Institute's estimate of non-Hispanic whites tends to be lower than that of the U.S. Census figure for various technical reasons.)

In the end, Americans have to ask themselves very specific questions about the immigration flood unleashed upon their country by the politicians in 1965:

- *Has the mass immigration triggered by the 1965 reform made me and my family better off? Has it made it easier or more difficult for us to work, to educate our children, to live our lives? Has it resulted in more or less congestion? pollution? racial tension? crime? Do I feel it has made America respected for its generosity—or despised for its gullibility? Are we stronger because immigration brought diversity? Or weaker because it brought divisiveness? Has the post-1965 immigration enabled us to achieve more—or nothing that we could not have managed on our own? What if the 1965 Act had worked as promised and there were fewer immigrants? Or if immigration had been stopped completely in 1965?*

Would America be a happier or unhappier place than it is today?

Well?

5

WHY DID IT HAPPEN?

The supreme function of statesmanship is to provide against preventable evils.

In seeking to do so, it encounters obstacles which are deeply rooted in human nature. One is that by the very order of things such evils are not demonstrable until they have occurred: at each stage in their outset there is room for doubt and for dispute whether they be real or imaginary. By the same token, they attract little attention in comparison with current troubles, which are both indisputable and pressing: whence the besetting temptation of all politics to concern itself with the immediate present at the expense of the future.

Above all, people are disposed to mistake predicting troubles for causing troubles and even for desiring troubles: "if only," they love to think, "if only people wouldn't talk about it, it probably wouldn't happen." Perhaps this habit goes back to the primitive belief that the word and the thing, the name and the object, are identical.

At all events, the discussion of future grave but, with effort now, avoidable evils is probably the most unpopular and at the same time the most necessary occupation for the politician.

Those who knowingly shirk it, deserve, and not infrequently receive, the curses of those who come after.

—**ENOCH POWELL,**
speech on immigration, Birmingham, England, April 20, 1968

Why? Why did it happen? Why did the 1965 Act's supporters get it so wrong?

And why didn't *you* know about this?

One obvious reason:

- *Because the 1965 Immigration Act was passed in such a deceptive way.* There was little public interest in the issue at the time. If anything, the legislation just seemed like a harmless tribute to President John F. Kennedy, who had published a book advocating immigration reform. The Act's supporters were able to evade all serious challenge to their claims. As a result, there was no general recognition of the policy's profound effect as it subsequently occurred.

Like a Chinese executioner's sword, the 1965 Immigration Act flashed through the American body politic so fast that nothing seemed to have been altered—until, after a pause, the country's head fell off.

Another, less obvious but intensely human reason that the immigration imbroglio has been allowed to fester so far:

- *Because of sheer intellectual inertia.* Very few people can absorb new realities after the age of twenty-one. And two generations of American political leaders—from those who passed the 1965 legislation to those in their fifties today—spent their formative years in one of the greatest lulls in the history of American immigration, the four decades between the 1920s and the 1960s.

It's worth remembering the amazing numbers (see Chart 1, pages 30–31). In 1933 only 23,068 immigrants entered the United States, the lowest figure for 102 years. Overall, there was probably a net loss. In the whole of the 1930s, only about 500,000 legal immigrants entered the country. (At that time, there was virtually no illegal immigration.) And only about a million entered in the 1940s—including World War II refugees.

By contrast, of course, the United States is currently accepting about 1 million immigrants, counting refugees and asylees, every year. And in the single year of 1990 alone, it accepted 1.8 million.

Naturally, we *should* be able to think things through in prospect. And certainly we should be able to recognize them in *retrospect.* But *actually,* we find it very difficult.

Which is why generals always refight the last war. And why politicians go on campaigning for the last cause (which in the case of an important section of today's U.S. political elite happens to be the Civil Rights movement of the 1960s—something else that seriously inhibits the developing immigration debate; see pages 102–104).

The implication of this time lag in political perception is very grave. It means that, before the issues raised by immigration can be confronted, an entirely new generation of politicians may have to come to power—which could easily be too late.

IGNORING THE FLOOD

But, even so, why are we not supposed to notice the impact of immigration *now*?

Because it's unmistakable: the American political elite—liberal, moderate and conservative—shows every sign of not wanting the subject raised at all.

The immigration scuttles were opened, apparently by accident, in 1965. Since then, opinion polls have consistently shown that most Americans want them shut again. Recently, they have been wanting them shut even more.

In 1993, a *Newsweek* poll showed that fully 60 percent of Americans thought immigration levels were bad for the country. A *Los Angeles Times* poll showed that 86 percent of Californians thought illegal immigration into their state was a "major" or "moderate" problem; 47 percent of them thought the same about legal immigration. An *Orlando Sentinel* call-in poll showed 95 percent of respondents endorsing a ban on all immigration for a few years. And *The New York Times* reported an Empire State Survey that showed a solid majority (51 percent) *of immigrants themselves* thought immigration was bad for the city. Their view was shared by 66 percent of native-born New Yorkers.[1]

Nothing surprising about those immigrant attitudes, incidentally. Immigrants, as Samuel Johnson said about the Irish, are a fair people: they rarely speak well of one another. (Look at me!) Immigrants know too much to share the immigration enthusiasts' romanticism.

Similarly, in 1992 the Latino National Political Survey found that the proportion of Mexican Americans and Puerto Ricans "agreeing or strongly agreeing" that "there are too many immigrants" was actually higher (75 percent and 79 percent) than the proportion of non-Hispanic whites (74 percent). Still more striking, this feeling was even more intense among Hispanics *who were not U.S. citizens,* i.e., were immigrants themselves. For example, among non-citizen Mexicans the proposition that there were too many immigrants was approved by an astounding 84 percent to 16 percent.[2]

- **In nine surveys taken since 1955, no more than 13 percent of Americans have ever said they wanted immigration increased; recently, the proportion has been as low as 4 percent.**[3]

But immigration was increased anyway. There could not be a sharper contrast between what America wanted and what it got.

However, the political elite's reaction has been unexpectedly perverse. It stands around idly, alternately ignoring the situation, denouncing anyone uncouth enough to mention it, or, most frequently, indulging in romantic retroactive rationalizations. *("The more the merrier!" "Diversity is strength!")*

One example: as a New Yorker (by adoption—but some 28 percent of New York City's population is now foreign-born), I naturally think *The New York Times* is the voice of God.

At the end of 1992, God summarized the developing immigration debate, including my own contribution, quite accurately:

> CALLS TO RESTRICT IMMIGRATION
> COME FROM MANY QUARTERS

And Deborah Sontag's story did note, in passing, that critics of immigration policy now included some environmentalists, civil rights advocates, Democratic legislators, and a former Democratic presidential candidate, Eugene McCarthy.

But the subhead was still "Rudeness Goes Public":

> Across the country, and particularly in California, Americans have felt freer to voice a rude inhospitality that at other times they might have considered racist or at least xenophobic. . . . Those who call for a freeze on immigration, however, saw the sour mood as a harbinger of a new conservatism ahead.[4]

Let's disregard pitiful conservative whimpering about Sontag's casual smearing of "conservatism" with racism, xenophobia, sourness, etc. In today's America, conservatives are a minority it's OK to oppress.

More important, however: note that *nowhere in this article was there any mention of*

1. the record levels of legal immigration in 1991–92
2. the record levels of *illegal* immigration
3. the record levels of asylum applications . . . even though it was at New York's John F. Kennedy International Airport that the scandal of fraudulent asylum applicants' overwhelming immigration controls had just broken

Immigration apparently just didn't exist as a factual issue in late 1992, in the view of *The New York Times*'s editors. And because it did not exist as a fact, any public concern about immigration must naturally be irrational. It had to be explained, and of course disparaged, in the vulgar psychoanalytic terms *("anxiety attacks . . . frustration")* that Sontag employed.

And the crowning piece of evidence that concern about immigration amounted to no more than an expression of "racist discomfort" was . . . me. Because I had noted in my *National Review* cover story that INS waiting rooms were "an underworld that is almost entirely colored."

I had. They are. I do it again on page 28. (Patrick J. Buchanan was also indicted by Sontag, for noting during his 1992 presidential campaign that white Americans could be in a minority by 2050. And that's true too—as we have seen. In fact, when they think they're safe, multiculturalists actually boast about it—look at Henry Cisneros on page 25 or Ada Deer on page 137.)

IMMIGRATION POLICY AND THE STRANGELOVE SYNDROME

This points to one reason the immigration debate has been so deeply flawed:

- *Because of the extraordinary difficulty American intellectuals and politicians have with any issue remotely connected with race*

Watching them struggle with this topic always reminds me of "Dr. Strangelove," one of the menagerie of characters played by Peter Sellers in the 1963 Stanley Kubrick comic movie *Dr. Strangelove; or, How I Learned to Stop Worrying and Love the Bomb.*

Remember? Strangelove was a German immigrant who advised the U.S. president on nuclear strategy. He would appear to be totally sane and rational, if rather creepy. And then suddenly, in the middle of conversation, his right arm would start to give the Nazi salute and he would start to rant. He would wrestle his arm down and get control of himself. But a few minutes later, it would happen again.

You have to be constantly on guard for a similar sort of explosive reflex when you talk to some Americans about these sensitive topics. They can converse calmly up to a point. Then, without warning, they snap. Their arms start to jerk and the ranting about "racism" begins.

These Americans would be deeply hurt by the comparison, of course. But it does convey the irrational character of this Strangelove Syndrome—and the extent to which it has paralyzed debate.

Take this *New York Times* piece, for example. What I said was a fact. And what Buchanan said was logical. But Deborah Sontag clearly took it for granted that our comments were so self-evidently scandalous that she had merely to report them to reduce her audience to quivering pools of shock and horror.

In this situation, facts and logic are no defense. We are dangerously close to a taboo—the point at which it is impossible to discuss race-related topics at all.

This would be funny if it were not tragic. Here, for example, is *The New York Times* in May 1993 describing a man wanted for raping, sodomizing and robbing two young women in the Chelsea area of Manhattan:

> The attacker is alleged to be between 25 and 30 years old, muscular and 5 feet ten inches to 6 feet tall. He is wearing a red long-sleeved sweatshirt, the police say.

And here is the *New York Post*'s description: "A muscular black man, 5–10 to 6-feet tall, wearing a red sweatshirt and dark pants."[5]

Journalists sometimes justify not reporting race on the grounds that *"What difference does it make?"*—as if making a difference was the test they apply to any other fact they report. In this case, however, there was (even in New York City) a chance that a truthful description could have helped the rapist to be recognized and captured. And prevented from raping again.

Well, *The New York Times* does bear on its masthead the famous slogan: "All the News That's Fit to Print." News about the race of criminals is definitely not fit to print—in the judgment of the *Times* and of all the American establishment media. And news about immigration is pretty suspect too.

All this "sensitivity" is a big change since 1965. At that time, the Immigration Act's supporters did not hesitate to discuss the American ethnic balance in fairly explicit terms.

What they said was totally wrong, of course. But they did not suggest that the subject itself was illegitimate—yet.

That has come later, by degrees. It's part of the intellectual shell game that is typical of the evolving U.S. immigration debate.

IMMIGRATION POLICY AS EMOTIONAL SPASM

Which brings us to another reason for the peculiar failings of the debate on the 1965 Act:

- *Because the 1965 Immigration Act was not a policy: it was a national emotional spasm.*

Both the Act itself, and the mass immigration it unleashed, have powerful symbolic and psychological associations for important groups of Americans. These profoundly affected the debate in 1965. And they continue to distort it.

Unlike many immigration enthusiasts, I don't think that psychoanalyzing the other side is the same as refuting it. You can run from a rational argument in that way easily enough. But you can't really hide. Ultimately, whatever the argument's sinister hidden motivation, you have to deal with it on a rational level.

Moreover, some of these psychological reflexes are honestly acquired and sincerely felt. They have to be accommodated in some manner.

But what if argument has ceased to be rational? If facts and logic no longer count? Obviously, in view of The Wedge (page 47) and The Pincers (page 63), most conventional immigration commentary is absurdly unrealistic. There is something unmistakably odd about the tenacity with which immigration enthusiasts have clung to the notion that immigration is not high by historical standards, and about the hysteria with which they respond to news of indisputable facts like the tilting U.S. ethnic balance. Under these circumstances, we have to worry about why this intellectual market so persistently refuses to clear—why opinions so stubbornly ignore facts.

This irrationality was already glaringly obvious back in 1965. Secretary of State Dean Rusk, testifying about the diplomatic problems allegedly caused by the national-origins system, admitted that Asians *"were not complaining about numbers but about the principle which they considered discriminatory."* (Indeed, it's clear from the national origins of immigrants as revealed by Chart 11 that, by the 1950s, immigration policy had been significantly relaxed.) Senator Sam Ervin, debunking the alleged need to reorient immigration policy toward family reunification rather than skills, noted that there were in total only five or six thousand outstanding cases of family separation and pointed out that *"we could cure any such injustice* [by special legislation] *without changing the status of all the countries of the earth."*[6]

But the bill's supporters would not listen. They were determined on their radical solution; the actual problems were secondary.

Occasionally, immigration enthusiasts will frankly tell you that they just can't handle the subject. One eminent case: Michael Kinsley, the liberal costar of CNN's *Crossfire* television shout show, opposite Pat Buchanan.

Writing *New Republic* magazine's celebrated "TRB" commentary column, Kinsley started to twitch at my *National Review* article. He described it as "suggesting that free market capitalism itself . . . may depend on the continued predominance of Anglo-Saxon stock." It didn't [*patient sigh!*], and anyway I was just quoting the Nobel laureate economist Milton Friedman. (See page 176.)

But then Kinsley got his Strangelove Syndrome under control and concluded:

> There are counterarguments to all these points, and others. And counter-counterarguments. No one can know the effect of future large-scale immigration on our country. It has always been beneficial in the past, but that's no guarantee it will be so in the future. The previous tenant of this column, the late Richard Strout, believed passionately that America's achievement of a liberal welfare state depended on levels of both affluence and social cohesion that were threatened by large-scale immigration.
>
> Immigration is a subject, I suspect, on which very few opinions are changed because of arguments or statistics. It's almost a matter of faith. Your views on immigration depend on your sense of what makes America America. For some it's endless open spaces. For some it's a demographic image frozen in time. For some that stuff on the Statue of Liberty still plucks a chord. All these visions of America have a large component of fantasy. But I know which fantasy I prefer.[7]

As I've said, I find people do change their opinions in response to argument about immigration. Putting that aside, however, Kinsley's column is a remarkably honest confession of intellectual and emotional bankruptcy. He admits that *no one knows what the effects of current immigration policy will be*—enough to make any normal person want to call a halt. And he makes it clear that, although he recognizes there are serious arguments against immigration, he just can't bring himself to think the issue through.

Just one question, though:

- *Why does he persist in attacking those of us who can?*

IMMIGRATION POLICY AS REVENGE

Another factor inhibiting the immigration debate:

- *Because the 1965 Immigration Act represented revenge for the humiliation inflicted on some of the groups that had been cut back in 1921–24,* and an affirmation of their status in American society.

By a pleasing coincidence, this was personified by the House sponsor of the 1965 Act, Representative Emanuel Celler (D.-New York). Celler was the only then current member of the House who had been in Congress when the quota system had been enacted in 1924. He had made his maiden speech opposing it. In 1965, speaking with emotion that still suffuses the transcript, he said:

> I am glad I am living today and have lived to see that my theories have been vindicated, that we are now to obliterate and nullify and cancel out this admonition [*sic—presumably* abomination] called the national theory [*sic—presumably* national origin theory] of immigration.

Celler also published in the *Congressional Record* a statement "designed to correct mistaken notions" about his bill. He claimed it would not let in "great numbers of immigrants from anywhere," including Africa and Asia. The effect of the bill on the U.S. population, he said, would be "quite insignificant."[8]

So much for Emanuel Celler.

It is very common to hear Americans who trace their ancestry back to the 1890–1920 First Great Wave Era citing this folk memory to shame each other out of doubts about the current immigration. For example, in the *New Republic* column quoted above, Michael Kinsley quipped pointedly that if the restrictionists had triumphed earlier, "it might have spared us [FAIR executive director] Dan Stein." Stein is Jewish, and his forebears came here in the early 1900s.

(An extreme form of this tactic is to invoke the Holocaust and blame American immigration restrictions for hampering the escape of Hitler's victims. Since restriction happened in the 1920s when Hitler was residing in jail and the Nazis were apparently eliminated as a political force, this is hardly reasonable. But it is also an impossible basis for immigration policy. There is no limit to the foreign tragedies that theoretically could have been avoided if their victims had been in the United States instead of wherever they happened to be.)

There are various responses to this appeal to ancestors. Lawrence Auster, author of *The Path to National Suicide,* always replies frankly that he thinks Americans had a right to preserve their nation regardless of the effect on his own family. Dan Stein has patented another answer.

While I was writing this book, *National Review* editor John O'Sullivan and I arranged a dinner in New York to introduce Ira Mehlman, FAIR's Director of Media Outreach, to Norman Podhoretz, the celebrated editor of *Commentary* magazine. Podhoretz, a neoconservative, is deeply committed to immigration. Eventually, he invoked their common forebears.

Mehlman, of course, spends all his time collecting arguments against immigration. He smiled the serene smile of one who knows his boxing glove is loaded with lead. Then he hit Podhoretz between the eyes with Stein's stunner:

- Saying you can't object to current immigration because your great-grandparents were immigrants in 1900 is just like saying that, because you were once a fetus, therefore you should be against abortion.

Norman Podhoretz is a heavyweight brawling champion in the toughest dinner-debate city in the world. You don't just knock him down. He clinched, and the exchange ended in an inconclusive flurry.

But he was shaken. Watching closely, I could see him thinking, hard.

IMMIGRATION POLICY AS CIVIL RIGHTS REFLEX

Another factor that explains the flawed immigration debate:

- *Because of the prolonged national trauma over Civil Rights legislation*—and the resulting generalized revulsion against anything thought to smack of "discrimination."

The Civil Rights Act was passed the year before the Immigration Act, in 1964. The related Voting Rights Act was passed in 1965. Both were the culmination of a long and bitter battle over the treatment of American blacks, which had been raging at least since the imposition of the "Jim Crow" segregation laws of the 1890s.

Eliminating the national-origins immigration quota system was part of that battle's aftermath—like shooting the wounded. (Or, in this case, since the national-origins system had no historical connection to segregation, a civilian bystander.)

The Civil Rights battle has left deep and permanent scars on America. It has imbued important sections of the political elite, and of public opinion, with a powerful conditioned reflex: that "discrimination" is the primary manifestation of evil in society, to be rooted out wherever it is detected.

(I'm not exaggerating about this. When Alexander was a few months old, Maggy took him to a mothers' meeting at Manhattan's 92nd Street YM-YWHA. The librarian gave a talk about children's books. She warned against books encouraging racism, sexism, . . . and *speciesism.* For example, if you read to your child about Little Red Riding Hood and the Big Bad Wolf, you must balance it with a book showing that wolves are loving, caring parents. Fortunately, Alexander is more interested in fire trucks.)

The national-origins quotas were just the beginning for the Civil Rights reflex. Eventually, a wide range of social questions, far removed from black-white relations, have come to be handled as problems of "discrimination."

Take Washington's decision to help the handicapped in the late 1980s. From an economist's standpoint, this is a welfare program, a subsidy. It could have been organized as a welfare program quite simply, by taxing money away from the public and spending it on this (or any other) worthy cause.

But, instead, helping the handicapped was converted to a Civil Rights issue. The handicapped have been invested with "rights"—of access, of employment. Landlords and employers have been required to observe these rights on pain of public and private litigation. Which is why you see all those wheelchair ramps that never get used. The motive may be noble. But it's very expensive. And (as a matter of fact) not particularly effective.

The difficulty is that not all social questions fit into this Civil Rights framework. Immigration is a classic example.

Firstly, it's unclear that foreigners have any right to immigrate to whatever country they want. And to compare any such "immigration right" to the civil rights of black American citizens surely risks trivializing the latter.

Secondly, immigration policy is *inherently discriminatory.* Some people are allowed in. Others are not. There is no way to avoid this. Not even removing all border controls would avoid it—that would discriminate, in effect, in favor of those in neighboring countries and against those whose journey would be longer and more expensive.

The only question is: *by what criteria do we discriminate?* But this question was acutely embarrassing for the antidiscrimination legislators who framed the 1965 Immigration Act. So, after abolishing the national-origins quotas, they gave no coherent answer. In fact, to the maximum extent possible, they avoided the question altogether, by making immigration itself a sort of "civil right"—extended to an accidentally selected, self-perpetuating group of foreigners: the relatives of citizens and resident aliens.

The result is the chaos that now constitutes U.S. immigration policy. And, needless to say, real discrimination against those foreigners not among the (accidentally selected, self-perpetuating) favored few.

The emotion that underlay this policy incoherence is quite easy to understand and, indeed, respect. For a significant number of American whites, the Civil Rights movement was a genuine crusade. It drew on two of the most powerful moral traditions shaping the modern world: the evangelicism of the descendants of the New England Puritans, and the messianism of the descendants of the Eastern European Jews. Its triumph remains fundamental to their sense of moral order. To the extent that the 1965 Immigration Act is seen as part of the Civil Rights triumph, it is above criticism—let alone reform.

But there is a terrible irony here. For it is at least arguable that the immigration unleashed by the 1965 Act has significantly worsened the plight of American blacks. And that plight, despite the Civil Rights triumph, has deteriorated sharply and shockingly. (See pages 173–75.)

IMMIGRATION POLICY AS "ALIENISM"

A further factor, uncharted but powerful, affecting the U.S. immigration debate:

- *Because, just as everyone has heard of "nativists" and their dislike of foreigners, so there are also "aliens" who dislike the natives, and the America that the natives built.* To these "aliens" (who are quite often not immigrants, but the disgruntled, "alienated" native-born) mass immigration offers potential reinforcement and support.

This fierce current swirling beneath America's bland multicultural surface was first charted and named in *National Review* by the columnist Joseph Sobran—himself of Ukrainian stock, and therefore fully entitled to complain about the 1921–24 Restriction if he felt like it. Sobran pointed out that contemporary American political language

> . . . abounds in words for the hostility of the native for the alien, the majority for the minority, the respectable for the marginal, white for black, Christian for Jew, and so forth. We have prejudice, bigotry, racism, anti-Semitism, nativism, xenophobia, bias, discrimination and so forth. But these words are themselves prejudicial: They sum up, one-sidedly, a vast range of sentiment and behavior without admitting reciprocal moral realities: the hostility of Jew for Christian, black for white, marginal for respectable, minority for majority, alien for native, abnormal for normal. . . .
>
> . . . If we can sum up the worst attitudes of one side in the term "Nativism," then we ought to have some such term as "Alienism" (with apologies to the psychiatric profession) to sum up those of the other.[9]

This concept of *alienism* is crucial to understanding American politics—and, indeed, American culture. Because the American immigration debate has been so one-sided, "alienists" are quite often startlingly open, or unguarded, about their agenda.

Here, for example, is Raoul Lowery Contreras writing in the Sacramento weekly paper *El Hispaño.* Contreras is angry about a syndicated column by George Will, raising questions about current immigration policy. Will had been nice enough to quote a point I made in my *National Review* cover story: *"The onus should not be on critics of current* [*immigration*] *policy to explain their motives. Instead, supporters of current policy must explain why they wish to transform the American nation as it had evolved by 1965."*

Obligingly, Contreras explains why:

> In their precious 1965, I was 24 years old and, though I was a veteran of six years service in the American armed forces and a life-long U.S. citizen, I could not vote in some Texas counties. Fellow Marines, black Marines, couldn't vote in at least ten states of the land of the brave and of the free.
>
> . . . In 1965, Black children were murdered by white males in many ways, in many places, in the South. Black male adults were beaten, killed and castrated in Mississippi, Alabama, Arkansas and other Southern states for the crime of having a black skin. . . . In 1965, though a veteran, college graduate and political professional, a bartender refused to serve me a drink in a Texas bar because, he said, "We don't serve foreigners."
>
> That was Brimelow's and Will's 1965 America. Unfortunately, it was my 1965 America also. *That's the America that needed to be transformed and that's exactly what's happening,* Brimelow, Will and Metzger notwithstanding.[10] [Italics added]

(Tom Metzger is the leader of the neo-Nazi White Aryan Resistance. In a 1990 case, he was held liable for civil damages on the theory that his views had inspired three of his followers to murder an Ethiopian immigrant. Contreras seems to have thrown him in to keep us company.)

This column would certainly cow most Americans. But, with an immigrant's insensitivity to national customs, I say: bunk! Even at the height of the Jim Crow Era, the United States was not Hitler's Third Reich. And by 1965, lynching had long been suppressed and the federal government was intervening massively throughout the South to prevent voting fraud.

However, the factual accuracy of Contreras's argument is not important here. What is important is his profound alienation from America—and his conscious support of immigration as a way of striking back.

Let me emphasize: given his emotional attitudes, Contreras's policy prescription is entirely logical.

I just think that, when he urges his prescription on the American people, he should explain his motives to them.

IMMIGRATION POLICY AND THE SILENCE OF THE CONSERVATIVES

By this point, it's obvious why American liberals have been determinedly, even devoutly, incurious about immigration. As a foreigner, you quickly learn never to raise with them anything that could remotely be connected with race or ethnicity.

But the silence of the American conservatives—broken only by strong characters like *Washington Times* columnist Samuel Francis and *Chronicles* magazine editor Thomas Fleming, in striking contrast to the aggressive Americanism of Republicans from Henry Cabot Lodge to Theodore Roosevelt last time around—has a more complex cause.

In his first volume of autobiography, *Making It,* Norman Podhoretz describes the "brutal bargain" by which he says the children of Eastern European Jews were accepted into WASP society at the price of repressing their ethnic *mores.*[11] Similarly, the American conservative movement has reached what might be called a "bland bargain" with the liberal establishment that has been so powerful in the United States since the New Deal of the 1930s.

Conservatives are now somewhat more likely to be allowed into public debate than in the dark years of the 1950s. But they still must not say anything that impinges upon the truly sacred liberal taboos—above all, of course, anything that might be remotely connected with ethnicity or race. And immigration is inextricably so connected.

Slaves naturally try to curry favor with their masters. Some conservatives, fixated on the issue of economic growth, have apparently calculated that, by emphasizing the (assumed) need for more immigration, they can establish their nonracist credentials and possibly even advance their limited agenda with the liberal elite.

Other slaves can grow to love their chains. These are conservatives who have internalized the prohibitions under which they must operate. An example, alas, seems to be Paul Gigot, the *Wall Street Journal* editorial page's very readable Washington columnist. Writing about the question, which became an issue early in the 1992 presidential election cycle, of whether a million Englishmen or a million Zulus would assimilate more easily into Virginia, Gigot expressed good inside-the-Beltway distaste. Then he added an economic-growth twist: *"The Zulus . . . would probably work harder than the English."*[12]

This comment reveals an utter innocence about the reality of ethnic and cultural differences, let alone about little things like tradition and history—in short, the greater part of what would normally be regarded as the conservative vision.

Even in its own purblind terms, it is totally false. All the empirical evidence is that immigrants from developed countries assimilate to the American economy better than those from underdeveloped countries. As George Borjas puts it

> . . . the per capita GNP in the United Kingdom is more than six times greater than the Dominican Republic. It is not surprising that immigrant households originating in the Dominican Republic are about five times more likely to be on welfare than those in the United Kingdom.[13]

But it should not be necessary to explain that the legacy of Chaka, founder of the Zulu Empire, who among other exploits killed all his concubines' children, sometimes with his own hands, massacred some seven thousand of his own subjects to mark his mother's death, sliced open a hundred pregnant women to satisfy a fleeting interest in embryology, and ordered executions at whim daily until his assassination in 1828[14]—about the time de Tocqueville was getting ready to visit the United States to research *Democracy in America*—is not that of Alfred the Great, let alone that of Elizabeth II or any civilized society.

Let's spell it out with an anecdote. A year or so ago, the South African police was perplexed by an epidemic of murders on the black commuter trains from Johannesburg. Naturally, Nelson Mandela's African National Congress blamed the white government. But the victims were from all factions. Now it has emerged that the black operators of the semilegal private cab services competing with the railroad had paid gangs of those hardworking Zulus to influence consumer preferences by going on board and throwing passengers from the moving trains.

IMMIGRATION POLICY AS PSYCHOTHERAPY

A final, highly personal reason that U.S. immigration debate is blocked:

- **because much commentary about immigration is quite clearly the projection of personal values, fears, phobias and fantasies.**

This is something, of course, that is regularly taken for granted about immigration critics—see Deborah Sontag, page 95, above. But it is less often applied to immigration enthusiasts. Yet, as we have seen, immigration critics have in fact been right and enthusiasts wrong.

An example of the phenomenon, freely admitted except for the part about being wrong, is the leader of the immigration enthusiasts (economists' division): Julian Simon himself. Simon has dominated the immigration debate so much, and in such a personal way, that it's worth examining his statements on the subject carefully.

In *The Economic Consequences of Immigration,* Simon makes an admirable effort to be honest about his underlying emotions:

> Perhaps a few words about my tastes are appropriate. I delight in looking at the variety of faces I see on the subway when I visit New York; . . . [telling innocent schoolgirls visiting from Ireland] about the Irish in New York—and about other groups too—I get tears in my eyes, as again I do now in recalling the incident.[15]

This is obviously somewhat different from my own reaction to the New York subway, although presumably we are both studying those faces to see if their owners plan to mug us—the interest that unites subway-riding New Yorkers of all races.

However, although Simon presents his preference as a matter of personal "taste"—different strokes for different *volks*?—in debate he is notoriously quick with accusations of "racism" if anyone dares mention America's shifting ethnic balance. Talking in 1990 to Jim Cook of *Forbes* magazine, Simon was flatly dogmatic:

> The notion of wanting to keep out immigrants in order to keep our institutions and our values is pure prejudice.[16]

The intensity of this reaction goes beyond "taste" and into the realm of psychology.

When I reread this *Forbes* interview in mid-1993, I was quite surprised. I had just had dinner with Simon near his home in suburban Washington. "Why do you worry about immigration?" he had said thoughtfully, fixing me with a psychoanalytical eye. "I think it's like wanting your children to look like you," he answered himself helpfully. "Which is OK," he added kindly. "It's just a matter of value judgments."

I wasn't sure I agreed with this dissection of me. But when I reread that interview, I certainly wanted to know if my suspected value judgment was, in fact, OK or not, should I wish to confess to it.

So I called Simon up and asked him about his *Forbes* fulmination.

"Oh," he said without batting an eye, "I was probably too harsh."

Simon is the sort of engagingly frank fellow who will tell you what he thinks about sex before you've reached the main course of your first dinner together. (He's in favor.) Accordingly, his remarkable explicitness about the relationship between his work and his underlying emotions should be no surprise. But it appears to have stunned his academic peers into silence: they never mention it.

For example, in his widely praised 1981 book on population, *The Ultimate Resource,* Simon wrote:

> When I began my population studies, I was in the midst of a depression of unusual duration. . . . As I studied the economics of population and worked my way to the views I now hold—that population growth, along with the lengthening of human life, is a moral and material triumph—my outlook for myself, for my family, and for the future of humanity became more optimistic. Eventually, I was able to pull myself out of my depression. This is only part of the story, but there is at least some connection between the two sets of mental events—my population studies and my increasing optimism.[17]

In his riveting 1993 book, *Good Mood: The New Psychology of Overcoming Depression,* Simon—who majored in psychology at Harvard before taking his Ph.D. in business economics at the University of Chicago—offers a step-by-step course in self-therapy, with extensive reference to his own experience.

He was severely depressed, he writes, for thirteen years. He refrained from killing himself only because he believed his young family needed him. He traces this depression in part to the way his parents pressured him as a child. And (in a passage rending to a middle-aged new father's heart) he reports:

> When I was an infant, my parents put me into a large box-like structure hung outside a second floor window, well-checked by an architect friend for safety. In accord with the theory of the times, they taught me independence by refusing to accede to my cries when I sought attention and company.[18]

They did *what*? You begin to wonder if you really want to challenge Simon's ideas face-to-face—and not only because, at a famous cocktail party, he threw not one but *three* gin and tonics over a faculty colleague who had disparaged him at an Earth Day teach-in.[19]

It's safe, actually. He's charming. But there, in microcosm, is a considerable slice of America's inhibited immigration debate.

THE GRIDLOCKED IMMIGRATION DEBATE

For all these and other reasons, by the late 1980s American immigration debate was blocked by a sort of intellectual gridlock. The number of immigrants was building. Public disquiet was rising. But every major magazine and newspaper, and the leaderships of both political parties remained adamantly in favor of immigration. Even alarming new evidence was not being considered.

Such was the grip of the American elite's pro-immigration consensus, for example, that when George Borjas's book *Friends or Strangers* appeared in 1990, reviewers simply assumed Borjas must be pro-immigration too. They completely failed to pick up on what he described as his "worrisome" evidence that problems were developing with the post-1965 immigrant flow. Thus *Business Week*'s associate economics editor Michael J. Mandel reviewed both Borjas's and Simon's books under the drum-beating heading DOES AMERICA NEED MORE "HUDDLED MASSES"? YES.[20]

Possibly provoked by such total misreadings, Borjas in the following year spelled out his position in the preface to his paperback edition:

> . . . it is almost certain that during the 1990s *new immigrants will make up at least a third of all new labor market entrants.* In view of the available empirical evidence, there is *no economic rationale* to justify this huge increase in the size of the foreign-born population.[21] [Italics added!]

(He's right, incidentally. For more on the economic aspects of immigration, see Chapters 7 and 8.)

Even more significant, given his elevated position in the American media food chain, was this recent outburst from longtime *New York Times* editor A. M. Rosenthal. Like Julian Simon, Rosenthal harks back to his childhood:

> Almost always now, when I read about Haitians who risk the seas to get to this country but wind up behind barbed wire, I think of an illegal immigrant I happen to know myself, and of his daughters and his son.
>
> Then a shiver of shame and embarrassment goes through me . . .

The illegal immigrant was—guess!—Rosenthal's father. He came here from Russia via Canada.

> Many years later, when his children told the story of their father and his determination to find work in America, to hell with borders, people smiled in admiration of this man. And always, his children were filled with pride about him. . . . I know that if he had been born in Haiti or lived there, he would have broken every law that stood between him and work in the U.S.

In short, because one generation of Americans failed to catch an illegal immigrant, their children must accept more.

> Imagine what a quick pickup [a] lobby, or parade, demanding succor for the Haitians could do if it were headed by a few Irish-American Cardinals, a batch of rabbis and the presidents of Eastern European, Greek, Italian, Arab and Turkish organizations. American Blacks and Wasps welcome too! . . .
>
> . . . Even reluctantly recognizing some economic limitations, this country should have the moral elegance to accept neighbors who flee countries where life is terror and hunger, and are run by murderous gangs left over from dictatorships we ourselves maintained and cossetted.
>
> If that were a qualification for entry into our golden land, the Haitians should be welcomed with song, embrace and memories.[22]

(Be careful about those embraces, Mr. Rosenthal, sir. Some 3 percent of the Haitian refugees at Guantànamo tested HIV-positive.[23])

The search for an explanation for the paralysis of the American immigration debate need go no further than this raging psychodrama in the mind of the man who, as the longtime editor of *The New York Times,* substantially set the national media agenda.

Actually, Rosenthal is unfair to Jewish organizations. They have generally supported immigration. FAIR's Ira Mehlman looks depressed at the thought.

"They still think it's 1939," he says. "But even if we took all the Soviet Jews, and all the Israelis, that would still only be 6 million people."[24] As it is, FAIR expects 10 to 15 million immigrants in the 1990s.

CONCLUSION: DESERVING THE CURSES . . .

The reasons for America's flawed immigration debate are varied. Beyond any question, cowardice, corruption, and stupidity on the part of politicians and pundits play a major role. But so too does a sincere, if misplaced, moral sentiment—and an honest perplexity in the face of issues that are as difficult as any that have faced a free society. On a human level, the hesitations and evasions of the American elite are all too easy to understand.

But not to forgive. No one ever said it was easy to defend a great nation. And this applies as much to civilians as to soldiers.

In 1927, the French writer Julien Benda published a book condemning France's intellectuals for their fascination with politics rather than culture and art—*La Trahison des Clercs,* or "Treason of the Clerks," using "clerk" in its medieval sense to mean the educated classes.

This phrase exactly describes the behavior of America's elite as the disaster of the 1965 Immigration Act has become apparent. The evils that this policy has inflicted upon the country will still be felt in a hundred years, quite probably even more intensely with the passage of time. Yet they were always preventable. The American political elite could have prevented them. It failed in its supreme function, for reasons about which the best that could be said is that they were self-indulgent.

And this, in its own way, was a species of treason.

Needless to say, elite members aren't very enthusiastic about this criticism. They are still to be found denying that immigration has any negative consequences. Above all, they deny that immigration's transformation of America is a proper subject for discussion.

In Chapter 3, page 66, I identified this as the "So What?" reaction. We examine it in the next chapter.

6

SO WHAT?

Without fully realizing it, we have left the time when the nonwhite, non-Western part of our population could be expected to assimilate to the dominant majority. In the future, the white Western majority will have to do some assimilation of its own.

—**MARTHA FARNSWORTH RICHE,**
director of population studies, Population Reference Bureau, in *American Demographics,* October 1991; now director, Bureau of the Census, in the Clinton administration

One winter afternoon early in 1990, I attended a seminar for assorted journalists and what were just beginning to be called "policy wonks" at New York's Manhattan Institute to hear Julian Simon talk about his just-published book, *The Economic Consequences of Immigration.*

Simon and I hadn't met before. But, living in the little catacomb of free-market writers, we knew each other's work. He greeted me warmly, quizzed me about my rumored deviationism on immigration, and kindly inscribed my copy of his book:

FOR PETER,
WHO WRITES SO INTERESTINGLY AND SO WELL,
JULIAN
MARCH 14, 1990

How very nice! It made me feel quite guilty that it was just a free review copy I'd been sent by *National Review*.

Author seminars of this sort are extremely valuable in stimulating ideas—even in this case, where most members of the audience were (as usual) Simon groupies.

One, however, was emphatically not. The demographer Michael S. Teitelbaum, a program officer at the Alfred P. Sloan Foundation, put down a heavy barrage on Simon that I found enthralling. Much of it is reflected in Chapters 2 and 3. Among other points, Teitelbaum noted that Simon in his brief talk had neglected to mention the fact that current immigration *is* historically high—*compared to native-born Americans' birthrates.* (See pages 43–45.)

Being nasty to one another at point-blank range across a seminar table is apparently quite normal in the academic world, where both Teitelbaum and Simon have their roots. It just shocks sensitive journalists like me. Simon's response probably wasn't exceptional in form. But its content made it explosive.

Look, he said in effect, from an economic standpoint the only important issue is the overall *size* of the population. The relationship between immigration and native-born American birthrates doesn't tell you anything new. It only tells you about how immigration is going to change the *composition* of the population.

And why would the population's composition be important? Unless you care about . . . race?

"SO WHAT?" IN PERSPECTIVE

Race! *RACE!!* As an immigrant, I was fascinated, once again, to watch the mere threat of an accusation of racism send the native-born Americans scattering for cover like hightailing rabbits. Except for Teitelbaum. He bravely stood his ground, although I don't remember exactly what he said.

Similarly, as we saw in Chapter 3, an implicit accusation of racism is the common reaction of a vocal minority of Americans to news of their country's shifting ethnic balance: *"So what?"* And, given prevailing sensitivities, it is the most dangerous response to answer.

I say a vocal minority because I think the vast majority of Americans regard as just a matter of common sense that the composition of a country's population cannot, in fact, be changed without risking dramatic consequences. You can tell from the momentary perplexity that comes into their eyes when confronted with the "So What?" reflex.

But they lack the language to express their concerns. So they hesitate and fall silent. Time and again, the "So What?" reflex succeeds in effectively crippling all discussion of America's impending ethnic revolution in particular—and, indeed, of immigration in general.

This happens although there are some extraordinary aspects of the impending ethnic revolution that, by any standard, deserve discussion in a democracy:

- *It is unprecedented in history.* No sovereign state has ever undergone such a radical and rapid transformation. (See pages 124–33.)
- *It is wholly and entirely the result of government policy.* Immigration is causing both the shifting American ethnic balance and also the projected massive increase in overall population. Left to themselves, pre-1965 Americans would be stabilizing both their ethnic proportions and their overall numbers.

In other words: let's suppose that it would indeed be impolite to raise the question of ethnic balance—if a shift were occurring due to the unaided efforts of one's fellow Americans, resulting in different birthrates for different groups.

But how can it be impolite to mention it when the shift is due to the arrival of unprecedented numbers of foreigners—arbitrarily and accidentally selected by a government that specifically and repeatedly denied it was doing any such thing?

UNFAIR TO FAIR

Nevertheless, the "So What?" reflex is usually decisive. It is sufficiently powerful, for example, that Dan Stein's Federation for American Immigration Reform has deliberately steered away from any mention of ethnic balance in its arguments against immigration. FAIR concentrates very firmly on immigration's role in swelling U.S. population, and on the various ways in which it hurts native-born Americans, such as displacing them from jobs, consuming tax dollars and so on.

These arguments are perfectly reasonable. And they do reflect the concerns of FAIR's founders. FAIR was founded in 1979, primarily by representatives of the environmentalist and population movements. Sheer population size is a worry for them because it undeniably does put pressure on the ecology. (See pages 187–90.)

Needless to say, FAIR gets no particular credit for its restraint. One amusing example: look at Deborah Sontag's disparaging body language—no doubt quite unconscious—in her *New York Times* article from which I've already quoted:

> Mr. Stein is *usually careful* to base his fear about increasing immigration on arguments about scarce resources. He often *voices concern* about immigrants displacing black and Hispanic Americans from jobs. But others, Mr. Buchanan for example, *also* resent the "dilution" of their European heritage.[1] [Italics added—but insinuative paragraphing retained!]

REFOCUSING THE QUESTION

The "So What?" reflex is perhaps the most important example of the way in which the American immigration debate has stalled because everyone is looking at the wrong thing.

A key thesis of this book is that *immigration has consequences.* In Part 2, we will examine some of these consequences. A number of them do relate to sheer population size and the impact on native-born Americans. But others do require us to boldly go into the composition of the immigrant flow, for a variety of reasons, including economic.

However, the "So What?" reflex demands a more general response.

The entire question needs to be refocused as follows:

- **The onus should not be on critics of current immigration policy to explain their motives. Instead, supporters of current policy must explain why they wish to transform the American nation as it had evolved by 1965.**

In other words, the answer to the "So What?" reflex is "So why?"

Why does America have to be transformed? *What have you got against it?*

As we saw in Chapter 5, pages 105–7, there is a class of people in America who absolutely, positively (as it says in the Federal Express TV ads) do want to transform America. And they look to immigration to help them achieve this object. Their alienation from America as it currently exists is so powerful as to justify calling them "alienists"—the opposite of the much-denounced "nativists" whose attachment to America is so intense that they distrust anyone who might conceivably change it.

Alienists, therefore, do have answers to the question "So why?" One common alienist answer: *because American whites must be swamped by immigration to make it impossible for them to act on their racist impulses.*

Sound extreme? Listen to Earl Raab, of Brandeis University's Institute for Jewish Advocacy and columnist for the San Francisco *Jewish Bulletin.* Denouncing the Great Restriction of the 1920s, Raab wrote:

> It was only after World War II that immigration law was drastically changed to eliminate such discrimination. In one of the first pieces of evidence of its political coming-of-age, the Jewish community has a leadership role in effecting those changes.[2]

And calling for the German government to ban neo-Nazi groups, he noted happily that—

> The Census Bureau has just reported that about half of the American population will soon be non-white or non-European. And they will

> all be American citizens. We have tipped beyond the point where a Nazi-Aryan party will be able to prevail in this country.
>
> We have been nourishing the American climate of opposition to ethnic bigotry for about half a century. That climate has not yet been perfected, but the heterogeneous nature of our population tends to make it irreversible—and makes our constitutional constraints against bigotry more practical than ever.[3]

This is, of course, almost laughable in its apparent confirmation of anti-Semitic stereotypes. And it tends to make those prominent critics of U.S. immigration policy who are Jewish, some of whom we have already met, very angry indeed.

But it is an internally consistent answer to the question "So why?" In order to prevent it from discriminating against minorities, the historic American majority must be destroyed.

It's consistent, all right. However, as in the case of Raoul Lowery Contreras, I think it is an answer that should be clearly explained to the American majority, when they come to consider whether they should allow the current transformation of their country to continue.

ARE DIVERSE SOCIETIES LESS "BIGOTED"?

Actually, Earl Raab's argument is foolish even on its own terms. It is precisely in the most diverse societies that people are the most conscious of ethnicity and race. It was in the Austro-Hungarian Empire, where the Germans were a minority exposed to Slavs, Magyars and Jews from the shtetls of Galicia, that anti-Semitism first became a viable electoral force—and Adolf Hitler was born and spent his formative years.

Conversely, Norman Podhoretz, writing in his autobiography *Making It* about his years with the U.S. army in Germany, much of it spent with white Southerners, reports his "amazement" on discovering that a "hillbilly buddy" had simply never realized that he, Podhoretz, was Jewish.

This emerged one night outside a Frankfurt bar. Podhoretz was trying to explain why he had felt obliged to insist they both leave after he had got into a row (in German, which of course only Podhoretz understood) with a former Waffen SS man.

"He was both fascinated and shocked," Podhoretz says of his friend, "but it took him exactly one second to recover. 'Let's go back in there and kill the dirty kraut bastard,' he said."[4]

To this day, the counties of the Appalachian South are among the most ethnically homogeneous in the United States. They consist very largely of British-origin whites. Amazing though it must appear to a native New Yorker, it would be quite normal for people from such a background not to notice whether any individual is Jewish. Apart from anything else, why waste the effort? Nobody ever is.

Similarly, when I was at Stanford, a Chinese student once told me that she was always in trouble with her American roommate for being unable to describe the various hopeful males who came patrolling by their door.

"She asks, 'What color eyes? What color hair?' " my friend said. "But I don't notice—in China, why would we look?"

The mountain Southerners would, of course, notice if the individual was black (or Chinese). But, as it happens, there are relatively few blacks in the area.

Which in turn meant that black-white relationships were not quite the pressing problem they have been elsewhere in the South. The abolition of slavery was an issue that meant much less to the mountain counties. And, for precisely that reason, they were most inclined of all the South to support the Union side in the Civil War—in a great arc stretching from West Virginia, which actually seceded from Confederate Virginia, down to Winston County in northern Alabama, which declared itself "the Free State of Winston" and sent several companies of troops to fight, as Alabama units, in the Union army.[5]

Once again: ethnicity, and demography, is destiny in American politics. The homogeneous group can afford to be secure in its liberalism toward outsiders.

You can see the logic of ethnic politics in a diverse society easily enough. Ethnic identity is always the simplest way to organize support. This is particularly true when it reflects genuine cultural differences, which mean there are even more irritating points of friction to get angry about.

When supreme power in the society is in strong hands, these ethnic differences often remain quiescent. Greek and Turkish Cypriots fought relatively little when Britain ruled Cyprus, for example. The Armenians and Azerbaijanis put up with each other, more or less, when the Caucasus were under the Soviet Union.

Trouble began when these imperial umpires quit. Then each ethnic group saw a chance of grabbing power for itself—or a threat that its rivals might.

The United States, of course, is not part of a greater empire but is an independent country. Nevertheless, it faces the direct equivalent of being abandoned by an imperial umpire: *the breaking of what on page 58 we saw called "the racial hegemony of white Americans."*

As that white voting bloc is reduced in relative size, ever more intense incentive will be offered enterprising politicians of all ethnic groups, including, perhaps, the almost-majority whites, to whip their own supporters into line in order to marshal their vote. Supreme power in American politics will have come within grabbing range—no longer for any one bloc but for an unstable, jockeying combination of them.

This is the situation that Raab thinks will diminish "ethnic bigotry." Actually, of course, it will put a premium on it.

The point at which that "racial hegemony of white Americans" will be broken is not easy to estimate. (Although the Census Bureau has said flatly that whites will go below half of California's population as early as 2000.[6]) American politics have always been sectional. The uneven distribution of immigration will tend to force the country's regions ever further apart. (See map, pages 70–71.) Additionally, the American federal-election system is complicated. It can produce paradoxical results.

But foreign experience suggests that the breaking point could come well before whites slip below half of the overall U.S. population. In Canada, although the French-speaking minority has never been much above a quarter of the population, it has been able to dominate national politics for most of this century by voting as a bloc. English-speaking Canadians have been typically so split that federal governments based solely on their support have been elected very rarely, although they have comprised around three quarters of Canada's population.

To some extent, this sort of ethnic rotation has happened before, in many of America's cities. Arguably, it began with the Irish displacement of the Colonial-stock Yankees in New York and Boston, confirmed when the first Irish Catholic mayors were elected in 1881 and 1885 respectively.

But the ethnic differences the United States confronts now are exceptionally deep—perhaps unbridgeable. Here, too, previous American experience might be suggestive. No transfer of power at City Hall from one European immigrant group to another ever produced anything equivalent to the "white flight" that has followed the election of black mayors in cities like Detroit and Newark.

And now the prize is so much larger—the whole country. This time, moreover, there will be no suburban enclaves to which to flee.

All of which leads us to a follow-up question for immigration enthusiasts:

- *While explaining why they want to transform America, supporters of current immigration policy should also explain just exactly what makes them think multiracial societies work.*

WELL—*DO* MULTIRACIAL SOCIETIES WORK?

Over three years after I first met Julian Simon, I was having dinner with him to debate our differences. We got on to the question of whether multiethnic and multiracial societies can work.

"Yugoslavia . . . ," I began, thinking of the Serbo-Croatian-Bosnian war that had exploded into the headlines.

"Yes! Yugoslavia!" he interrupted gleefully. "That supports my case, doesn't it?"

I was so surprised that I felt my jaw drop—something that really happens, I find, and not just in cartoons. It took me several seconds to realize what he meant:

- The former Yugoslavs are fighting *despite* the fact that they are all the same race (white). Indeed, they are all members of the same

> general ethnic group (South Slav). Even the language spoken by the two major contestants (Serbs and Croats) is basically the same (although written, respectively, in Cyrillic and Roman script).

So—Simon is saying—you can't blame all civil conflict on the divisive results on nontraditional immigration. Homogeneity is no guarantee against strife.

All right, all right! For the record, let me admit (in fact, assert): you can't blame *everything* on immigration or on racial differences.

But who said you could? The fact remains that the Yugoslav spectacle can only be seen as chilling—and as a Horrid Warning about current U.S. immigration policy. The differences between the Yugoslavs are indeed relatively minor—certainly compared to the differences between the American nation of 1965 and the immigrants who are now arriving. *And that's the point.* Those minor differences were still enough to tear the country apart.

I've never doubted Simon's debating skills, and this episode left me with even greater respect for his ingenuity.

I just worry about whether he's right.

MULTIRACIAL SOCIETIES: THE EVIDENCE

Of course, our follow-up question, about whether multiracial societies work, is a fairly shocking one.

It's actually much more shocking than the original question—why do the immigration enthusiasts want to transform America? No one ever thinks to ask that. But asking about whether multiracial societies work is quite obviously a direct challenge to America's recently established religion. And, since America has been biracial since Colonial times, it appears to imply a pessimistic view of the prospects for black-white harmony—the greatest problem of American life (until the post-1965 immigration).

But there's a plain fact to be considered: the evidence that multiracial societies work is—what shall we say?—*not very encouraging.*

There have, of course, been multiracial societies (strictly speaking, usually multiethnic) in the past. Famous examples are the Roman Empire, or the Arab Caliphate, which briefly ruled from

Spain to Samarkand in the name of Muhammad. But these were old-fashioned despotisms, not modern democracies. And, even so, ethnic divisions still kept surfacing. The ancestors of the modern Iranians repeatedly rebelled against Arab rule, although they tended to justify their revolts in terms of a convenient Islamic heresy.

Heterogeneous empires that lasted, such as the Eastern Roman Empire of Byzantium, which survived until 1453, were generally based on a core ethnic group—distinctly like our old friend, the "racial hegemony of white Americans." In the case of Byzantium, for instance, this core group was Greek.

In modern times, there has been a lot of seductive murmuring about internationalism, united nations, new world orders, and so on. But, meanwhile, the role of ethnicity and race has proved to be elemental—absolute—fundamental. Look at the record, working back from the present:

- *Eritrea,* a former Italian colony ruled by Ethiopia since 1952, revolt begins in 1960s, finally splits off 1993.
- *Czechoslovakia,* founded 1918, splits into Czech and Slovak ethnic components, 1993.
- *Soviet Union,* founded 1922, splits into multiple underlying ethnic components, 1991. (Some of the underlying components are themselves promptly threatened with further ethnic fragmentation—Georgia, Moldova.)
- *Yugoslavia,* founded 1918, splits into multiple underlying ethnic components 1991. (An earlier breakup averted by imposition of royal dictatorship, 1929.)
- *Lebanon,* founded 1920, progressive destabilization caused by its Muslim component's faster growth results in civil war, effective partition under Syrian domination, after 1975.
- *Cyprus,* independent 1960, repeated violence between Greeks and Turks results in military intervention by Turkey, effective partition with substantial ethnic cleansing, 1974.
- *Pakistan,* independent 1947, ethnically distinct eastern component rebels, splits off after Indian military intervention, 1971.
- *Malaysia,* independent 1963, political conflict between ethnic Malays and Chinese, Chinese-dominated Singapore expelled, 1965.

And these are just the cases where ethnic and racial differences have actually succeeded in breaking a country up. Many other cases are not yet resolved, because of often-bloody repression.

Here's a partial list: *India*—protracted separatist revolts by Sikhs, Kashmiris, northeastern hill tribes. *Sri Lanka*—protracted separatist revolt by Tamils. *Turkey, Iraq, Iran*—separatist revolts by Kurds. *Sudan, Chad*—endemic warfare between Arab north, black south. *Nigeria*—secession of Ibo-majority "Biafra" crushed in 1967–70 civil war. *Liberia*—English-speaking descendants of freed American slaves overthrown by tribal forces 1981, civil war renders more than half the population refugees. *Ulster*—protracted campaign by members of province's Catholic Irish minority to force the Ulster Protestant ("Scotch-Irish") majority to accept its transfer to the Irish Republic. Some of these conflicts have been very violent—over 1 million deaths each in Nigeria and Sudan.

And there's a whole further category of disputes that are being conducted, mostly, through political means. For example: *Belgium*—Flemish and Walloon; *Canada*—French and English; even *Brazil*—a movement in the predominantly white southern states Rio Grande do Sul, Santa Catarina and Paraná to separate from the mixed-race north.

What a record! You would think it would inspire at least some caution about the prospects for multiethnic, multiracial, multicultural harmony within the same political framework.

But you would be wrong. The recent record seems to have made very little impression on the American political elite. (Nor, to be fair, on the Canadian or Western European political elites either. Both have remained fanatical about their respective transnational federations.) Which suggests the sheer power of their will to believe. On this subject, wish has replaced thought.

Indeed, despite all the failed federations and multiethnic mayhem of the past few decades, the most frequent reaction to any questioning of the possibility of multiethnic harmony is still *"What about Switzerland?"* The recent record just doesn't count.

OK, what about Switzerland?

- Its ethnic groups, German, French, Italian and Romansh, are racially identical and culturally very similar.

- The Swiss ethnic groups are fragmented into a number of small, separate political units called "cantons," each of which is firmly under that group's control. It's as if American whites, blacks, Hispanics, and Asians all lived in and controlled several separate U.S. states. All but four of the twenty-six Swiss cantons and "half-cantons" are unilingual.
- Religion cuts across ethnic lines. For example, during the debate that led to the creation in 1979 of a new French-language canton in the Jura region of the German-language Berne canton, the substantial minority of French Protestants were notably less enthusiastic than were the French Catholics.
- In Switzerland as a whole, the German speakers safely predominate. They constitute some 65 percent of Switzerland's population and control seventeen cantons. The French speakers, the next largest group, comprise less than 20 percent and control four of its cantons. Italian speakers, less than 15 percent, control one canton. Romansh speakers, about 1 percent, share the one trilingual canton. Three cantons are bilingual.
- The Swiss ethnic balance has been stable.
- And anyway, there *was* a Swiss Civil War (in 1847). Furthermore the establishment of the French-language canton in the Jura was preceded by years of minor, but nasty, terrorist violence.

Conclusion: *Switzerland is hardly a practical model for U.S. ethnic policy.*

MULTIRACIAL SOCIETIES: HOPELESS BUT NOT (NECESSARILY) SERIOUS?

Sound gloomy? Not particularly. For two reasons:

- UNGLOOMY REASON #1: In politics, problems with no answers don't always have to be answered. Sometimes they can just be accommodated.

There are circumstances in which people's differences can be forgotten, or at least contained. The United States has actually been quite good at getting moderately diverse immigrant groups to live together. It was working on its black-white problem.

But this relative American success did not amount to a Declaration of Independence from history. It depended on time, numbers, degree of difference . . . and, above all, on some very specific policies, like "Americanization," which tended to swamp all difference with a common American civic culture.

And these policies have now been largely abandoned. (For more on this, see Chapter 11, pages 216–19.) Still, they can be restored.

- UNGLOOMY REASON #2: Most human impulses have good and bad applications. The impulse that causes men to go to war over their racial etc. differences is closely related to the impulse that causes them to protect and feed their families.

The difficulties posed by human differences are depressing only if you find human nature itself unacceptable. Unfortunately, much of the American political elite does. So, through immigration, they insist on making the country's problems worse—quite unnecessarily.

It's tempting to say that their passionate will to believe in the likelihood of multiracial and multiethnic harmony is noble. At least, they say so themselves. Repeatedly.

But what is so noble, or moral, about insisting on gambling the future of a nation on an immigration policy that reflects a patently flawed view of human nature? Particularly when the alternative policy is perfectly practical and moral.

Good fences do make good neighbors—in every sense of the word "good." (For more on the moral issues raised by immigration, see Chapter 13.)

THE SIMON SOLUTION

Julian Simon keeps rather odd hours. As I understood it, he had to break up our dinner early in order to go home and sleep for a few hours. Then he planned to get up in the middle of the night and work.

I still hadn't cornered him on the possibility of multiracial harmony. As we moved toward the door, I tried again.

"What makes me think multiracial societies work?" he echoed. "Well, look at this restaurant." He waved his hand around vaguely. "It's French, the waiters are Indian, the customers . . . it works OK, doesn't it?"

Somehow, this didn't seem quite enough.

AMERICA'S UNPRECEDENTED ETHNIC REVOLUTION

Simon's answer, however, had better be enough. Because current immigration policy, as we saw in Chapter 3, is turning the United States into a multiracial society—not to mention a multilingual, multireligious and multicultural society—with extraordinary speed. To repeat:

- **There is no precedent for a sovereign country undergoing such a rapid and radical transformation of its ethnic character in the entire history of the world.**

The Modern Era

The twentieth century is really the aftermath of the great European expansion that began around the time of the Renaissance in Italy some five hundred years earlier. In the rest of the world, this European expansion established two main types of immigrant societies:

- those in territory that was originally sparsely populated that are now essentially white. These are mainly, but not entirely, English-speaking. (The Argentine constitution of 1853, as amended in 1957, says specifically that "the Government will promote and encourage immigration from Europe."[7])
- those in territories with substantial native populations. In Latin America, these tend now to be ruled by white elites of varying sizes, with much of the population of mixed blood. In Africa, the white elites have been overthrown; and the mixed-blood population is much smaller. Typically, all these societies have been undemocratic.

In both types of immigrant-created societies, the ethnic balance now seems relatively stable. Absolutely nothing comparable to the U.S. ethnic revolution is on the horizon.

Both Australia and Canada began to admit Third World immigrants in the 1960s, at about the same time as the United States. But they remain about 93 percent and 89–90 percent white respectively. In the nineteenth century, Brazil's whites did grow from about a quarter to above a half of the population because of immigration. But, as Brazil was run by a small white elite through all of this period anyway, it hardly mattered.

(Immigration enthusiasts like to trap naive critics as follows: *"The foreign-born populations of several European nations are higher than that of the United States. So there."* And it's true: for example, France had a 9.5 percent foreign-born population in 1993, compared with 8.9 percent in the United States.

(But it's also deceptive. These countries usually do not have birthright citizenship, so children born to foreign residents are counted as foreigners, whereas the children of immigrants and transients in the United States are counted as native-born citizens.

(And many foreign-born populations in Europe are due to special circumstances, particularly the aftershocks of empire. The British acquired most of their Caribbean and Indian populations by inadvertently defining their citizenship to include newly independent countries that were still members of the post-imperial "Commonwealth." The French, apart from a similar post-imperial Third World influx, experienced an unusual immigration from Europe in the 1930s and also acquired over a million whites from the settler community in its former colony of Algeria in the 1960s. Germany automatically accepts the descendants of the historic German colonies in Eastern Europe and Russia—an echo of Israel's "Law of Return," which offers citizenship to Jews throughout the world. And, of course, Germany suffered the asylum disaster of 1992–93, when an influx like that at New York's John F. Kennedy Airport [see page 27] reached an astonishing sixty thousand a month before the politicians dared to act.

(Furthermore, what the immigration enthusiasts don't add is this: *every Western European nation is officially committed to preventing further immigration.*)

There are some modern examples of massive influxes by one ethnic group into territory historically occupied by another. For example, Han Chinese have settled in Manchuria, Inner Mongolia, Tibet and East Turkistan; Russians have settled in Estonia, Latvia and elsewhere in the former Soviet Union; Bangladeshis (the former East Pakistanis) have settled in the Chittagong Hill Tract.

But in all these cases, the influx was imposed on the resident population by somebody else. In several cases, the influx was clearly intended to swamp the resident population. In some cases, it has led to serious strife.

The Middle Ages

Once we go back beyond the modern era, comparisons with the current U.S. situation become difficult. Medieval peoples were mostly illiterate peasants and medieval governments were autocratic. The relationship between the two was, well, feudal.

But one medieval immigration is worth noting: the steady influx of Germans into Eastern Europe, particularly from the eleventh century to the fourteenth century. This movement was mostly peaceful. It was often actively encouraged by Slavic and other princes in the region, who hoped to benefit from the increased economic activity stimulated by German peasants and merchants. Thus King Otakar II of Bohemia—heartland of the Czech-speaking Slavs—established more than sixty German cities in his realm between 1253 and 1278.

But, however much it added to princely coffers in the short run, this immigration did result in the outright Germanization of much previously Slav territory. Eventually, it was Hitler's effort to incorporate this territory into his Third Reich that triggered World War II.

The Ancient World

In some ways, the nearest thing to a precedent for today's world in motion appears to be the famous *Volkwanderung*—the great "movement of peoples" in the fifth century that saw Germanic tribes overrun the Western Roman Empire. Europe as we know it was shaped by these invasions. Historic names like England, France, Burgundy, Lombardy—all derive from these areas' German conquerors in this period.

Just as the current influx seems likely to do in the United States, this Germanic influx appears to have produced considerable ethnic change in some areas, for example in England. Just as in the United States today, this was magnified by demographic trends within the Roman Empire—population was declining, partly because excessive taxation had resulted in economic stagnation.

And, just as in the United States today and in Eastern Europe during the Middle Ages, the Germanic influx was connived at, to some extent, by the authorities. Rome repeatedly allowed tribes to settle on lands within her frontier as *foederati*—allies—sometimes at the expense of the Roman citizens already living there.[8] In return for these lands, the *foederati* were supposed to accept Rome's overlordship and come to its defense.

Remember this if you ever corner an immigration enthusiast about historical precedents. They tend to get tricky when (understandably) desperate.

For example, *Time*'s April 9, 1990, cover story on what it called "The Browning of America" uncomfortably acknowledged that there essentially is no precedent for a successful multiracial society. But it quickly supplied an ingenious, if ludicrously flimsy, excuse for complacency.

". . . comparisons are flawed," it argued, because the United States was not created by conquest but by "voluntary immigration." The point, presumably: all the multiple races must really want to be American, and this will hold society together. (What about illegal immigrants—will they retain their contempt for U.S. law? *Time* didn't say.)

Well, the German *foederati* immigrated to Rome voluntarily. Unfortunately, they just didn't stay loyal very long.

But there are differences between the *Volkwanderung* and today's immigration. Despite the impression given by understandably depressed Roman historians, the numbers of Germans were relatively much smaller than today's Third World overhang. There were perhaps 31 million people in all of Europe—and somewhere up to three quarters of them were subjects of Rome. In what is now Germany, there were only an estimated 3.5 million Germans. The German war bands averaged around 80,000, of whom only perhaps 20,000 were warriors.

The German demographic impact was significant where invasion could be followed up by continued immigration. But, overall, it supplemented rather than swamped the existing population.[9]

Additionally, of course, the Germans were Western Europeans. They were virtually identical to the populations they conquered and with whom, in most cases, they proceeded quickly to merge.

Conclusion: the current U.S. situation really is unprecedented, even by comparison with the *Volkwanderung.*

Oh, and there's a final point:

Rome fell.

PART TWO

Consequences

7

IMMIGRATION HAS CONSEQUENCES: ECONOMICS

Now looking ahead to the twenty-first century—this is my social work coming out in me now—in the twenty-first century, and that's not far off, [minority] racial and ethnic groups in the U.S. will outnumber whites for the first time. The browning of America will alter everything in society from politics and education to industry, values and culture. . . . And as I talk with the faculty and the staff here at Ripon they're aware of this and they're helping prepare for this.

—**ADA DEER,**
lecturer, School of Social Work and Indian Studies, University of Wisconsin at Madison, and former chair of the Menominee Indian tribe, Clinton administration nominee for Assistant Secretary of Indian Affairs, in her commencement address to Ripon College, May 15, 1993

Ripon, Wisconsin, is the site of the Republican party's founding in 1854 and heart of an area that is currently 98 percent white. Nevertheless, Ada Deer, cited above, was apparently able to talk its credulous college teachers into "helping prepare" for something that may never happen.

(Er—what, exactly, does Ms. Deer mean by "prepare"? Well, the Associated Press reported her adding that "everyone in the hemisphere should know Spanish.")

As we have seen, however, there is no certainty at all that minorities will "outnumber whites" in the twenty-first century. That can occur only in one extraordinary circumstance: if massive Third World immigration is allowed to continue at its current unprecedented rate.

Ms. Deer is right about one thing, however. The ethnic

shift brought about by such immigration would indeed inevitably "alter everything in society."

Multicultural enthusiasts happily proclaim this vital point at the very time that immigration enthusiasts are trying to play it down. In the symposium in response to my *National Review* cover story, Julian Simon even proposed "a general theory"—

> . . . explaining why immigrants have had so little noticeable effect on American life patterns. The pattern of civic life remains what it was before a wave of immigration, unless the immigrants are greater in numbers or riches than the prior residents. The chances that any immigrants into the U.S. will meet these conditions is nil.[1]

As we have seen, of course, if immigration is allowed to continue, the post-1965 immigrants and their descendants are likely to outnumber pre-1965 Americans in large areas of the United States. And it is quite possible that some groups, perhaps the Cubans of Miami and the Asians of California, will be wealthier—just like the Jews of New York have become.[2]

But the "general theory" is, well, distinctly divorced from reality anyway. Nearly half a century ago, the philosopher Richard Weaver published a book the title of which convinced many Americans, at least in the conservative movement: *Ideas Have Consequences.* Similarly, if they consider the evidence fairly, they cannot evade a further truth: *Immigration Has Consequences*—especially in their own, much-blessed country.

IMMIGRATION AND ECONOMICS

"The business of America is business," President Calvin Coolidge once famously remarked. Many of his countrymen still wince at his crassness. But, curiously, when asked about immigration, they very quickly start talking about economics.

Even many immigration critics have been muscled into assuming unquestioningly that the economic consequences of immigration must necessarily be good. They just try to block. *("There's more to a country than its gross national product.")* Then they change the subject to issues like culture, crime and crowding.

Quite right, too. There is indeed much more to a country than its GNP. But GNP matters—particularly in a society like America, which has tended to justify itself because of its material success.

And the assumption that there are vast and vital economic benefits from mass immigration deserves to be questioned. Typical of the one-way U.S. immigration debate, it turns out to be a myth. Put it this way:

- **For the United States, immigration is not an economic necessity. It is a luxury. And like all luxuries, it can help—or it can hurt.**

You can see why many people assume immigration must be economically beneficial. Just as they tend to think that the sudden mushrooming of minorities in the United States is a natural phenomenon, they also assume vaguely that immigration must have been ratified by some sort of free-market process. Immigrants must be moving to wherever their labor is best rewarded, as Americans do within the United States. It must be part of what economists call the "efficient allocation of resources."

"You have to accept the free movement of people if you believe in free trade/free markets." You do? It's a more radical proposition than appears at first sight. Third World populations are very large and their wage levels very low—Mexican wages are a tenth of those north of the border, and Mexico is relatively advanced. So calculations of the market-clearing wage in a United States with open immigration necessarily imply that, even with capital accumulation and productivity gains, it must be some fraction of its present level.

This arrangement might optimize global economic utility. But it can hardly improve American social harmony.

However, a calculation of this sort requires impossible assumptions. The fact is that a belief in free markets does not commit you to free immigration. The two are quite distinct. Even Julian Simon, although he favors immigration, says explicitly that "contrary to intuition, the theory of the international trade of goods is quite inapplicable to the international movement of persons."[3]

In fact, on a practical level, free trade tends to operate not as a complement for immigration but as a substitute. If you have free trade, you don't need immigration.

Hence the Japanese have factories in the Philippines rather than Filipinos in Japan. Victorian Britain, with its foreign policy of "splendid isolation" from the quarrels of Europe, combined total free trade with almost no immigration, a policy that satisfied Liberal "Little Englander" isolationists and Tory Imperialist global interventionists alike. And in 1993 a popular argument for the North American Free Trade Agreement with Mexico was that it would help reduce the current immigrant flood by providing alternative employment south of the border.

(However, "free-trade negotiations"—a paradox: what's to negotiate?—often get captured by political elites seeking to skew things in favor of contributors and constituencies. There's a nasty possibility this might have happened with NAFTA. Early rumors were that it would lead to an *increase* in immigration, absurdly, because of its inevitable short-term dislocation of the Mexican economy. Apparently, the American negotiators were prepared to tolerate this in their eagerness to see Mexico rapidly remove agricultural price supports and other barriers to powerful U.S. export interests.)

"You have to accept the free movement of people . . ." Oh, yeah? You mean completely open borders?

Even immigration enthusiasts gulp at this. Except *The Wall Street Journal* editorial-page editors under their intrepid leader R. Bartley. They periodically suggest it as a constitutional amendment: "There shall be no borders."[4]

Julian Simon has quietly declined to go this far. And it's important to note why.

Firstly, he says (quite rightly) that the numbers and type of potential immigrants is unknown. So he would prefer to raise immigration step by step, to see what happens. But, secondly, he is concerned about what he calls *"negative human-capital externalities."* Most immigrants have lower skill levels than natives, he acknowledges. If enough of them were to arrive, they could overwhelm and render less effective the higher skills of the natives.

> In other words, if there is a huge flood of immigrants from Backwardia to Richonia, Richonia will become economically similar to Backwardia, with loss to Richonians and little gain to immigrants

> from Backwardia. . . . So even if *some* immigrants are beneficial, a *very large* number coming from poorer countries . . . may have the opposite effect.[5]

This is a crucial theoretical concession. It means that there is a point at which intervention to stop immigration is justifiable *on economic grounds*—not just because there's a backlash from the dreaded nativists.

Of course, Simon insists that immigration levels could be *much* higher than at present. But Richonians in California, Florida and New York City might not agree.

IMMIGRATION, THE 1965 IMMIGRATION ACT (NOT THE SAME THING), AND ECONOMICS

Needless to say—and not for the first time—this discussion of immigration in principle has little to do with immigration in practice, as governed by the 1965 Immigration Act. Today, immigration to the United States is not determined by economics: it is determined—or at least profoundly distorted—by public policy. *Current U.S. immigration is not an economic phenomenon; it is a political phenomenon.*

As we saw in Chapter 4, pages 78–84, the effect of the 1965 reform has been *to uncouple legal immigration from the needs of the U.S. economy.* A low point was reached in 1986, when less than 8 percent of over 600,000 legal immigrants were admitted on the basis of skills—of whom about half were accompanying family members.

The 1990 Immigration Act was allegedly designed in part to rectify this situation. But in 1992, only 13 percent of the 914,000 non-IRCA legal admissions were employment-based—of whom half were accompanying family. Most legal immigrants, 55 percent, entered under the law's various "family reunification" provisions. And this proportion does *not* include the accompanying family members of humanitarian or "diversity" immigrants.[6]

Of course, some of the family-reunification immigrants will have skills. But it is purely an accident whether their skills are wanted in the U.S. economy.

The family-reunification policy inevitably contributes to two striking characteristics of the post-1965 flow:

- **Firstly: the post-1965 immigrants are, on average, less skilled than earlier immigrants.** And getting even less so. As George Borjas put it in his *Friends or Strangers:* "The skill level of successive immigrant waves admitted to the U.S. has declined *precipitously* in the past two or three decades."[7] (My italics—but you see the point.)
- **Secondly: the post-1965 immigrants unmistakably display more mismatching between what they can do and what America needs.** They seem not to be fitting as well into the economy as did earlier immigrants. Instead, they are showing a greater tendency to become what used to be called a "public charge."

Let's look at both of these characteristics (see Chart 13, below) in turn.[8]

POST-1965 IMMIGRATION: SKILL LEVELS DOWN

Put another way, in 1970 the *average* recent immigrant had 0.35 less years schooling than native-born Americans. By 1990, the average recent immigrant had 1.32 years less schooling.

(And note that "native" here includes American blacks and

Chart 13

IMMIGRANT SKILLS: LOSING GROUND

High-school-dropout and college-graduation rates among native-born Americans and immigrants

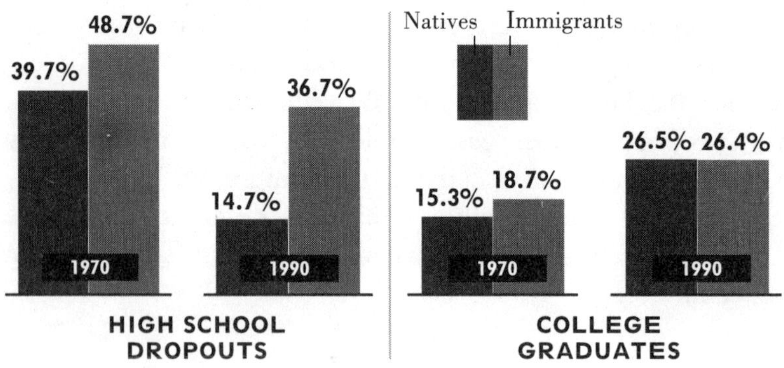

Puerto Ricans. Both these groups systematically lag American whites in educational achievement. If we were to look only at native-born, non-Hispanic American whites, average educational attainment might increase by as much as a year. Which makes the immigrant performance appear really grim.)

"But everyone knows American education is going down the tube—a high school diploma just doesn't mean what it used to," immigration enthusiasts extemporize desperately.

Maybe. But economists, in their unromantic way, view earnings as a proxy for skills. And the relative decline in immigrant education seems to be confirmed by the relative decline in their earnings that has occurred over the same period.

In 1970, immigrants on average actually earned some 3 percent more than native-born Americans. (That slight inferiority in average education was apparently counterbalanced, perhaps by higher average age.) But in 1990, this immigrant achievement had disappeared: immigrants on average earned 16.2 percent less than native-born Americans.

Examined more closely, the trend is even more alarming. In 1970, immigrants who had just arrived—within the previous five years—earned some 16.6 percent less than the native-born population. But by 1990, the gap had nearly doubled: immigrants who had arrived within the previous five years earned some 31.7 percent less than natives.

In other words, the decline in *average* immigrant earnings masked an even sharper deterioration in the earnings of the *most recent* immigrants.

The evidence, George Borjas has concluded, no longer supports another of the immigration enthusiasts' favorite claims: *"Immigrants soon catch up with and outstrip native-born Americans in earnings"*—thus proving what desirable citizens they are (at least economically). He says:

> My research indicates that if a particular immigrant cohort is tracked across Censuses, there is relatively little wage convergence between the immigrants and natives. Because more recent immigrant waves start off poorly, *it is unlikely that the earnings of the "new immigrants" will ever catch up with those of natives.* In fact, the wage differ-

> ential between immigrants and natives may exceed 20 percent even after two or three decades after immigration. [My emphasis again.]

Borjas, incidentally, thinks that the skill decline would have occurred even apart from the 1965 Immigration Act's preference for family reunification above skills. This is because of a paradox in the way the 1965 reform works:

- Besides favoring "family reunification," the 1965 Act also allowed immigration from the Third World. And Third World countries typically have comparatively unequal income distributions. By contrast, First World countries, such as the welfare states of Western Europe, have relatively equal income distributions, reinforced by government policies that tax the rich and spend on the poor.

  So a skilled worker in the Third World has less incentive to emigrate, relative to his unskilled countrymen—who have enormous incentives. Whereas in egalitarian Western Europe, skilled workers have relatively more to gain by emigrating to the United States . . . if they could get in.

Borjas's theory seems to work: First World immigrants are indeed disproportionately skilled and successful. As he puts it, Third World immigrants tend to be *"negatively selected."*

Thus current immigration is tending to

1. *lower the average quality* of the U.S. workforce; and
2. *stratify it,* with the post-1970 immigrants tending to the bottom.

Now look again at Chart 13. Some further comments:

- *The chart* is (more accurately, was) *bipolar.* That is, it peaks at both extremes—immigrants cluster both at the low-skill end and at the high-skill end.

This is why immigration enthusiasts have been able to get away with arguing that immigrants are more highly skilled than native-born Americans. It's true. They are. But they are also, simultaneously, lower-skilled.

You hear a lot about Ph.D. immigrants working in California's

Silicon Valley computer complex. Just under 3 percent of recent immigrants had Ph.D.s, as opposed to just over 1 percent of native-born Americans. But that's only, say, 30,000 immigrant Ph.D.s a year. And have you heard that surveys show some 10 percent of Mexican illegal immigrants (suggesting, say, 30,000 to 50,000 of the net illegal influx each year) were *totally illiterate in any language*?[9]

You haven't? Oh.

Note also this: *by 1990, the immigrant advantage in college graduates had disappeared.* This reflects the sharp relative deterioration in immigrant skills in the most recent years. It happened at the other, unskilled pole too: at various times in the 1980s the proportion of newcomers who had not graduated from high school was running in excess of 40 percent.

- *Chart 13 shows* relative *skills.* Immigrants' education levels are improving in absolute terms (rather slowly, at the unskilled pole). But not as fast as the education levels of native-born Americans.

"Immigrants have never been more educated," immigration enthusiasts sometimes argue. Maybe not. But in a rapidly developing and increasingly competitive world, *relative* skill levels are what count.

"The 1890–1920 immigrants were fairly unskilled"—although actual illiterates were banned in 1917—*"and they did fine, didn't they?"* (Well, not all of them, as a matter of fact—see Chapter 8.) You can immediately see the fallacy of this further favorite argument of immigration enthusiasts if you think about the issue of the *relative* skill levels of native-born Americans and immigrants.

Most people realize that the U.S. economy at the beginning of the twentieth century was much less skill-based. It could use laborers and sweatshop workers. But few people realize, in addition, that native-born Americans were, on average, much less skilled.

For example, only 13.5 percent of the over-twenty-five adult population had four or more years of high school in 1910.[10] The ideal that everyone should go through high school came surprisingly late in American history—really after World War II.

So the contrast with unskilled immigrants was not as sharp as it is today.

- Chart 13 shows proportions, *not absolute numbers.* Thus the proportion of immigrants in the United States who are unskilled is lower in 1990 than it was twenty years earlier. But, because the absolute number of all immigrants is higher, the absolute number of unskilled immigrants in the American workforce is higher too.

Question: *Why doesn't the United States just lop off the unskilled-immigrant pole?*

Answer: *Good idea. Why don't you suggest it?*

POST-1965 IMMIGRATION: WELFARE UP

The second striking characteristic of the post-1965 immigrant flow: *increased mismatching with the U.S. labor market.* This shows up in immigrants' increasing tendency to go on welfare.

In the early 1980s, immigration researchers were generally pretty complacent about immigration's impact on the United States. It became an article of faith, still echoed by some of the less alert immigration enthusiasts, that immigrants earned more, and went on welfare less, than native-born Americans.

The reason for this complacency, of course: the researchers were looking at old data. It still substantially reflected the pre-1965 immigrants.

By the early 1990s, the scene had changed completely. It was becoming clear that, among the post-1965 immigrants, welfare participation rates were sharply higher. *Immigrant welfare participation was, on average, higher than native-born Americans (9.1 percent vs. 7.4 percent).* And what's more, *immigrant households on welfare tended to consume more, and increasingly more, than native-born households on welfare.* (In 1970, 6.7 precent of all welfare cash benefits went to immigrants; in 1990, 13.1 percent.) Some immigrant groups, such as Dominicans (27.9 percent on welfare), were far above the welfare participation even of American-born blacks (13.5 percent).

(And note that "welfare" means just cash programs like Aid to Families with Dependent Children, Supplementary Security Income, and other general assistance—not non-cash programs like

Food Stamps and Medicaid, for which there are no good numbers.)

Even pro-immigration researchers like the Urban Institute, while downplaying immigrant welfare participation, have reported that the immigrant proportion of those people living in areas of concentrated poverty had nearly tripled in twenty years, to over 10 percent in 1990.

The Urban Institute's solution: more public spending—"to put it bluntly, [to] avert the formation of a new urban underclass."[11]

Question: *Why not just cut out immigration?*

Answer: *?????????????*

Chart 14 (below) shows how George Borjas assessed the situation, using data from the 1990 Census.

Again, note that "natives" here includes American blacks and Puerto Ricans. Both are disproportionately heavy users of welfare. One estimate suggests that looking only at native-born, non-Hispanic American whites, might drop the welfare-participation rate by more than two percentage points, to somewhere above 5 percent.[12]

Which makes the immigrant performance appear, once again, really grim.

Chart 14

IMMIGRANTS AND WELFARE: SINKING DEEPER

Native-born and immigrant household welfare participation; proportion of total cash welfare payments going to immigrant households

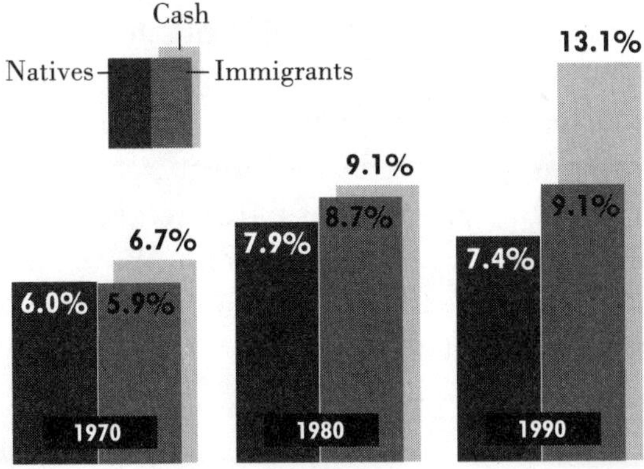

AS PERCENTAGE OF POPULATION

And, as with immigrant skill levels, examining the welfare participation of just the most recent immigrants makes the trend more alarming. The 1990 Census reported that those arriving in the previous five years were significantly more likely to be on welfare (8.3 percent) than were their counterparts in 1970 (5.5 percent).

Which is particularly interesting news. Because according to the law, legal permanent residents are liable to be deported as a "public charge" *if they use public benefits during their first five years in the United States.* But as a practical matter (look at the numbers!), the whole concept of a "public charge" has collapsed. Only some forty-one people were deported on these grounds from 1961 to 1982. At that point, the INS just stopped bothering to report the category separately.[13]

Similarly, U.S. authorities now make no real effort to enforce the guarantees given by the sponsors of any immigrants—not just refugees—who then become public charges.

This passivity is unprecedented in American history. When immigration was handled by the states, prior to the 1875 Supreme Court ruling establishing federal jurisdiction, they legislated repeatedly and frantically to block European countries from dumping their "paupers"—potential welfare cases—in America. (Historians used to dismiss the Know Nothings' complaints about pauper-dumping as propaganda, but recent research has shown that they were, in fact, right.[14])

In Massachusetts in 1639, the Pilgrims, who themselves had landed only nineteen years earlier, set fines for shipmasters who discharged criminals and paupers. Two centuries later, in 1839, after it had been discovered that three quarters of the residents of the New York municipal almshouse were foreign nationals, popular reaction forced the return of a number of Scottish paupers whose passage had been paid by the city of Edinburgh and most of whom had arrived still wearing Edinburgh poorhouse uniforms.[15]

When the federal government took over immigration, its rigorous (if quick) screening process was partly to keep out likely public charges. At the height of the First Great Wave of immigration through Ellis Island, more than half of the 2 percent of arrivals sent back were potential charity cases.[16]

But even if the American authorities were enforcing the law, they would have to deal with rampant fraud. One indicator: an INS study found that *83 percent* of illegal immigrants amnestied under IRCA had false Social Security numbers.[17] But local agencies are now essentially forbidden by confidentiality laws from reporting fraud to the INS.[18]

Similarly, the Internal Revenue Service makes no effort to prevent illegal aliens from receiving Earned Income Tax Credit refunds, which are sometimes payable even if no income tax is due and can exceed two thousand dollars. Of course, the IRS computers often choke on those false Social Security numbers. If necessary the IRS *will then assign a temporary number.*

Got to get that check in the mail![19]

Unquestionably, the largest loophole in welfare-eligibility provisions, however, is the birthright-citizenship provision of the Fourteenth Amendment. Whole nations are coming through it.

It works like this: the minor "citizen children" of illegal immigrants have the full entitlements of American citizens—for example, to cash payments under the federal Aid for Families with Dependent Children (AFDC) program. Naturally, their illegal parents collect it for them. And, equally naturally, no U.S. government is going to deport the parents of an American citizen. So having a child in the United States gives the illegal immigrant a secure, taxpayer-funded foothold here. And when the child turns eighteen, it can sponsor the legal immigration of its relatives.

Examining the group of immigrants arriving in the five years before 1970 reveals even more depressing news: welfare participation actually *increased* the longer they were in the United States. Originally, their rate was 5.5 percent; the 1990 Census reported it at 9.8 percent. All waves of immigrants show a similar drift. The conclusion is unavoidable: *immigrants are assimilating into the welfare system.*

Immigrants from different countries differ enormously in how likely they are to go on welfare. Cambodians and Laotians show astonishing welfare-participation rates—close to half (48.8 percent and 46.3 percent, respectively). Vietnamese are above a quarter (25.8 percent).

The apparent reason for these extreme welfare-participation rates: many members of these groups are refugees. And refugees are immediately entitled to welfare. And it's addictive.

Even after twenty years, refugees are still more likely to be on welfare than either native-born Americans or other immigrants. Even refugee groups that Americans think of as successful, such as the pre-1980 non-*Marielito* Cubans or refuseniks from the former Soviet Union, in fact participate heavily in welfare (15.3 percent and 16.3 percent, respectively).

One startling account of the refugee policy's consequences appeared in the April 1994 issue of *Atlantic Monthly* magazine. Author Roy Beck reported that in the late 1970s, local church groups in Wausau, Wisconsin, sponsored some Hmong refugees from Southeast Asia. This began a typical chain migration, as the refugees sponsored their own relatives.

Today, Hmong comprise *almost a quarter* of Wausau's elementary school enrollment and could conceivably become a majority. Some *70 percent* of the Hmong receive public assistance—sixteen times the average for native-born Americans in the county. (Sponsoring church groups must pledge to care for their guests only for thirty days.) Wausau school-district taxes are rising at three times the rate of neighboring districts with few immigrants; crime has become a problem; busing is a bitter political issue.

Still, says county welfare official Phyllis A. Bermingham, "This was a rather sterile community, and we needed ethnic diversity."[20]

Unavoidable conclusion, looking at these numbers:

- **The post-1980 approach to refugees has created a catastrophe—even by the generally disastrous standards of immigration policy.**

Still, Borjas says, the refugee presence is not enough to account for the immigrant slide into welfare. That trend remains even after refugee households are factored out. (Non-refugee immigrants are 7.8 percent into welfare, as opposed to native-born American participation of 7.4 percent.)

And immigrants from different countries still differ sharply in their likelihood to go on welfare even when none are refugees. The basic pattern: immigrants from developed countries are significantly less likely to go on welfare (the United Kingdom, 3.7 percent; Germany, 4.1 percent) than immigrants from the Third World (Haiti, 9.1 percent; Mexico, 11.3 percent).

Borjas's conclusion echoes that of the Urban Institute: a significant number of recent low-skilled immigrants now go to swell the ranks of the underclass.

> Question: *Aren't immigrants supposed to be "young and healthy"* [Julian Simon, "The Nativists Are Wrong," *The Wall Street Journal,* August 4 1993]*? Why are they on welfare at all?*
>
> Answer: *Address queries to J. Simon, c/o University of Maryland, College Park, MD 20742*

POST-1965 IMMIGRATION: "AN EXCELLENT INVESTMENT"?

So the post-1965 immigrants are less successful economically and more inclined to use welfare. Does that mean they are now taking more from the various levels of American government than they pay in taxes—that immigration is a net cost to the public purse?

Immigration enthusiasts deny it vehemently. They are fighting a desperate battle to defend the proposition that, as Julian Simon put it in *The Economic Consequences of Immigration,* "an immigrant family is an excellent investment."[21] But they are clearly losing.

In part, the immigration enthusiasts are being driven back by the sheer volume of horror stories slowly emerging from the local level. For example, in California, *fully a third of all public assistance* goes to immigrant-headed households.

And Californians are reacting. Which is why the state's two Democratic senators, Dianne Feinstein and Barbara Boxer, have spoken out against illegal immigration. And why, in mid-1993, Republican governor Pete Wilson launched perhaps the broadest challenge yet made by an elected official to the immigration taboo—even advocating the abolition of birthright citizenship. (Ironically, as a U.S. senator, Wilson worked hard for the 1986 amnesty for illegal immigrants favored by agricultural interests. But maybe that shows he's not prejudiced.)*

Also in mid-1993, Donald Huddle, emeritus professor of economics at Rice University, published a report arguing that the net costs of immigration to government, including the welfare costs of native-born workers displaced by immigrants, exceeded $40 billion in 1992.[22] His work was fiercely attacked. But at least it got the debate going—at last.

And the debate needs to get going. For example, I've several times had quoted at me this factoid: "Business Week *says immigrants pay $90 billion in taxes and get only $5 billion in services.*" And the magazine did report that, in its July 13, 1993, cover story "The Immigrants: How They're Helping the U.S. Economy," a classic example of America's one-way immigration debate.

The $5 billion, however, referred *only to cash welfare benefits received by immigrants*—not to other means-tested programs, like Medicaid, Earned Income Tax Credits, housing subsidies, food stamps.

More important, the $5 billion implicitly assumes that no immigrant taxes should go to pay for the rest of the services provided by all levels of American government, from roads to defense. (*"But those services would have to be provided anyway—immigrants' using them makes no difference,"* say immigration enthusiasts. Tell that to drivers on Southern California's freeways.)

But the factoid floats on. Clearly, it's what a lot of people want to believe.

George Borjas suggests that a back-of-the-envelope cost-to-government calculation should look like this:

---

* This lack of prejudice helped Wilson to return from the political dead and be reelected in the 1994 midterm elections, an astonishing turnaround. Even more astonishing was the landslide victory of California's Proposition 187, an initiative designed to clamp down on illegal immigrants' access to taxpayer funding. Although 187 was immediately put on hold by a liberal judge—as presaged on page 260—its triumph in the face of the overwhelming opposition of the American political and media elites makes it the most remarkable election result for many years (and that definitely includes the Republican capture of the House and Senate). This sort of intense popular sentiment confronts the political elite with a stark choice: they can bend, or they can break. But they cannot do nothing.

- Assume immigrants are charged a proportionate "fair share" of all government expenditures. Assume also that they take the same proportion of non-cash benefits as cash benefits (13.1 percent). Thus in 1990, about 8.9 percent of government revenues are used to fund cash and non-cash programs. And in 1990, immigrants earned about $285 billion (net of welfare payments) and, combining federal, state and local taxes, probably face an estimated 30 percent tax rate. That adds up to some $85 billion in immigrant tax payments. So 8.9 percent of immigrants' $85 billion taxes ($7.6 billion) can be set against their use of cash and other benefits (about $23.8 billion). **Net cost to native-born American taxpayers: over $16 billion.**

THREE BIG QUESTIONS: EDUCATION, SOCIAL SECURITY, AND UNEQUAL IMPACT

Note that Borjas's calculation doesn't include the immense costs of educating immigrant children. A year for one student in the New York City public school system, for example, involves an average annual expenditure of nearly $7,400.[23] By comparison, the annual per capita national income of Mexico is about $4,000. In Haiti, it's just $320 per capita.[24]

Arguably, some of that cost will be paid back, as the immigrant children's skill levels are improved and they eventually earn more than they would otherwise have done. And, on the other side of the ledger, some immigrants arrive already educated and presumably benefit native-born Americans with their skills—although capturing much of the surplus in their own earnings. So the net impact of education costs is hard to figure out.

But meanwhile, *education costs money now.*

Note also that Borjas is not taking into account immigrants' payments into the Social Security system. Which may seem surprising, because for many workers these payments now exceed income taxes. But (as with education) there's another side to the question: *immigrants paying into the system also represent a future claim upon it.*

Amazingly, there have been no full-blown academic studies of the net impact of immigration on the Social Security system. But, since the median age of immigration is thirty, many immigrants will pay into the system for a much shorter period than will the native-born. Yet the benefits they receive will be substantially the same. If you work fifteen years, you receive only slightly less than for working thirty years. So it looks ominous.

"But immigrants are going to bail out the Social Security system!" This is a favorite claim of immigration enthusiasts. It works like this. Social Security is not really an insurance system: it's actually a direct hand-over, via the government, from working Americans to retired Americans. The benefits that retired Americans receive far surpass the value of their earlier payments. While working Americans far outnumber retired Americans, as they do while the Baby Boom generation is in the labor force, the system teeters in balance. But what happens when the Baby Boomers retire—and the succeeding Baby Bust generation is all that's available to support them?

"IMMIGRANTS!" say the immigration enthusiasts. Of course, they are being irresponsible (not for the first time). What happens when the *immigrants* retire?—more immigrants? And the spectacle of poor young workers of color being taxed to support rich old white retirees is a social San Andreas Fault in English, Spanish or anyone's language.

But (again not for the first time) the immigration enthusiasts' numbers don't add up. The Dallas-based National Center for Policy Analysis has calculated that to keep payments constant and the Social Security payroll tax at current levels, the U.S. workforce would have to be doubled by immigration in less than three decades. Since parents will bring children, this could involve the departure of *about half the nonelderly population of Latin America.*[25]

There is, however, a third point in the cost-to-government debate on which everyone agrees:

- *Whatever the overall balance between immigrant taxes and costs, the impact on specific states and cities is severe.*

This is because many of the taxes that immigrants pay go to Washington—for example, their Social Security deductions—

whereas the services they receive are paid for by the local community.

It's easy enough to argue that Washington must step in with money to repair the damage. But this almost certainly means further loss of control by the state governments, further erosion of the founding American principle of federalism in favor of centralization in Washington.

This has already happened, dramatically, when the nation faced war against external enemies.

But what enemy is America fighting now?

Regardless of the academic argument, Wall Street, in its unideological, money-grubbing way, has already made up its mind about this "excellent investment." And it's pulling back its snout. As the investment firm Sanford C. Bernstein commented tersely in downgrading the state of California's bond rating in 1991:

> The primary reasons for the state's credit decline are above-average population growth and shifting demographics. . . . The degree of public assistance required by two of the fastest growing groups, Latinos and political/ethnic refugees (most of whom are Southeast Asians), is substantially higher than that of the general population . . .[26]

George Borjas has drawn the inevitable moral as well as it can be done:

- **A welfare state cannot afford the large-scale immigration of less skilled persons.**[27]

8

IMMIGRATION HAS (MORE) CONSEQUENCES: ECONOMICS II

I do not know what I may appear to the world; but to myself, I seem to have been only a boy playing on the sea-shore, and diverting myself in now and then finding a smoother pebble or a prettier shell than ordinary, whilst the great ocean of truth lay all undiscovered before me.

—**SIR ISAAC NEWTON,**
discoverer of the principle of gravity

I can never read without emotion this quotation from Newton—despite his humility in it, one of the greatest scientific minds in history. For, of course, Newton was right. Inconceivable as it must have seemed just a few decades ago, Newtonian physics, upon which the entire Industrial Revolution was built, has been overshadowed by Einstein and the theory of relativity.

It's a Warning to us all.

Just look at the American immigration debate. It has been playing, albeit rather ineffectually, with a smooth pebble—the issue of government bookkeeping. Yet this pebble is not only disgustingly technical; it's really quite trivial. Even Donald Huddle's estimated $40 billion loss is small compared to the $6 trillion U.S. economy—less than six tenths of 1 percent. (Although, we should remember, it's certainly substantial when a few states and cities have to pay it all.)

And this quibbling about bookkeeping is indeed causing us to overlook the ocean of truth. The immigration debate should not center on: *What, if anything, is immigration costing the taxpayer?* Instead it should be refocused as follows:

- **Is immigration actually necessary for economic growth?**

The answer, perhaps surprisingly, is: *certainly not.* Immigration does very little that the host country cannot achieve, possibly better, by other policies.

THE ULTIMATE QUESTION: IS IMMIGRATION NECESSARY?

What does "economic growth" mean anyway? Basically it can be viewed three ways:

1. *growth of overall national income*—literally, any increase in the size of a country's output. Of course, if immigration increases the workforce at all, it must cause such an increase, even if it's just one immigrant mowing lawns.
2. *growth in national income per capita*—increase per head of the population, including the new heads that have just immigrated. This could happen, for example, if all immigrants earned more than the national average . . . as perhaps they might if they were just those Ph.D.s. Immigration of this sort would be a real economic luxury. Government policy could easily arrange it. It just hasn't.
3. *growth of the national income received by native-born Americans*—that is, the Americans already here increase their standard of living because of the presence of immigrants, even if the immigrants themselves don't rise to the same level.

Thus the American lawn-owner is happy to pay to have his lawn mowed. The lawn-mowing immigrant is happy too (presumably). And national output will rise by the amount of the wages he receives. But national income *per capita* will fall—because those wages are far below the national average.

Obviously, immigration that results in point 2, everyone getting richer on average, is the easiest to defend. And immigration that results in point 3, native-born Americans getting richer, is at least rational in economic terms. But it might be socially disturbing if it led to a racially distinct, lawn-mowing servant caste.

Immigration that just results in point 1, some (possibly minimal) growth in overall output, is the most questionable. How much growth are we talking about anyway? One mowed lawn's worth? And why should native-born Americans put up with immigration at all if they themselves don't get significant—make that *significant*—benefits?

Unfortunately, point 1, some (possibly minimal) growth in overall output, is just about the only thing we can be sure that immigration achieves. It does generate instant population growth. The host country can't achieve *instant* population growth by other policies. And an instantly larger population can be very useful if you are seizing a continent or fighting a war (at least before high-tech weapons).

Thus it's possible to imagine all kinds of awful things if the United States had not increased its population quickly in the late nineteenth century. Just think: *the Southwest might have been reoccupied by Mexico!*

But, from an economic standpoint, instantly acquiring more people is not so obviously useful. A country's living standard is expressed by its output per capita, not just by its sheer output. The economies of Britain and China had about the same output in the early nineteenth century. But Britannia could afford to rule the waves while China was starving, because British output was fifteen times higher *per capita* than Chinese output.

In short, just acquiring more people is not enough. In an increasingly technical age, what will count is not the quantity of people but their quality—and the quality of their ideas.

This insight casts a stark new light on much American immigration history. For example, Professor Richard A. Easterlin, writing in the *Harvard Encyclopedia of American Ethnic Groups,* has argued that the vast immigration into the United States in the nineteenth century "probably did not alter substantially the growth of output per capita."

The innovations that drove American economic growth such as mass production in manufacturing, Easterlin points out, were already celebrated worldwide by 1850, when mass immigration was only just getting under way. In the next hundred years, both France and Germany outstripped the United States in per capita output growth.[1]

"Immigrants built America." Well, not quite, as it turns out. The Colonial-stock Americans had things rolling along pretty well before mass immigration began.

Still, the immigrants of the nineteenth century did contribute to the total size of the United States when it smashed onto the global scene during World War I. They did help fill the trenches of the Western Front.

But what if large numbers of immigrants arrive who are far less skilled than the host population? Even if they enter the workforce smoothly and cause total output to grow, their greater numbers must cause output *per head* to fall. And if their marketable skills are minimal, and their entry is not smooth but causes social stress, it's possible that even total output may not grow much more than it would have anyway. Even, perhaps, less.

- *This is the specter haunting the United States in 2050*—that the American population may be 30 percent larger than it would have been without immigration; but its overall national income may be little greater than it would have achieved anyway.

Just spread thinner. Over a more strife-torn society.

In fact, the specter may already be visible. As we have seen, immigration has exploded since 1965. *But overall economic growth has slowed.* The United States grew at an average rate of 4 percent in the immigrantless 1950s. In the quarter century from 1969 to 1993, with immigrants, its average growth rate has been just 2.5 percent.[2]

Which is not to say that immigration has hurt. But wasn't it supposed to help?

HOW MUCH ECONOMIC GROWTH ARE WE TALKING ABOUT ANYWAY?

Oddly, American economists have made very little effort to measure the overall economic benefits of immigration. But the answer seems to be clear: *immigration doesn't contribute that much to economic growth.*

How much? George Borjas suggests another back-of-the-envelope calculation, using a standard applied-economics technique called a "Harberger triangle." (It's too horrible to reproduce here, but appears in Appendix 5.) It's crude, but it makes possible a simple estimate of point 3, the growth of the national income of native-born Americans through immigration—the additional economic "surplus" generated by immigrants and accruing to native-born Americans.

- **In 1992, the economic surplus generated by immigrants and accruing to native-born Americans was very small:** about one to three tenths of 1 percent of total U.S. economic output, or between $6 billion and $18 billion.

That's 0.2 or 0.3 percent! In an economy whose long-run average annual growth is about 2 percent anyway!! Within the normal margin of error for economic projections—*so it may be, for practical purposes, infinitesimal!!!*

And even if this economic surplus exists, other policy measures could potentially generate far more. For example, the Environmental Protection Agency has estimated that federal clean-air and clean-water regulations alone depressed U.S. GNP below the level where it would otherwise have been—what economists call the "opportunity cost"—by no less than 5.8 percent in 1990.

Of course, we need clean air and clean water. But if they can be achieved more efficiently—and there is evidence that they can be—the potential economic benefits are enormous.[3]

Another point:

- **If immigration is indeed causing a net loss to taxpayers of $16 billion**—as George Borjas estimates—**that means its economic effects are neutral.** It's a wash!!!

America is being transformed for—*nothing?*

Yep. That's what it looks like.

However, note that this Borjas back-of-the-envelope calculation has a subtle but ugly implication:

- *The overall economic surplus generated by immigrants and accruing to native-born Americans might be very small—but immigration might still be causing a significant redistribution of income* within *the native-born American community.*

This happens because the small amount by which immigrants drive down the wages for all American workers, nationwide, adds up to a sizeable sum—which goes to American owners of capital. Borjas estimates it could be 2 percent of GNP, or as much as $120 billion. It's a technical argument that you can inspect in Appendix 5.

However, this is the ugly implication: the American elite's support for immigration may not be idealistic at all, but self-interested —as a way to prey on their fellow Americans.

"But what about that poll from the de Tocqueville Institution showing that all reputable economists favor immigration?" The Arlington, Virginia–based immigration enthusiast think tank did indeed publish a 1990 poll of "38 leading U.S. economists, including seven Nobel laureates," of whom 80 percent opined that twentieth-century immigration has had "a very favorable impact" on U.S. economic growth. Almost two thirds thought increased immigration would increase U.S. living standards.

And this certainly is an interesting result. Is it because economists are part of the elite benefiting at the expense of their fellow Americans? Say it ain't so!

A kinder interpretation: the economists were being asked about immigration *in principle,* which we have seen is quite a different matter than immigration *in practice,* as it has developed after the 1965 Act.

Moreover, economists (contrary to the general view) are human—up to a point. They can be swayed by the same passions as everyone else. And immigration is a subject that much of the American elite gets emotional about. Similarly, polls of economists have been known to give the wrong technical answer to questions about rent control, because rent control is often a sacred cow to the sort of political parties that academics tend to favor.

Nevertheless, a small immigration surplus is exactly what you would expect given the logic of applied economics. And, when cornered in their professional mode, even pro-immigration economists like Julian Simon quickly admit that immigration is not, in fact, necessary for the American economy at all. (See below!)

HOW CAN THE IMMIGRATION SURPLUS BE SO SMALL?

There's an irony here. Immigrant enthusiasts often boast: *"Most studies show that American workers' wages have been driven down only very slightly by competition from immigrants."* And that's basically true—as yet. (There's evidence that the impact on wages of the First Great Wave of immigration in 1890–1920 began to show up much more strongly as time passed, stimulating the labor-union agitation that helped bring about the Great Restriction.[4])

But it's exactly because wages have not been driven down that Borjas's Harberger calculation reports such minimal overall economic benefits.

- The formal economic logic of immigration is that *only if* wage rates are driven down—meaning that American owners of capital can hire workers more cheaply and make an increased profit for themselves—can the economy derive an overall benefit.

That increased profit is the *basic* way in which native-born Americans are supposed to benefit from immigration. If it can't be shown to exist, then native-born Americans are just not benefiting.

In other words, the very wage stability that helps the immigration enthusiasts' political argument also works to undermine their economic argument.

Naturally, immigration enthusiasts have trouble accepting this. They are shocked to hear that the gains from immigration are so trivial. Particularly if they live in New York or California, where its effects are very visible. *How can it be?* they ask. And they start telling stories about immigrant entrepreneurs.

Well, you can fit a lot of Korean convenience stores, and even Silicon Valley electronics firms, into $6 billion to $18 billion.

(Indeed, even if immigrants ran *the entire computer industry,* software and hardware, that would account for only just over 2 percent of GNP—some $120 billion annually.[5])

And remember, because of the one-way American immigration debate, anecdotes about immigrants on welfare, in jail or in the hospital at public expense don't get really equal time.

Ironic evidence in support of Borjas's back-of-the-envelope calculation: a study by two Julian Simon–sympathizing economists. They argued that, by 1912, immigration since 1790 had generated social savings that had increased the capital stock of the United States by between 13 and 42 percent, depending on the discount rate used. (The lower is more likely.)

Sounds like a lot? They thought so too. *But, by their own calculations, it would have taken the U.S. economy only five to eighteen years more to achieve the same capital stock if there had been no immigration at all.* Hardly "building America"—in fact a shockingly small increment, given the magnitude of the population movement involved.[6]

Other immigrant countries have similar stories:

- *Canada.* A 1991 study by the very establishment Economic Council of Canada modeled the effects of doubling gross immigration to Canada from the average of the past twenty-five years to an annual 1 percent of the current population (equivalent to 2.5 million immigrants a year entering the United States). Result: "very small" gains—an infinitesimal increase in economic growth that by the year 2015 would increase native-born Canadians' per capita income only by about 1.4 percent above where it would otherwise have been.

And most of that projected gain would come from the economies of scale possible in a larger market—an effect which, the Economic Council pointed out, will be achieved through the 1988 Free Trade Agreement with the United States anyway.

Significantly, the Economic Council went ahead and recommended increasing immigration anyway, saying it would "make Canada a more interesting and exciting society." Even *Canadian* economists are human.[7]

- *Australia.* A 1985 study by the Committee for Economic Development of Australia found that immigration had no clear beneficial effects on output per capita at all.

Again, the Australian study noted tersely that it "at no stage supposed that immigration was the best or only means of securing the results that are reputed to flow from it."[8]

And, really, it makes sense, when you think about it, that immigration would have only a minimal effect on economic growth. After all, the U.S. economy is huge and deeply capitalized. Immigrants make up only just over 9 percent of the workforce. And the contribution of labor is itself only a relatively small element in economic growth (see below). So the role of immigrant labor must obviously be minor—without even considering the fact that so many immigrants are now unskilled.

Trying to boost economic growth through immigration is, to borrow a phrase from another economists' quarrel, like pushing on a string.

WHY IMMIGRATION ISN'T NECESSARY: THE [????] FACTOR

Why is labor only a small element in economic growth?

Audiences always burst out laughing at one apparently gagless scene in the 1985 hit movie *Back to the Future:* the time-transported hero drove up to a gas station in the 1950s, and an army of uniformed attendants leaped forth to pump the gas, clean his windshield, fill his tires, polish his hubcaps, offer him maps and so on.

The joke was in the shock of self-recognition. It was only yesterday—and yet completely forgotten, so accustomed is everyone now to self-service.

"We need immigrants to meet the looming labor shortage/do the dirty work Americans won't do." This further item from the immigration enthusiasts' catechism seems to be particularly resonant for American conservatives, deeply influenced by libertarian ideas and open, somewhat, to the concerns of business.

But it has always seemed incongruous, given persistent high levels of unemployment among some American-born groups. These groups, after all, obviously eat. Unless they are all criminals, they must be living on government transfer payments. Public policy is subsidizing their choosiness about work, thus artificially stimulating the demand for immigrants.

And *if* there is a looming labor shortage—hotly disputed—it could *in theory* be countered by "natalist" policies. That is, Americans could be encouraged to step up their below-replacement birthrate. Even the current high immigration inflow is exceeded by the 1.6 million abortions in the United States each year. Arguably, some of those abortions are due to economic worries that government could relieve.

Examples of natalist policies: the tax deduction for a dependent child could be increased. In 1950, this exempted the equivalent of $7,800 in 1992 dollars from federal income tax. Now, after forty years of inflation, it exempts only $2,100.

Or the "marriage penalty"—by which two individuals living together pay less tax than a married couple—could be abolished. Or something could be done to reduce the crushing costs of educating a child.

(Or—*immigration could be reduced.* There is some evidence that economic insecurity, for example the insecurity caused by job competition, motivates people to restrict family size.[9] So, if immigration increases job competition, particularly for entry-level jobs, it could be indirectly suppressing the reproduction of native-born Americans. Ironically, this echoes the "Walker Thesis" that immigrants tend to replace rather than reinforce the native population—an argument made during the First Great Wave of Immigration and much-denounced ever since.[10])

Note carefully: I'm not advocating natalist policies, necessarily. I merely point out that they are the more normal response of nations worried that their populations are not growing fast enough.[11] It's an interesting question why the American political elite prefers to import foreigners.

But *Back to the Future* makes a more fundamental point about economics: labor is not an absolute. Free economies are infinitely ingenious at finding methods, and machinery, to economize on labor or any other scarce resource.

The implicit assumption behind the popular economic argument for immigration appears to be something like this:

LABOR × CAPITAL = ECONOMIC GROWTH

So, for any given capital stock, any increase in labor (putting aside the question of its quality) must result in some significant increase in output.

This assumption is just wrong. "However surprising it may seem to laymen, capital and labor are relatively minor as factors of production," I was told in an interview by the famous British development economist Professor Peter Bauer (created a peer by Prime Minister Margaret Thatcher, with the title of Lord Bauer of Market Ward). "For example, the work of Simon Kuznets [such as his *Modern Economic Growth: Rate, Structure and Spread*] showed that increases in capital and labor together accounted for no more than 10 percent of the West's increase in output over the last two hundred years, and possibly less.[12] The balance was caused by technical innovation—new ideas."

Although it has been ignored in the current immigration debate, there is an entire "Accounting for Growth" industry among applied economists that attempts to isolate and measure the causes of economic growth. Invariably, it finds that *increases in labor and capital together* account for *at most half, and often much less, of increases in output.*

The rest seems to be attributable to changes in organization—to technological progress and ideas. Or:

ECONOMIC GROWTH = LABOR × CAPITAL × [???]

And [???] is dominant.

Back to the Future illustrates this process in action. On the face of it, gas stations have simply substituted capital (the self-service pumps) for labor (gas jockeys). But actually what has happened is more complex: the cost of making the pumps, and of designing the computer system behind them, is far exceeded by the savings on labor, which extend indefinitely into the future. It is reorganization that has resulted in a permanent increase in productivity.

Or think about that lawn-mowing immigrant. If he were not around, maybe local kids would organize lawn-mowing services. Maybe better lawn mowers would be invented. Or maybe house owners would stop demanding their very own putting greens and adopt gardening styles better suited to local conditions—desert flowers in the Southwest, for example. It would save on water bills too.

And it's happened before. When British aristocrats began to run short of gardeners in the late nineteenth century, they substituted perennial flowers for annuals and invented the herbaceous border—now recognized as one of the glories of what Noël Coward hymned as "The Stately Homes of England."

From an economist's standpoint, *the factors of production are not absolutes. They are a fluid series of conditional interacting relationships.*

This insight won Julian Simon one of the famous debating victories of recent years. In 1980, he bet Paul Ehrlich, the well-known environmentalist commentator and Stanford University entomologist whom we met earlier, that several commodities Ehrlich claimed were running out would, in fact, be lower in price in 1990, the economy having adjusted in the meantime. They were, and Ehrlich had to pay up.

But, paradoxically, when it comes to immigration, Simon seems to revert to a classic non-economic view: labor is good, more labor is better.

The economist's view of labor has influenced the current immigration debate only in (as usual) one direction. It is triumphantly produced by the immigration enthusiasts to refute an assumption often made by unwary critics of immigration: that native-born workers must inevitably be displaced by immigrants coming in and taking their jobs.

Which does seem plausible, right? After all, because British-born

Harold Evans is the president and publisher of Random House, whose imprint is on this book, a native-born American is not.

But in fact studies of the workplace both in the United States and other immigrant-receiving countries rarely detect increased unemployment among the native-born. (One exception: Donald Huddle's surveys of Texas construction workers, part of his estimate of immigration's fiscal burden—see Chapter 7, page 152. Naturally, these are disputed.)

The apparent reason: the native-born aren't displaced, necessarily, in aggregate, because the economy adjusts. And because the increase in the factors of production tends to create new opportunities. "Immigrants not only take jobs," writes Julian Simon, "they make jobs."[13]

In other words, Harry Evans's superior publishing decisions generate more sales and more enlightenment for Random House and for American society.

All right. But missing from the current immigration debate is the fact that this effect operates in the other direction too. On the margin, the economy is probably just as capable of getting along with less labor.

Within quite wide boundaries, *any* labor-supply change can be swamped by the much larger influence of innovation and technological change.

The economy's use of more or less labor is like the early automobile manufacturers' use of paint when they decided to break with Henry Ford's practice and allow customers a choice of colors. Labor doesn't matter a lot: paint doesn't cost a lot. But, in other respects, sociologically and perceptually, they sure make a difference.

THE [???] FACTOR AND THE JAPANESE MIRACLE

The [???] factor is the explanation for the great counterexample hanging like the sword of Damocles over the immigration enthusiasts' polemics: the extraordinary economic success of Japan since World War II. Despite its population of only 125 million and virtually no immigration at all, Japan has grown into the second-largest economy on earth. GDP (Gross Domestic Product—the measure of an economy's size preferred by some international agencies) is up nearly ten times since 1955, and is now about perhaps half that of the United States, which has barely tripled in the same period (see Chart 15, page 170).

The way immigration enthusiasts have handled the Japanese counterexample tells you a lot about the one-way American immigration debate: they ignore it. Americans, after all, worry a lot about Japan. Acres of books have been published about How the Japanese Do It. (Is it management? social organization?) But no attempt is ever made to look for lessons in Japan's immigration policy.

Incredibly, although his book is called *The Economic Consequences of Immigration,* Julian Simon does not mention the Japanese experience at all. Directly asked about it in 1990 by *Forbes* magazine's Jim Cook, he in effect struck out. "How Japan gets along I don't know," he said. "But we may have to recognize that some countries are *sui generis.*"[14]

In the early 1990s, the Japanese economy has been having something of a hiccup, by Japan's standards. The reasons have nothing to do with immigration. Perhaps it won't recover (although don't bet on it). *But the fact that Japan already grew so fast for so long without immigration proves: It Can Be Done.*

Still, some immigration enthusiasts cling to the hope that Japan must now rejoin the human race and allow immigration . . . mustn't it?

Not any time soon, judging by the recent reaction of an anonymous Japanese consular official in New York when asked about the procedures for immigrating to Japan and obtaining Japanese citizenship:

> ANONYMOUS JAPANESE OFFICIAL [*complete surprise and astonishment*]: "Why do you want to emigrate to Japan? . . . There is no immigration to Japan. [*Asked if there aren't political refugees or asylum seekers.*] There might be three people a year who become Japanese. [*Chuckles.*] And even they don't stay long, they try to emigrate elsewhere, like the U.S."

Chart 15

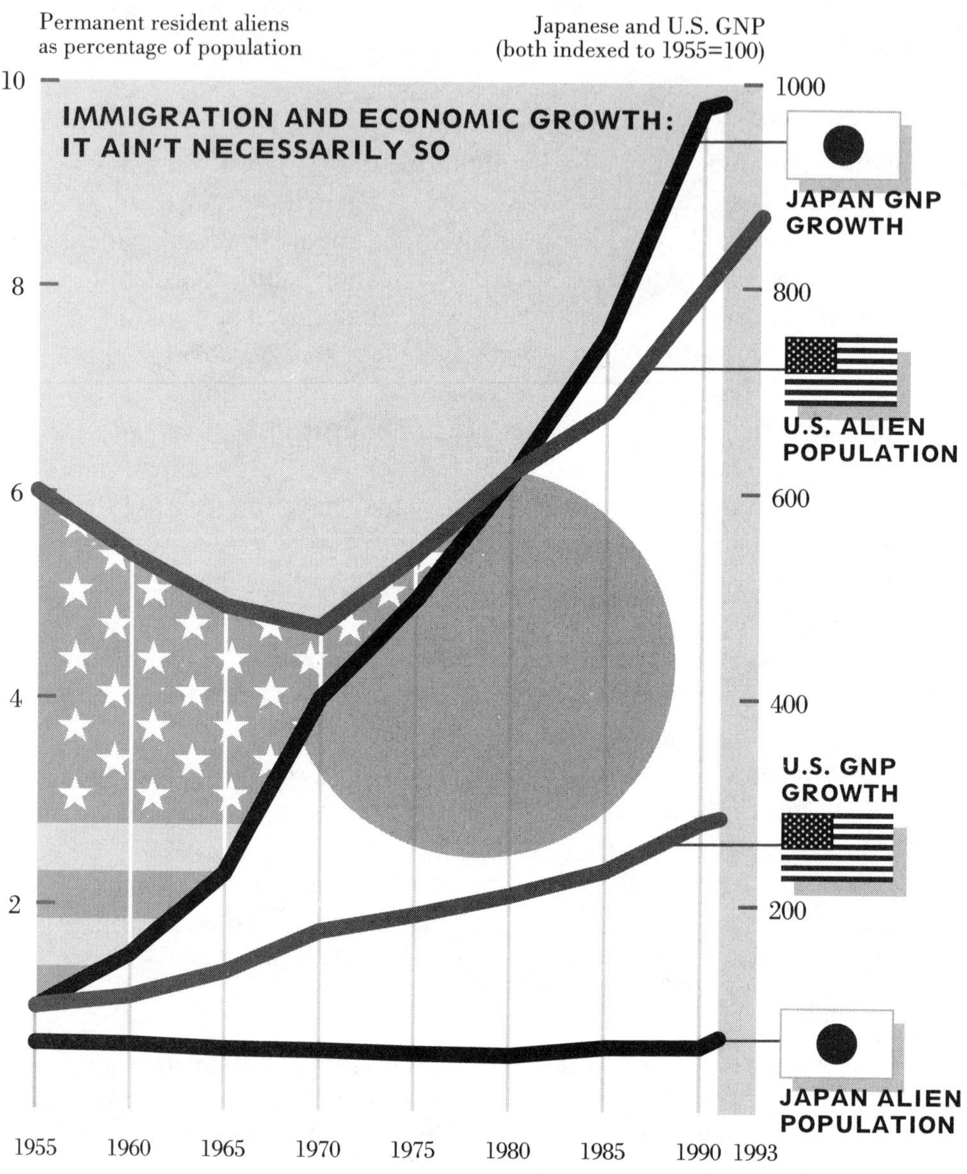
Permanent resident aliens
as percentage of population
Japanese and U.S. GNP
(both indexed to 1955=100)
IMMIGRATION AND ECONOMIC GROWTH:
IT AIN'T NECESSARILY SO
10
8
6
4
2
1000
800
600
400
200
JAPAN GNP
GROWTH
U.S. ALIEN
POPULATION
U.S. GNP
GROWTH
JAPAN ALIEN
POPULATION
1955
1960
1965
1970
1975
1980
1985
1990
1993

(In 1992, incidentally, almost 11,000 immigrants from Japan entered the United States—about twice the recent average.)

He's not joking. Japanese entry statistics don't even seem to recognize the concept of an immigrant, as opposed to a visitor. So Chart 15 uses legal foreign residents in Japan, excluding students, as a proxy for immigration. In 1991, there were about 900,000, less than 1 percent of Japan's population. This proportion has remained remarkably stable. Japan's illegal population was reportedly increasing but still minute at perhaps 250,000.

By contrast, according to Washington, D.C.'s Center for Immigration Studies, working from census numbers, foreign residents are almost 9 percent of the recent 260 million U.S. population. And rising rapidly—to an estimated 12 percent by 2010, according to the Urban Institute. (The Center includes illegal immigrants, but thinks this may well wash with the undercount of legals, a chronic problem for the Census Bureau.)

A mere 222,000 people have acquired Japanese citizenship since 1945—including those who have married Japanese. By contrast, in the same period over 8 million have acquired U.S. citizenship.

How have the Japanese done it? One partial answer: capital investment. The Japanese do save and invest more than Americans. According to the Organization for Economic Co-operation and Development, Japan's gross-savings ratio in 1990, almost 35 percent, was 20 points above that of the United States. And its Gross Fixed Capital Formation had averaged 9 percent growth over the previous five years, more than three times the American rate.

But other countries come significantly nearer the Japanese savings and investment rate without matching its growth. Moreover, Japan achieved even more impressive growth rates before World War II, although its savings rate was then much lower. Japanese manufacturing output increased six times between the two world wars. U.S. output increased only about two thirds.[15]

The basic reason for Japan's immigrantless expansion: the [????] factor—innovation.

"There's no question that the key to Japanese economic growth is not the savings rate but institutional innovation," Professor Chalmers Johnson, a prominent Japan-watcher at the University of California at San Diego, said recently. One example: when Japan's textile industry began to agitate for immigrant labor in the 1960s, the government quietly clamped down on it. Instead, the industry automated, focused on higher value-added synthetics, and ultimately moved low-skill production offshore.

Like other observers, Chalmers Johnson expects marginal increases in Japan's use of contract foreign labor, long-term "trainees" and other subterfuges. But no fundamental change.

Japan does have a demographic problem. Its population is aging rapidly. But it also still has surprisingly large reservoirs of underutilized Japanese labor. (Which shows how effective innovation in the efficient parts of its economy must be.)

More than 7 percent of Japan's workforce is still in its highly protected farming sector, two or three times the proportion of that in the United States or the United Kingdom. In other words, just allowing more food imports would free labor for business—besides benefiting the long-suffering Japanese consumers. Japanese women of childbearing age drop out of the workforce more often than women in other industrial economies. Japanese women who do work are notoriously restricted. And Japan's fragmented distribution sector—the shops and warehouses that get goods to the consumer—is heavily overstaffed.

Chalmers Johnson quotes a Japanese observer: "Demographics are important, but much more important than demographics is good strategy." By combining innovation with better use of native-born labor, Japan probably need never resort to mass immigration. It's as if the United States were somehow able to tap its unemployed underclass—and also get better value from its spending on schools.

Or, as Chalmers Johnson, as a resident of Southern California, adds acidly: "Americans sit around counting on all these young Mexicans [to boost the economy]. But they have no idea how to educate them or employ them."

I asked Julian Simon: given Japan's apparent demonstration that growth through innovation is a viable alternative, is immigration actually necessary for the U.S. economy?

"I've never said it's *necessary,*" Simon replied.

He just thinks it helps. But how much? And with what side effects?

ECONOMIC CONSEQUENCES FOR BLACKS

As it happens, the United States contains one particular group that is clearly vulnerable to competition from immigration: American blacks.

This question has attracted attention for years. In New York City in the 1830s, before mass immigration began, most domestic servants were black; twenty years later, they were Irish.[16] Later, and more dramatically, immigration from Europe after the Civil War is often said to have fatally retarded the economic integration of the freed slaves. For example, blacks were apparently crowded out of skilled jobs they had been working their way into both in central Pennsylvania steel mills and in northern Michigan logging and lumber mills.[17]

Prominent black leaders certainly saw immigration this way. "Every hour sees us elbowed out of some employment to make room perhaps for some newly arrived emigrants, whose hunger and color are thought to give them a title to especial favor," said Frederick Douglass, escaped slave and abolitionist orator.[18]

"To those of the white race who look to the incoming of those of foreign birth and strange tongue and habits for the prosperity of the South, I would repeat what I say to my own race, *Cast down your bucket where you are,*" the founder of the all-black Tuskegee Institute, Booker T. Washington, powerfully urged in his famous speech at the 1895 Atlanta Exposition. "Cast it down among the eight millions of Negroes," he continued, in a pointed reference to immigrants' radical political habits,

> . . . who have, without strikes and labor wars tilled your fields, cleared your forests . . . nurs[ed] your children, watch[ed] by the sick-beds of your mothers and fathers, and often follow[ed] them with tear-dimmed eyes to their graves.[19]

In later years, Washington's argument that acquiring basic skills was more important for blacks than contesting segregation was remembered and often reviled. His complementary plea that they be protected from immigrant competition was forgotten, as the First Great Wave surged to its crest.

More recently, no less an authority than Simon Kuznets endorsed this analysis of immigration's impact. He felt that the Second Great Immigration Lull after the 1920s enabled Southern blacks to begin their historic migration to the cities and the economic opportunities of the North.[20]

How can this happen if immigrants make more jobs than they take? Because of important qualifications that immigration enthusiasts often miss—native-born workers are not *necessarily* displaced *in aggregate.*

Julian Simon, to his credit, does not miss these qualifications. In *The Economic Consequences of Immigration,* he frankly and repeatedly acknowledges that "[a]ny labor-force change *causes some groups to suffer some harm in the short run* . . . It is true that some particular groups may be injured by a particular group of immigrants . . ."[21] (my italics).

Naturally, if you are in the particular group displaced, knowing that the economy is benefiting overall may not be much consolation.

(This effect works in reverse too. Agribusiness lobbies for cheap immigrant labor rather than mechanize itself, regardless of the overall cost to the economy. Ironically, agribusiness is often itself an unnatural bloom—subsidized by federal water projects.)

In *Friends or Strangers,* George Borjas found that blacks living in areas of immigrant concentration did not seem to have suffered significantly reduced incomes compared with those living elsewhere. The reason, he theorized, is that during the years in question—the 1970s—the effect of immigration was overwhelmed by the effects of baby boomers and women entering the labor market. Now, of course, these factors no longer apply.

But studies of specific high-immigrant areas may fail to capture a tendency for native-born workers to be repelled from them because of the increased competition. Across the entire country in the 1980s, the wages of native high school dropouts fell by 10 percent relative to the wages of more educated workers. Borjas has more recently calculated that about a third of that decline is due to immigration.[22]

Since the Great Society reforms, a significant part of the black community has succumbed to social pathology. As Andrew Hacker put it in his 1992 bestseller, *Two Nations: Black and White, Separate, Hostile, Unequal,*

> . . . fewer blacks now have steady jobs of any kind and their unemployment rates have been growing progressively worse relative to those recorded for whites.[23]

There is at least a possibility that this is related to the simultaneous opening of the immigration floodgates. Which is why it is to current policy, and not to critics of immigration, that the charge of "racism" might best be applied.

IMMIGRATION AND THE METAMARKET

I said in Chapter 1 that an interest in free markets is a hazard of my occupation. But I have to admit that some of us in the free-market ghetto are "semi-skilled intellectuals," in the scathing phrase of Irving Kristol (himself a true idea craftsman). What this means is that we take ideas crafted by others and fit them into place. If they don't fit, well, we bash them in anyway. And on the subject of immigration, there's a great deal of bashing indeed.

It's wrong. A commitment to free trade and free markets does not mean that you would sell your mother if the price were right. The free market necessarily exists within a societal framework. And it can function only if the institutions in that framework are appropriate. For example, a defined system of private property rights is now widely agreed to be one essential precondition.

Economists have a word for these preconditions: the "metamarket." *Some degree of ethnic and cultural coherence may be among these preconditions.* Thus immigration may be a metamarket issue.

At the very least, a diverse population increases what in economics-speak are called "transaction costs." Dealing with people whom you don't know and therefore can't trust requires expensive precautions. I suspect this is one factor behind the legalism infesting business practices in the United States as compared with Britain.

Beyond this, capitalism generates inequality and, therefore, envy.

And such emotions can be much more intense across ethnic and racial lines—witness the fate of Los Angeles's Korean storekeepers, burned out during the Rodney King riots.

This is not an unprecedented insight. Friedrich von Hayek, the first classical liberal to win the Nobel Prize for economics, used to advance a sort of sociobiological argument for the apparently immortal appeal of socialism. Cities and civilization have come very late in human history, he pointed out. Almost all mankind's experience has been in small hunter-gatherer bands. Face-to-face relationships are still much more comprehensible to us than impersonal ones. Thus, for example, an increase in rent provokes an irresistible urge to bash the greedy landlord with rent controls, despite all the evidence that this reaction leads merely to shortages and inequity.

And, to extend Hayek's argument, it is obviously easier to demonize a landlord if his features—language, religion—appear alien.

Another classical liberal economics Nobel laureate, Milton Friedman, has speculated that the culture of the English-speaking world itself may be, from an economic standpoint, *sui generis* . . . in Simon's phrase. I interviewed him for *Forbes* magazine in 1988:

> FRIEDMAN: . . . The history of the world is the history of tyranny and misery and stagnation. Periods of growth are exceptional, very exceptional.
>
> BRIMELOW: *You've mentioned what you see as the institutional prerequisites for capitalism. Do you think there might be cultural prerequisites too?*
>
> FRIEDMAN: Oh, yes. For example, truthfulness. The success of Lebanon as a commercial entrepôt [before its long-repressed ethnic divisions finally exploded into civil war] was to a significant degree because the merchants' word could be trusted. It cut down transaction costs.
>
> It's a curious fact that capitalism developed and has really come to fruition in the English-speaking world. It hasn't really made the same progress even in Europe—certainly not in France, for instance. I don't know why this is so, but the fact has to be admitted.[24]

It's a simple exercise in logic:

1. *Capitalism (and no doubt every other economic system) needs specific cultural prerequisites to function.*
2. *Immigration can alter the cultural patterns of a society.*

THEREFORE—

3. *Immigration can affect a society's ability to sustain capitalism.*

Let's leave the last word to George Borjas, again. "*The economic arguments for immigration simply aren't decisive,*" he says. "You have to make a political case—for example, does the U.S. have to take Mexican immigrants to provide a safety valve?"

9

IMMIGRATION HAS CONSEQUENCES: CULTURAL, SOCIAL, ENVIRONMENTAL . . .

The most obvious fact about the history of racial and ethnic groups is how different they have been—and still are. . . .

Human differences are often assumed away in social theories. . . . But this fashionable view of society ignores the fact that groups may carry their own messages with them from country to country—a very different message from those who live cheek-by-jowl with them in the same society and sit next to them in the same school rooms or on the same factory assembly line.

—**THOMAS SOWELL,**
The Economics and Politics of Race: An International Perspective

Perhaps because he is himself black, or because his formidable reputation deters critics, Hoover Institution economist Thomas Sowell, quoted above, has not felt the usual inhibitions about studying the varying achievements of different ethnic groups.

His work, begun in his *Ethnic America: A History* (1981), conclusively demonstrates that cultural patterns are pervasive, powerful and remarkably persistent. Traits like attitudes toward work and education are intrinsically related to economic success. Thus Germans, Japanese and Jews are successful wherever they are in the world.

In addition, Sowell has shown that these ethnic differences persist *even after generations of living together under common institu-*

tions, as in the United States. What he calls the "messages" that different groups carry still come through loud and clear.

"Ethnicity matters," agrees George Borjas, "and it matters for a long time." His own analyses of census data show that educational achievement, economic success and welfare recipiency differ systematically between ethnic groups. And the disparities last for generations—the effects of the different groups arriving in the 1890–1920 Great Wave of Immigration are still discernable in America today.

THE CULTURAL CONSEQUENCES OF IMMIGRATION

In a sense, economists are just rediscovering what historians have always known. The Brandeis University historian David Hackett Fischer recently struck a massive blow for cultural history with a monumental work: *Albion's Seed: Four British Folkways in America* (1989). It ingeniously traced America's dominant sectional traditions all the way back to four distinct waves of colonial immigration from different regions of Britain into four American "cultural hearths":

- *New England:* 21,000 East Anglian Puritans to Massachusetts, 1629–41
- *the South:* about 45,000 gentry and indentured servants from the south and west of England to Virginia, 1642–75
- *the Middle Atlantic:* 23,000 North Midland Quakers to the Delaware, 1675–1725
- *the Mountain South:* about 250,000 Border English and Scots, Ulster Protestants ("Scotch-Irish") to the Appalachian "Back Country," 1717–75

Subsequent migration from these four "cultural hearths" across the continent can still be detected in the four American "speech regions" delineated by linguistic geographers in the mid-twentieth century:

- *Northern:* New England; upstate New York; northern Ohio, Indiana, Michigan, Wisconsin; northern Plains; Pacific Northwest; some urban islands like Denver, San Francisco
- *Midland:* middle latitudes from Pennsylvania to Pacific Coast, widening at the Mississippi Valley
- *Coastal South:* Virginia through Florida and Gulf of Mexico
- *Highland Southern:* Appalachia, lower Mississippi Valley, Texas, New Mexico, Arizona, Southern California

I recommend Fischer's book as a Christmas present for Americans who visibly belong to one or another of these traditions—often nowadays without realizing it.

Which involves more Americans than might appear at first sight, because these traditions are assimilative. As Fischer writes: "The author's Protestant stereotypes about the culture of Judaism were utterly exploded by his Brandeis students who have included Yankee Jews, Philadelphia Jews, southern Jews and, most startling of all, backslapping Texas Jews in cowboy boots and ten gallon hats."

But he adds, "Their culture was a *product* of *ethnicity* and *region*"[1] (my italics). Clearly, immigration can alter the balance of this equation, and will.

Thus the culture of a country, exactly like its ecology, turns out to be a living thing, sensitive and even fragile. Neither can easily be intruded upon without consequences.

Curiously, Congress has shaken off its general paralysis to recognize that immigration can have cultural consequences—*for Pacific Islanders.* Five U.S. territories—American Samoa, the Federated States of Micronesia, the Republic of the Marshall Islands, the Commonwealth of the Northern Mariana Islands, and Palau—have been granted local control over immigration to protect their ethnic majorities. In American Samoa and the Northern Marianas, U.S. citizens cannot even own land unless they are Samoan, Chamorro or Carolinian.[2]

"But aren't these consequences good?" Naturally, there isn't anything in the immigration enthusiasts' script about cultural consequences. However, this is their usual reaction if you insist on raising the point.

Francis Fukuyama, author of *The End of History and the Last*

Man, and one of the country's most celebrated intellectuals after a controversy he provoked about the universal application of American values, made this argument in a piece he wrote for *Commentary* partly in response to my *National Review* cover story. Fukuyama is a sophisticated commentator who acknowledged that there is a ("Christian Anglo-Saxon") core to America. But he argued that American culture was actually being reinforced by the strong "family values" of Hispanic immigrants. *Commentary*'s readers expect blood in the correspondence columns, but I was impressed with Fukuyama's subtlety and merely pointed out wimpishly that immigrants could have splendid family values and still not be Americans. (Sociologists have a name for this sort of indifference to the wider society: "amoral familialism.") Michael Lind of *National Interest* magazine was tougher. He noted scathingly that the data show Hispanic "family values" are another immigration enthusiast's myth—Mexican-American out-of-wedlock births, for example, are more than twice the white rate, at 28.9 percent.

You can't blame the immigration enthusiasts, necessarily. They are remembering all those endless newspaper columns about Vietnamese valedictorians and the delights of ethnic cuisine.

And it's embarrassing. In the current climate, it is impossible to discuss the failings of any ethnic group.

But look at it this way: there are two sides to every question. Thomas Sowell's work shows that cultural traits are related to economic success. Why wouldn't they relate also to economic failure—or worse?

In fact, George Borjas and others have already shown that national origin is an excellent predictor of economic failure, as measured by the propensity to go on welfare.

Thus there can be no doubt: the cultural characteristics of current immigrant groups will have consequences for the United States far into the future.

SOCIAL CONSEQUENCES OF IMMIGRATION: CRIME

For example, crime.

". . . the United States is in the grip of the third of three great crime waves," writes Ted Robert Gurr, professor of political science at the University of Maryland at College Park and editor of *Violence in America: The History of Crime.*[3] "They began about 50 years apart—approximately 1850, 1900, and 1960—and each has lasted for 20 to 30 years."

These waves, Gurr argues, contrast with a gradual decline of personal violence in Western societies generally, attributable to what he calls "the civilizing process." He adds:

> America's three great crime waves can be linked to *immigration,* economic deprivation and war, which all interfere with the civilizing process . . . *the first and second episodes of violent crime wound down as immigrants were incorporated into the expanding economy.*[4] [my italics]

Obviously, the current crime wave cannot ebb if immigrants continue to arrive as fast as they are incorporated—or faster.

Note carefully: immigration is not the *only* cause of crime. It may not even be the major cause of crime. But it is a *factor.*

And remember: this is immigration that has no economic rationale from the American point of view. Immigration enthusiasts have to find some other justification—and safe streets is not it.

News about immigrant crime is firmly in the unfit-to-print category. Researchers find that official figures on immigrant and ethnic crime patterns are rarely collected. Cities like New York, Chicago and San Francisco have even instructed their employees not to cooperate with the INS. *There has been no serious academic study of the impact on crime of the Second Great Wave of Immigration.*[5]

But here are a few pointers:

- *Criminal* aliens—*noncitizens who commit crimes—accounted for over 25 percent of the federal prison population in 1993.* They represent its fastest-growing segment. (And remember, this doesn't count naturalized immigrants who commit crimes.)

- *About 450,000 noncitizens have been convicted of crimes and are either in American jails, on probation or on parole.*[6]
- *In May 1990, a study showed that foreign-born criminals comprised 18 percent of the inmates passing through the Los Angeles County Jail Inmate Reception Center.* Some 11 percent of the inmates were foreign-born criminals whose offenses were sufficiently serious to qualify them as "deportable aliens."
- By May 1991, a follow-up study revealed, only half of these "deportable aliens" had been returned to their country of origin . . . *and over 40 percent of the "deportable aliens" had already been rearrested in the United States for further crimes.* (An average of about two crimes each, as a matter of fact.) Not only was this deportable group highly criminal, with a lifetime average of six arrests each, but some of them had clearly just turned around and come straight back to the United States after deportation—in itself a felony.[7]

This is what it means to have borders out of control.

- In 1989, when California Superior Court Judge David O. Carter allowed the INS to work in his Orange County courtroom, *some 36 percent of convicted criminals, many of them repeat offenders, turned out to be illegal aliens.* This did not include many individuals applying for IRCA amnesty; or individuals from countries refusing to accept deported felons, like Vietnam, Iran or Cuba—*whom the INS consequently ignores.* Up to 80 percent of the cases carried by some senior probation officers are estimated to be illegals.[8]

(*"But they're all in for drug offenses—they're international drug smugglers, not really immigrants at all!"* Some 81 percent of sentenced non-citizens in federal jails are indeed there for drug violations, but the wild claim by immigration enthusiasts that they are just smugglers and therefore somehow don't count is hard to take seriously. A more reasonable explanation: the fact that immigrants dominate the drug business inside the U.S. [see below].)

Still, in today's one-way immigration debate, immigration enthusiasts can get away with murder . . . almost literally, in this context. So for the record: only a fifth (18 percent) of those non-citizen inmates were sentenced for "drug importation." Over four fifths (81 percent) are in for "drug trafficking," which the Federal Bureau of Prisons says means selling drugs on America's street corners. Moreover, some 61 percent of *all* federal inmates are confined for drug violations. Are these American-born criminals "international drug smugglers" too?[9]

(I find more interesting the fragmentary evidence that the proportions of immigrant inmates in state-prison systems are sometimes less than the state's immigrant population. For example, in 1990 some 19.4 percent of California's state-prison inmates were foreign-born, as opposed to 21.7 percent of the state's population. Perhaps immigrant offenders are passed up to the federal level for deportation—deportation rates have shot up more than 1,000 percent since the mid-1980s—or congregate, as yet unreported, in county and city jails. Or perhaps they just Don't Tell: California has no foolproof way of checking status, but it does report that 15 percent of state-prison inmates were illegal aliens, although they make up anywhere from 3.5 to 7 percent—who knows?—of the state's population as a whole. In any case, immigrants in jail pose the same question for Americans as immigrants on welfare: *what's the point of immigrants who are no better than we are?*[10])

Of course, it is simply common sense that crime is a cost of immigration, if for no other reason than that immigrants tend to be young men, disproportionately inclined to crime in all societies. Immigration enthusiasts would do better to admit this cost honestly, and argue instead that it is outweighed by the benefits of immigration—whatever they are.

Equally, it is simply common sense that immigration can mean ethnic change, which can mean consequences for crime. For example, random street crime, the great scandal of American cities since the 1960s, is related to impulsiveness and what sociologists call "present-orientation," i.e., the inability to reckon with consequences. And this turns out to be a key cultural variable, differing significantly between ethnic groups.

Inevitably, therefore, certain ethnic cultures are more crime prone than others. The numbers can be staggering. For example: Blacks make up only 12 percent of the American population but 64 percent of all violent-crime arrests.[11]

However, less obvious but of urgent concern to the U.S. Department of Justice, is another ethnic-based criminal pattern: the propensity to develop forms of organized crime.

You can see why this has typically been ethnically based. Criminals prefer to deal with co-conspirators they understand and trust—in economist-speak, it reduces their transaction costs. And such tightly knit groups, operating in a foreign and sometimes obscure language, are notoriously difficult for the police to penetrate.

In recent years the Mafia or Cosa Nostra has been in decline, not least because of the acculturation of Italian Americans. But crime is "dirty work" that some of the post-1965 immigrant groups are positively anxious to do—more violently, particularly in the burgeoning drug business, than the Mafia ever was.

There are several such new "mafias," each with its own specialties: Colombians (cocaine); Mexicans (marijuana, auto theft, alien smuggling); Hong Kong Chinese (heroin, alien smuggling); South Koreans (prostitution) . . . and even lesser-known communities like the Chaldeans, Iraqi Christians whose heroically run convenience stores in the Detroit ghetto are reportedly centers of criminal activity (narcotics, gambling, coupon fraud).

You haven't read much about this because of the contemporary taboo that ensures only good things can be said about immigrants. One remarkable article shattering that taboo appeared in the January 1993 *Vanity Fair* magazine. Writer Robert I. Friedman quoted experts who believe that the predominantly Russian Jewish "Organizatsiya" is on the way to displacing La Costa Nostra and becoming "the largest criminal syndicate in the world."

"The Russians are just as crazy as the Jamaican drug gangs," a Ukrainian-speaking New York detective who had declined to work the Russian beat told Friedman. "They won't hesitate to go after a cop's family."

Friedman reported that the Soviet émigrés, the educated elite of a totally corrupt society, have created an unusually organized form of organized crime. For example, they have vastly expanded the bootleg-gasoline tax-evasion scam—formerly operated by "Turkish and Greek immigrants"—and have used it to penetrate legitimate businesses, like Getty Oil. They are bringing in Israeli ex-commandos. And they adroitly manipulate a good cause: "Jewish organizations have lobbied the Justice Department to downplay the Russian Mob," Friedman reports, "fearing that adverse publicity will jeopardize the mass exodus of Russian Jews to Israel."

"I never felt anti-Semitism [in the Soviet Union]," Marat Balagula—whom Friedman describes as "the Godfather of the Russian Mob"—told him frankly. ". . . I used that as an excuse when I applied for my visa."[12]

Another remarkable description of an ethnic mafia appeared in the spring 1993 issue of *Social Contract* magazine. David Simcox, a senior fellow at the Center for Immigration Studies, reported that U.S. law enforcement officials estimate an incredible *75 percent* of the 100,000 Nigerians now in the United States are involved in "an impressive and innovative variety of fraud schemes" using extensive countrywide networks. Cost to the United States in 1989: some $1 billion. Nigerian specialties: immigration and citizenship fraud; bank and credit card fraud; welfare fraud; insurance fraud; heroin. (The State Department estimates that 35 to 40 percent of all heroin entering the United States is imported by Nigerians.[13])

Interestingly, Nigerian criminals come from their country's privileged classes. They have education levels significantly above the immigrant norm. But as Simcox says bluntly: "[Nigeria] is notorious for corruption and non-existent business ethics even by African standards."

SOCIAL CONSEQUENCES OF IMMIGRATION: PUBLIC HEALTH

Whenever large numbers of people are on the move, disease has the opportunity to erupt. Cholera and smallpox returned to the United States with the Irish immigrants of the 1840s.[14] Awareness of this danger was one reason immigrants arriving at Ellis Island were so rigorously inspected by efficient batteries of doctors, the myth of "Open Borders" notwithstanding. Of the 24,000 refused admission in 1910, about 15 percent were carriers of contagious disease.[15]

- *With 2 to 3 million illegal entries every year, it is quite possible that the United States has never been so unprotected against immigration's impact on its public health standards.*

News about immigrant-borne disease is also firmly in the unfit-to-print circular file. But here are a few fragments:

- *Tuberculosis:* once the leading killer in the United States, tuberculosis was virtually extinct by the 1970s. Now it is surging. Partly this is because of new strains resistant to antibiotics, but largely it's because of immigration from regions like Latin America where the disease is endemic (foreign-born cases accounted for nearly two thirds of the increase in the last decade, according to the Centers for Disease Control and Prevention in Atlanta). In 1991, some 27 percent of U.S. cases were foreign-born; over 60 percent of California's cases, and 30 to 80 percent of the cases in some immigrant-heavy Washington suburbs.[16]
- *Leprosy:* of the six thousand patients in the United States in 1987, *90 percent* were refugees or immigrants from Southeast Asia or Mexico.[17]
- *Measles:* virtually eliminated in the United States during the 1980s, measles is flaring up—in Hispanic areas, particularly among recent arrivals from Latin America.[18]
- *Cholera, malaria, dengue fever* (what?—it's like yellow fever): all are widespread in Latin America, and all have been reported in the United States recently.[19]

Quite possibly, disease incubated in the teeming human petri dishes that Third World cities now comprise may be the chance factor that finally crystallizes immigration as a political issue in the United States. For example, the U.S. Institute of Medicine has recently predicted "*with some confidence*" that if yellow fever, the incurable mosquito-borne disease now resurgent in Africa and Amazonia, returns to New Orleans, public health defenses could be quickly overwhelmed: "100,000 people would become ill . . . and 10,000 would likely die within 90 days . . ."[20]

ENVIRONMENTAL CONSEQUENCES OF IMMIGRATION

Environmentalism has been one of the most powerful political forces of the last thirty years. It has provided an entirely new role for government. The federal Environmental Protection Agency was founded only in 1970. But it now accounts for a seventh of the staff and a third of the spending of the entire U.S. government regulatory apparatus.

In 1990, EPA officials estimated that complying with their pollution-control regulations alone caused Americans to spend about $115 billion a year. That was a remarkable 2.1 percent of the GNP.[21]

It's all wasted. Well, not *wasted* exactly (although there are some very critical critics) but possibly misdirected. *For the single biggest impact on the environment is the fact that the American population, almost uniquely in the developed world, continues to grow.* Increasingly, immigration is driving U.S. population growth. (See Chapter 2, page 46.) Washington's immigration and environmental policies are working in opposite directions.

This is a point that immigration enthusiasts have extraordinary difficulty grasping. *"And, environmentalists, please take note,"* Ben Wattenberg writes, *"immigration does not increase global population; it only shifts it around."*[22] Yeah. It shifts it to Southern California, which is being paved over as a result.

The relationship between population and pollution is a little more subtle than it looks—just like the issue of the impact of immigration on native workers. A primitive band of slash-and-burn agriculturalists can cause more devastation than a much larger community of modern exurbanites with sewage systems and manicured horse farms.

But this subtlety applies only within limits. Something has clearly got to give if the population of California grows from 20 million in 1970 to 60 million by 2020, which is Leon Bouvier's upper-limit projection. (His lower-limit projection: a mere 44 million. Phooey!)[23]

The fragile desert ecologies of the Southwest may not be utterly destroyed. But they must be transformed. California must cease to be the Golden State and become the Golden Subdivision.

This prospect is presumably anathema to true environmentalists, who value wilderness in itself. But although a few were active in founding FAIR, most members of the professional environmentalist establishment in Washington avoid the issue. Which, frankly, is a measure of the extent to which they have been seduced by their inside-the-Beltway alliances—just as the Civil Rights lobby never voices the anti-immigration sentiments widespread among the black masses. (Irritated grass-roots environmentalists have now formed new groups specifically to address population issues, such as Carrying Capacity Network and Population-Environment Balance.)

It is certainly true, as immigration enthusiasts sometimes argue, that there are still many places in the world more crowded than California. And perhaps it is even theoretically possible that California could sustain a population of a billion or so, and become a sort of Hong Kong writ large.

Environmentalists don't like to concede this. They tend to think there would be a catastrophic ecological breakdown that would actually threaten life. And there's no doubt that Hong Kongifornia would be pretty catastrophic for the current flora and fauna. But let's suppose it could be done by triple-parking human beings—*wouldn't it be horrible?*

- **Population growth is not simply an environmental issue: it is more urgently an amenity issue.**

Uncrowded ranges, empty beaches, mountain solitude—they may not sound as dramatic a rallying cry as the claim that food and water might run out. But there was a time, quite recently, when no one would have doubted they were just as necessary to the American soul.

Amenity issues are ultimately questions of values. And values, as we have seen, differ between ethnic traditions. You do meet environmentalists who mutter darkly about the post-Colonial immigrant groups' preference for cities (demonstrably true for some of them).

But here's a more concrete example:

Like most New Yorkers—at least the ones who work in the media—I am sentimental about Asian immigration. They seem law-abiding and hard-working (although I gather you aren't supposed to say this. And maybe it's just another immigration myth: there are growing reports of gangs and welfare dependency).

Still, the young female students I see every morning entering the Parsons School of Design, next to *Forbes*'s offices, are very charming, and fashionable.

But some years ago, on a radio call-in show in Vancouver, Canada, I was shocked to find, crackling through the microphones, an intense hostility to the developing influx of Hong Kong Chinese.

One symbolic reason: wealthy Chinese families are buying choice Victorian houses in wooded residential areas and—*cutting down all the trees.* (Supposedly, there's a Chinese superstition that evil spirits live in trees.) Then, often, they build enormous "monster houses," covering as much of the lot as possible.

This behavior is deeply shocking to Vancouver standards. Of course, it's not wrong in any profound sense (unless you like trees). But it is a genuine conflict of values, between groups who seem to have so much in common. *And it would not have happened without immigration.*

POSTSCRIPT . . .

> *The federal government has begun installing powerful floodlights along a four-mile stretch of the U.S.-Mexican border, west of the San Ysidro port of entry, where illegal crossings routinely occur. . . .*
>
> *The lighting project was approved in 1992, but it was delayed while experts studied whether the powerful lamps would disturb the nesting habits of the federally protected California gnatcatcher.*
>
> —*San Diego Union-Tribune,* January 22, 1994

What's wrong with this picture?

10

IMMIGRATION HAS CONSEQUENCES: POLITICAL POWER

. . . [immigrants] will bring with them the principles of the governments they leave, or if able to throw them off, it will be in exchange for an unbridled licentiousness, passing, as usual, from one extreme to the other. It would be a miracle were they to stop precisely at the point of temperate liberty.

—**THOMAS JEFFERSON,**
Notes on the State of Virginia (1782)

The safety of a republic depends essentially on the energy of a common national sentiment; on a uniformity of principles and habits; on the exemption of the citizens from foreign bias, and prejudice; and on the love of country which will almost invariably be found to be closely connected with birth, education and family.

The opinion advanced in [Thomas Jefferson's] Notes on Virginia *is undoubtedly correct, that foreigners will generally be apt to bring with them attachments to the persons they have left behind; to the country of their nativity, and to its particular customs and manners. . . . The influx of foreigners must, therefore, tend to produce a heterogeneous compound; to change and corrupt the national spirit; to complicate and confound public opinion; to introduce foreign propensities. In the composition of society, the harmony of the ingredients is all important, and whatever tends to a discordant intermixture must have an injurious tendency.*

The United States have already felt the evils of incorporating a large number of foreigners into their national mass; by promoting in different classes different predilections in favor of particular foreign nations, and antipathies against others, it has served very much to divide the community and to distract our councils.

—**ALEXANDER HAMILTON,**
response to Jefferson's message to Congress, January 12, 1802

"Immigration is the American tradition." In fact, as we saw in Chart 4, there was little immigration for long periods of American history. *Intermittent* immigration is the American tradition.

But immigration enthusiasts often make the more sweeping claim on the strength of one of the numerous charges leveled at King George III in the Declaration of Independence:

> *He has endeavoured to prevent the Population of these States; for that Purpose obstructing the Laws for Naturalization of Foreigners; refusing to pass others to encourage their Migrations hither. . . .*

(The rest of the complaint is rarely quoted: *"and raising the Conditions of new Appropriations of Land."* The real issue was the expanding Colonies' land-lust: the British authorities were afraid it would goad the outraged Indians west of the Appalachians into another uprising like Pontiac's Conspiracy of 1763. Even then, immigration had political consequences.)

However, despite the Founding Fathers' lip service to immigration—which at that time was purely a hypothetical issue in most of the Thirteen Colonies—even a cursory study of their attitudes reveals that their welcome was in fact highly qualified. They viewed immigration, as they viewed most things, with caution and skepticism.

"Put none but Americans on guard tonight," George Washington is supposed to have ordered at a key point in the Revolutionary War. His implicit doubts about the loyalty of the foreign-born are echoed in the Constitution, which requires the president and vice president to be "a natural-born citizen." Other examples abound.

Look again at the two quotations I've chosen to head this chapter, from Thomas Jefferson and Alexander Hamilton—himself an immigrant, from the British-ruled Caribbean island of Nevis. They show how the Founding Fathers' consensus on immigration went right across the political spectrum.

Jefferson and Hamilton led the two principal contending factions in the new American Republic. They favored, respectively, states' rights and a closer, more centralized union. They had differences on immigration, tussling over the residency requirement for naturalization because immigrants were thought to favor the Jeffersonians. But, basically, Jefferson and Hamilton shared the same reservations—*they knew immigration had political consequences.*

THE POLITICAL CONSEQUENCES OF IMMIGRATION

Many immigration enthusiasts are reluctant to admit that a shift in the distribution of political power is even a theoretical possibility. So it is worth emphasizing: *there are plenty of cases of immigrants and their descendants threatening a country's political balance.*

Two examples from either end of this century:

- *South Africa at the beginning of the twentieth century:* the Anglo-Boer (Afrikaans-speaker) War was raging in South Africa, triggered when the Afrikaans-speaking Republic of Transvaal was threatened by an influx of predominantly English-speaking *uitlanders* ("foreigners") attracted by gold discoveries. Transvaal refused to allow the *uitlanders* to vote; they attempted a coup.
- *Fiji at the end of the twentieth century:* the military ruler of Fiji has imposed a new constitution guaranteeing the prime ministership and a majority of legislative seats to "indigenous [racially Melanesian] Fijians." The Asian Indian minority, descendants of immigrant field-workers, had grown to virtually half the total population and had managed to elect an Indian-dominated government. It had promptly been deposed by the Fijian-dominated army.

And how about this chilling comment from the *Harvard Encyclopedia of American Ethnic Groups*?

> In obtaining land grants in Texas, Anglo immigrants agreed to become Mexican citizens, obey Mexican laws, accept the official Catholic faith, learn Spanish, and take other steps to become fully assimilated as law-abiding citizens. However, over the years, it became clear that these settlers, now Anglo-Mexicans, were not becoming integrated into the nation and that Anglo immigration had become a problem. . . . The strains and disagreements ultimately led to the Texas Revolution in 1835.[1]

Er, quite.

In the United States today, one glaring possibility is that the Mexican influx into Texas and the Southwest might eventually reverse this process. Groups like the campus-based MEChA, the Movimiento Estudiantil Chicano de Aztlan, are openly working for Aztlan, a Hispanic-dominated political unit to be carved out of the Southwest and (presumably) reunited with Mexico.[2] The technical term for this is *irredentism*—first applied by the newly united Italians in the nineteenth century to the "unredeemed" Italian-speaking areas in Switzerland and Austria-Hungary. Or *revanchism*—first applied to the French desire for revenge against the German Empire for seizing Alsace-Lorraine after the Franco-Prussian War of 1870–71.

How popular this irredentism may be among Mexican Americans is debatable—for now. But it should not obscure another development that already appears well under way: the Mexican government's claim to what amounts to extraterritorial rights over Mexican immigrants in the territory of the (former?) United States.

Recently, Mexico has opened "cultural institutes" and sponsored programs to teach Spanish to illiterate Hispanics from New York to California. It has, for example, reportedly donated textbooks and bilingual teachers to the Los Angeles school system. It has announced that it is "monitoring" death-penalty cases involving Mexican citizens and is lobbying for abolition of capital punishment in the states where they are held. And it is *supervising informal leadership elections in migrant communities to ensure that they "have proper representation before American city councils or county government."* (State Department's reported comment: "It is hard to object to people being shown how to avail themselves of the rights they have in this country." Beat me! Beat me!) Every major Mexican political party has opened offices in California.[3]

The plain fact is that this is a rational strategy for the Mexican elite. They can dump their poor in the United States—*and* become the tail that wags the geopolitical dog.

It's particularly interesting when you reflect that it is actually illegal for Mexican citizens to leave their country without official sanction. So the 2 to 3 million illegal immigrants each year are breaking not just U.S. law, but Mexican law as well. Moreover, *Mexican law views the American-born children of Mexican immigrants to the U.S. as Mexican citizens.*

Of course, these political consequences of immigration need not necessarily threaten the integrity of the country . . . just its foreign policy.

For example, in recent years Washington pursued totally contradictory policies toward the white settler communities of Southern Africa and the Middle East. It slapped economic sanctions on the former, but it supplied economic subsidies to the latter. Domestic ethnic-group pressure is the most obvious explanation for this striking difference.

Equally, what Alexander Hamilton called "predilections" among U.S. ethnic groups have influenced American attitudes toward foreign issues as diverse as the Greek-Turkish conflict and the Haitian military's domestic habits.

IMMIGRATION HAS PARTISAN CONSEQUENCES: REPUBLICANS

Ethnicity is destiny in American politics. This point was made definitively in Kevin Phillips's brilliant book *The Emerging Republican Majority* (1968), which demonstrated that immigrant settlement patterns had an amazingly persistent influence on subsequent American voting patterns.

Phillips predicted on the basis of demographic trends that the Republicans would replace the Democrats as the majority party. And he was undeniably right in the presidential contest—from 1968, the Republicans won five of the next six elections—even if timid and unimaginative leadership (and possibly the Democrats' advantages of incumbency) squandered the opportunity on the congressional level.

As a glance around any of their meetings will tell you, the Republicans are the party of the American majority; the Democrats are the party of the American minorities.

On its WASP foundation, the Republican party has been able to add the children of each immigrant wave as they assimilate. This was the unmistakable subtext of the 1988 presidential election. With a Greek American nominee, and implicitly anti-WASP attacks on George Bush's "preppie-ness," the Democrats hoped to hold the 1890–1920 immigrant wave. But they failed, just as nominating John F. Kennedy in 1960 did not prevent the continued defection of Irish Americans.

However, the post-1965 immigrants are overwhelmingly visible minorities. And these are precisely the groups that the Republican party has had the most difficulty recruiting.

What's more, it is important to note that, despite the hopeful rhetoric of "bleeding-heart conservatives" like former Secretary of Housing and Urban Development Jack Kemp, this failure is not necessarily a question of the Republicans' making nice, or nicer. *It may reflect the more divergent minorities' different values*—and their more radical feeling of alienation from white American society.

The numbers are indisputable: Current immigration policy is inexorably reinforcing Jesse Jackson's Rainbow Coalition.

That strained sound you hear is the conservative establishment whistling as they pass by the rainbow. Prohibited from discussing the problem by the "bland bargain" that has been the price of toleration by the liberal establishment—as we saw in Chapter 5—they have indulged in a frenzy of wishful thinking.

- *"We get quite a good vote from some Hispanic groups."* Well, Hispanics are not quite as Democratic as the blacks—that's a statistical impossibility—but the Republicans still face an uphill struggle. Even the much-lauded Cuban vote has actually been quite split, electing liberal Democrats like Claude Pepper and Dante Fascell to Congress.
- *"West Indians are different."* Some West Indians do appear to have been more economically successful than American blacks, although it must be said that nowadays part of their enterprise goes into drug "posses" and car-theft rings. However, the skill level of the post-1965 wave of West Indian immigrants has deteriorated sharply. And anyway, the political consequences were always illusory. Shirley Chisholm and Stokely Carmichael are both of West Indian descent.
- *"The Asians are small-business types, education-minded, family-oriented—they're natural Republicans."* So were the Jews, and look at their politics—still overwhelmingly and outspokenly Democratic despite the best efforts of a brilliant generation of conservative Jewish intellectuals. And Hawaii, where Asians predominate, is a Democratic stronghold.

The truth is this: *no one has the faintest idea how the Asians will vote.*

But since 1965 they have become a minority twice as large as the Jews—and potentially at least as influential.

IMMIGRATION HAS PARTISAN CONSEQUENCES: DEMOCRATS

Still, everyone has problems. If you look at it from an ethnic perspective, the Democrats' victory in the 1992 presidential election was somewhat less encouraging than it appeared at first sight.

The Democrats won because the white vote was split by the third-party candidate, Ross Perot. According to *The New York Times,*[4] Bill Clinton won with an astonishingly low 39 percent of the white vote (which was 87 percent of the total vote). George Bush got 41 percent—and Ross Perot, 20 percent. Clinton got 82 percent of the blacks (8 percent of the total vote) and 62 percent of the Hispanics (3 percent of the total vote).

(But, for what it's worth, he got only 29 percent of the Asians—1 percent of the total vote—as opposed to 55 percent for Bush and 16 percent for Perot.)

Among white Protestants (49 percent of the total), Clinton got 33 percent, Bush 46 percent (!) and Perot 21 percent. Among "white born-again Christians" (17 percent of the total), Clinton got 23 percent, Bush 61 percent (!!) and Perot 15 percent. *Remember—practically until the Civil War, white Protestants* were *America.*

But Clinton got a majority of the Jewish vote (78 percent: it's just 4 percent of the total vote). Bush got 12 percent; Perot, 10 percent. *As usual. Since 1980, Republican presidential candidates have never got more than 39 percent of the Jewish vote—and that was in 1980, Ronald Reagan's first election.*

The brutal truth is this:

- *the Clinton administration is a black–Hispanic–Jewish–minority white* (Southerners used to call them "scalawags") *coalition.*

If the immigration pincers continue to close on America, the Clinton administration's electoral coalition may be a harbinger of politics to come.

On the face of it, immigration looks good for the Democrats. The more minorities, the better their chance of locking in the presidency. And, if present trends continue, there will be a lot more minorities indeed. . . .

BUT—

- **DEMOCRATS' PROBLEM #1:** There's still some way to go. The immigration pincers may not even be closing fast enough to reelect Clinton—unless the white vote is split again. (Or unless he succeeds in dividing the whites on class lines. Which he well might—for example with his tax increases.)

This problem is made more serious for the Democrats by another factor: minorities tend to be ineligible, unregistered, or too young to vote. Note that the minority proportion of the 1992 vote lagged significantly behind their proportion of the population.

- **DEMOCRATS' PROBLEM #2:** As the pincers pinch, the backlash danger grows. The Democrats' strategy of uniting the minorities and dividing the majority increasingly runs the risk alienating the majority, so that none of it stays with the Democrats at all.

This is hardly an exaggeration. In 1992, Bill Clinton got just 34 percent of white Southerners. This is an astonishingly poor performance for a Southern candidate in what was, until well within living memory, the famous Democratic "Solid South." Moreover, across the country, Clinton's vote from white men systematically lagged his vote from white women (37 percent vs. 41 percent for Bush). This suggests that the proportion of *Southern* white men who voted for him must have been far lower. Yet this is a group that in the early years of the century, when virtually no one else could vote in the South, was almost unanimously Democratic.

Moral: *the Democrats have paid a significant price for their new supporters.*

To the Democrats' unite-the-minorities, divide-the-majority strategy, the Republicans have an obvious counter-stroke: they could aim to unite the majority, attracting former blue-collar Democrats, and marginalize the minorities. In effect, this has slowly been happening anyway.

But here the Bland Bargain plays its crucial role. Under its terms, Republicans cannot question the elite consensus on racial policies, nor can they make an open appeal to white interests. This leaves an open field for the Democrats' class appeal.

- **DEMOCRATS' PROBLEM #3:** The minority coalition may not coalesce. Some of the strains between components of the Rainbow Coalition, notably between blacks and Jews, have been widely publicized.

The ultimate danger for the Democrats: disaffected components of their coalition might actually secede and set up their own political parties. For example, one 1994 poll found fully half of American blacks supporting the creation of a separate black party, double the proportion of just a few years earlier. Half of all blacks viewed themselves as a "nation within a nation," with blacks below their mid-thirties especially inclined to separatism. For the Democrats, falling black-voter turnout may just be an ominous symptom.[5]

Forming splinter parties is a perfectly rational strategy. Minority leaders might reasonably hope to monopolize patronage through local elections—where their flocks are concentrated—and to use their splinter parties' nomination as a more valuable bargaining chip at the state and federal levels. This was the successful strategy of the New York Conservative and Liberal parties in the peculiar political conditions of the Empire State.

IMMIGRATION HAS PARTISAN CONSEQUENCES—FOR EVERYBODY IN SIGHT

Indeed, the threat of new parties is the ultimate danger for the entire American political elite. The opinion polls noted in Chapter 5 make it plain: *for nearly thirty years, official immigration policy has not merely systematically ignored, but has actually been diametrically opposed to, a popular opinion that has been as adamant and absolute as it is possible to reach in a democratic society.*

This may look clever in editorial offices and congressional committee rooms. But where government is supposedly based on the consent of the governed, it inevitably raises very real questions of moral legitimacy.

Third-party insurrections are usually contained when either or both of the major parties wakes up and accommodates the discontent. But eruptions in the 1850s permanently altered the political landscape, creating the two-party system Americans know and love today. And immigration played a vital role.

The Know Nothings' American party—formed in response to the unprecedented influx of immigrant Catholics (see pages 12–13)—turned out to be an acceptable halfway house for voters moving from the Whigs to the Republicans. Significantly, a key tenet in Know Nothing ideology was contempt for all political parties and professional politicians. They were suspected (rightly) of wanting to fudge the crucial issues of the day: immigration and slavery.[6] Not coincidentally, the same contempt has been surfacing again recently—in Ross Perot's 1992 presidential vote and in the burgeoning term-limit movement.

These things happen. Ignoring immigration has already proved extremely harmful to the health of the Canadian Progressive Conservative government. In the 1993 Canadian federal election, it was annihilated, going from 159 to 2 seats in the House of Commons. Its leader, Prime Minister Kim Campbell, was defeated in her own district. The party quite possibly will never recover.

Several factors were at work. But immigration was one. The leader of the newly founded Reform party, Preston Manning, broke with the Canadian all-party consensus and offered some (extremely moderate) criticism of the current massive influx. He was denounced as a racist, as usual. But Reform leapt from one to fifty-two seats and totally displaced the Progressive Conservatives in their historic stronghold of western Canada.

Abraham Lincoln, who himself indirectly benefited from the last great party disruption associated with immigration, authored one of his famous sayings on this subject:

> *If you once forfeit the confidence of your fellow citizens, you can never regain their respect and esteem. You may fool all of the people some of the time; you can even fool some of the people all of the time; but you can't fool all of the people all of the time.*

For the leaders of democratic political parties, this is no mere matter of principle. It is a matter of prudence.

II

IMMIGRATION HAS CONSEQUENCES: A LESS PERFECT UNION

It is commonly said that America is more than a nation; it is an idea. My thesis today is the precise opposite: America is more than an idea; it is a nation.

—JOHN O'SULLIVAN,
Boston University, March 31, 1993

There is no room in this country for hyphenated Americanism. . . . The one absolutely certain way of bringing this nation to ruin, of preventing all possibility of its continuing to be a nation at all, would be to permit it to become a tangle of squabbling nationalities.

—THEODORE ROOSEVELT,
speech before the Knights of Columbus, New York, October 12, 1915

"*Immigration isn't the sort of threat to us that it might be to other nations. America is exceptional.*" But is America exceptional enough?

We've all seen a speeded-up film of the cloudscape. What appears to the naked eye to be a panorama of almost immobile grandeur writhes into wild life. Vast patterns of soaring, swooping movement are suddenly discernable. Great towering cumulonimbus formations boil up out of nowhere, dominating the sky in a way that would be terrifying if it were not in real life so gradual that we are barely aware that anything is going on.

This is a perfect metaphor for the development of the American nation. America, of course, *is* exceptional. What is exceptional about it, however, is not the way in which it was created—but the speed.

On fast-forwarding film, the great cloud formations boil up so that they dominate the sky. But they also unravel and melt away. And just as the American nation was made with unusual speed, so it is perfectly possible that it could be unmade.

Historically speaking, the whole American episode could have come and gone in the twinkling of an eye.

NATION-STATE AND NATION

Let's start with a definition. What is a "nation-state"? It is *the political expression of a nation.* And what is a "nation"? It is an *ethno-cultural community*—an interlacing of ethnicity and culture. Invariably, it speaks one language.

In recent years in the United States, there has been a tendency to emphasize the cultural part of the equation. But this is to miss a critical point. The word "nation" is derived from the Latin *nescare,* to be born. It intrinsically implies a link by blood. A nation in a real sense is an extended family. The merging process by which all nations are created is not merely cultural, but to a considerable extent biological, through intermarriage.

In his recent book *Pandaemonium,* Senator Daniel Patrick Moynihan even used this rigorous definition, in an effort to capture both culture and ethnicity: a nation is "a group of people who *believe* they are ancestrally related. It is the largest grouping that shares that belief"[1] (Moynihan's italics).

Some American commentators, for various reasons, find the idea of a nation's common ethnicity deeply distressing. They regularly denounce references to the subject as "nativism" or "tribalism."

Ironically, when I studied African history in college, my tutor deprecated any reference to "tribes." These small, primitive and incoherent groupings should, he said, be dignified as "nations."

Which suggests a useful definition: *tribalism is nationalism of which the politically correct disapprove.*

In discussing nations and the nation-state, Americans suffer from a certain cultural deprivation. They have two peculiar difficulties, which might look minor but in fact have serious results.

Peculiar American Difficulty 1: Semantic

American editors are convinced that the term "state" will confuse their readers unless reserved exclusively for the component parts of the United States—New York, California, etc. So when talking about sovereign political structures, where the British would use "state," the Germans *"staat"* and the French *"l'état,"* journalists here are compelled to use the word "nation."

Thus in the late 1980s it was common to see press references to "the nation of Yugoslavia." Of course, Yugoslavia's problem was precisely that it was not a nation at all, but a state that contained several different small but fierce nations—Croatia, Serbia, etc.

(In my helpful way, I've been trying to introduce, as an alternative to "state," the word "polity"—defined by Webster as "a politically organized unit." But it's quite hopeless. Editors always confuse it with "policy." I've also tried "country," which is sometimes an alternative in British English. No good either. They seem to think that's a type of music.)

This definitional difficulty explains one of the regular blood sports of U.S. politics: uproar because someone has unguardedly described America as a "Christian nation." Of course, in the sense that the vast majority of Americans are Christians, this is nothing less than the plain truth. It is not in the least incompatible with a secular *state* (polity).

- RESULT: *Americans who confuse basic terms in this way must inevitably also get confused about what a nation-state is, what its function is, and what it requires in order to survive.*

  Specifically, they will tend to think that America is a purely political construct, with no particular ethnic or cultural content at all.

Peculiar American Difficulty 2: Perceptual

No discussion of U.S. immigration policy gets far without someone making this helpful remark: *"We are a nation of immigrants."*

As an immigrant myself, I always pause respectfully. You never know. Maybe this is what they're taught to chant in schools nowadays, a sort of multicultural Pledge of Allegiance.

But it secretly amuses me. Do they really think other nations sprang up out of the ground? ("Autochthonous" is the classical Greek word.) The truth is that all nations are nations of immigrants. But the process is usually so slow and historic—extending over hundreds and even thousands of years—that people overlook it. They take for mountains what are merely clouds.

This is obvious in the case of the British Isles, from which—including Ireland—the largest single proportion of Americans is still derived. You can see it in the place-names. Within a few miles of my parents' home in the north of England, the names are Roman (Chester, derived from the Latin for *camp*), Saxon (anything ending in *-ton,* town, like Oxton), Viking (*by,* farm, like Irby) and Norman French (Delamere).

At times, these successive waves of peoples were clearly living cheek by jowl. Thus among these place-names is Wallesey, Anglo-Saxon for "Island of the Welsh"—"Welsh" being derived from the word used by low-German speakers for foreigners wherever they met them, from Wallonia near the mouth of the Rhine to Wallachia near the mouth of the Danube. This corner of the English coast continued as home to some of the pre-Roman Celtic stock, not all of whom were driven west into Wales proper, as was once supposed.

Even the English language that America speaks today (or at least spoke until the post-1965 fashion for bilingual education) reflects the fact that the peoples of Britain merged, eventually. Their separate contributions can still be traced in it.

Every nation in Europe went through the same process. Even the famously homogeneous Japanese show the signs of ethnically distinct waves of prehistoric immigration.

But merging takes time. After the Norman Conquest of England in 1066, it was nearly three hundred years before the invaders were assimilated to the point where court proceedings in London were again heard in English. And it was nearly nine centuries before there was any further large-scale immigration into the British Isles—the Caribbean and Asian influx after World War II. (There was movement *within* the British Isles, of course: most English Catholics are of Irish stock, albeit totally assimilated.)

Merging takes time—except in America. Here the process has been uniquely rapid. Thus about 7 million Germans have immigrated to the United States since the beginning of the nineteenth century. Their influence has been profound. To my British eye it accounts for the odd American habit of getting up in the morning and starting work. About 58 million Americans told the 1990 census that they were wholly or partly of German descent. But only 1.5 million spoke German in their homes.

- RESULT: *Americans who take this "nation of immigrants" stuff too seriously tend to assume that they cannot share a common ethnic heritage. But this is false—at least, it was false until the Great Wave of Third World immigration unleashed by the 1965 Immigration Act.*

In fact, as we have seen,

1. At the time of the American Revolution, the white population in the Thirteen Colonies was 60 percent English, 80 percent British, 98 percent Protestant.
2. The United States population would still be at about half its current level if there had been *no immigration at all after 1790.*
3. As late as 1960, nearly 90 percent of the U.S. population was European, the great bulk of it closely related, from the British Isles, Germany and Italy.

A UNIVERSAL NATION?

It is because of these difficulties in the American debate that Ben Wattenberg is able to get away with talking about the United States becoming a "Universal Nation."

On its face, this is a contradiction in terms. A nation cannot be universal because it is, of its essence, specific—ethnically and culturally. Maybe you could have a universal *state* (. . . polity), although I'm skeptical—see below, page 208. But that's not the same thing.

It's possible, as Wattenberg variously implies, that he means the diverse immigrant groups will eventually intermarry, producing what he calls, quoting the English poet John Masefield, a "wondrous race." Or that they will at least be assimilated by American culture, which, while globally dominant, is hardly "universal." But meanwhile there are hard questions:

- *What language is this "universal nation" going to speak? How is it going to avoid ethnic strife? dual loyalties? collapsing like the Tower of Babel?*

Wattenberg is not asked to reconcile these contradictions, although he is aware of at least some of them, because the ideal of an American nation-state is in eclipse in the American political conversation.

Ironically, the same weaknesses were apparent in the rather similar concept of "cultural pluralism" which was invented by Horace M. Kallen at the height of the last great immigration debate, before the Quota Acts of the 1920s. Kallen, like many of today's immigration enthusiasts, reacted emotionally against the calls for "Americanization" that the 1890–1920 immigrant wave provoked. He argued that any unitary American nationality had already been dissipated by immigration (sound familiar?). Instead, he said, the United States had become merely a political state (. . . polity) containing a number of different nationalities.

Kallen left the practical implications of this vision "woefully underdeveloped" (in the words of the *Harvard Encyclopedia of American Ethnic Groups*).[2] It eventually evolved into a vague approval of tolerance, which was basically how Americans had always treated immigrant groups anyway—an extension, not coincidentally, of how the English built the British nation.

But in one respect, Kallenism is very much alive: he argued that authentic Americanism was what he called "the American idea." This amounted to an almost religious idealization of "democracy." Again, this was left underdeveloped, but it appeared to have as much to do with non-discrimination and equal protection under the law as with elections. Today, a messianic concern for global "democracy" is sometimes suggested to Americans as an appropriate objective for post–Cold War foreign policy.

AMERICA: IDEA OR NATION?

And Kallenism underlies another helpful remark that someone always makes in any discussion of U.S. immigration policy: *"America isn't a nation like the other nations—it's an idea."*

Once more, this American exceptionalism is really more a matter of degree than kind. Many other nations have some sort of ideational reinforcement. Quite often it is religious, such as Poland's Roman Catholicism; sometimes cultural, such as France's ineffable Frenchness. And occasionally it is political.

Thus—again not coincidentally—the English used to talk about what might be described as the "English Idea": English liberties, their rights as Englishmen and so on. Americans used to know immediately what this meant. As Jesse Chickering wrote in 1848 of his diverse fellow Americans:

> English laws and institutions, adapted to the circumstances of the country, have been adopted here. . . . The tendency of things is to mould the whole into one people, whose leading characteristics are English, formed on American soil.[3]

What is unusual in the current American immigration debate, however, is that Americans are now being urged to abandon the bonds of a common ethnicity so completely and to trust instead entirely to ideology to hold together their state (. . . polity).

This is an extraordinary experiment, like suddenly replacing all the blood in a patient's body. History suggests little reason to suppose it will succeed. The political form of the Estados Unidos Mexicanos is essentially that of the United States of America. But the content is Mexican, and the result very different. Conversely, the universalisms of Christendom and Islam have been long ago sundered by national quarrels. More recently, the much-touted "Soviet Man," the creation of much tougher ideologists using much rougher methods than anything yet seen in the United States, has turned out to be a Russian, Ukrainian or Kazakh after all.

Which is why Shakespeare has King Henry V say, before the battle of Agincourt, not "we defenders of international law and the dynastic principle as it applies to my right to inherit the throne of France," but

We few, we happy few, we band of brothers . . .

However, although intellectuals may have decided that America is not a nation but an idea, the news has not reached the American people—especially that 5.25 percent who sternly told the Census Bureau in 1990 that their ethnicity was "American."

(They seem usually to be of white Colonial stock, often from the mountain South. *Significantly, the tendency to self-identify as "American" diminishes very sharply wherever ethnic diversity appears.* Thus self-reported "Americans" are a high proportion of the homogeneous English-origin counties of Maine—but not in those counties that also have French-origin settlements.[4])

And any such talk about being an idea rather than a nation would have been viewed by Americans with amazement (probably something louder than amazement in the case of Theodore Roosevelt) throughout most of American history.

Notwithstanding the Declaration of Independence's charge that George III was hindering "Migration," it is highly (and consciously) culturally specific. In Thomas Sowell's terms, it was written out of awareness of a particular ethnic "message."

Thus another of the Declaration's charges is that George III had *abolished "the free System of English Laws in a neighbouring Province"*—meaning the British Parliament's 1774 Quebec Act, which obstructed American westward expansion and which also extended legal rights to Roman Catholics, so distrusted at the time that they were initially banned from holding office in seven of the thirteen new American states.[5] It referred to *"our British Brethren,"* reproaching them for ignoring *"our common Kindred"* and *"Consanguinity."* And it roundly denounced, without any sensitive multicultural mumbling about "Native Americans," *"the merciless Indian Savages, whose known Rule of Warfare, is an undistinguished Destruction, of all Ages, Sexes and Conditions."*

Symbolically, the Constitution announces its purpose is *"to form a more perfect Union . . . [for] ourselves and our posterity"*—the Founders' posterity, not posterity in general.

John Jay's first essay in *The Federalist Papers,* written as part of the campaign to get the Constitution ratified, began by laying down as an axiom that it was precisely America's ethnic and cultural homogeneity that made the great experiment possible. Americans, Jay wrote, were

> . . . one united people—a people descended from the same ancestors, speaking the same language, professing the same religion, attached to the same principles of government, very similar in their manners and customs . . . *a band of brethren* . . .[6] [my italics]

Some hundred years later, Theodore Roosevelt in his *Winning of the West* traced the "perfectly continuous history" of the Anglo-Saxons from King Alfred to George Washington. He presented the settling of the lands beyond the Alleghenies as "the crowning and greatest achievement" of "the spread of the English-speaking peoples," which he saw in explicit terms:

> . . . it is of incalculable importance that America, Australia, and Siberia should pass out of the hands of their red, black and yellow aboriginal owners, and become the heritage of the dominant world races.

(It's important to note that Roosevelt was personally a liberal on racial matters—particularly in the context of the 1890s, when the "Jim Crow" laws imposing segregation were being enacted, by his Democratic opponents, throughout the South. He believed that those "aboriginal owners" could and should be raised to the standards of the "dominant world races." He proclaimed that an individual of any race who could win admission to the "fellowship of doers" would be superior to a white man who failed. Of course, his language is unthinkably crude to our more delicate ears. But the balance he was trying to achieve, between ethnicity and culture, standards and tolerance, was daring and difficult. Having tried it, I sympathize.)

Roosevelt himself was an example of ethnicities merging to produce this new, crowning and greatest nation. He thanked God—he teased his friend Rudyard Kipling—that "there was not a drop of British blood in him." But that did not stop him from identifying with Anglo-Saxons or from becoming a passionate advocate of an assimilationist "Americanism."[7]

Above all, at the height of the last great immigration wave, Horace Kallen and his allies totally failed to persuade Americans that they were no longer a nation. Quite the contrary: once convinced that their nationhood was threatened by continued massive immigration, *Americans changed the public policies that made it possible.*

As the Great Restriction's national-origins quotas were being legislated, President Calvin Coolidge put it unflinchingly: "America must be kept American."[8]

Everyone knew what he meant.

THE REFRESHING ROLE OF PAUSES

"Pulling up the ladder"—this is exactly what Americans did with the Great Restriction of the 1920s, as described in another of those helpful lines that some immigration enthusiast uses in every immigration discussion.

But pulling up the ladder may be necessary—*if the lifeboat is about to capsize.*

And the American lifeboat undeniably did stabilize after the 1920s. It took time. As late as 1963, when Nathan Glazer and Daniel Patrick Moynihan published their seminal study *Beyond the Melting Pot,* the ethnic groups that had arrived in the 1890–1920 wave appeared not to be assimilating into the American mainstream. At best, as Will Herberg argued in *Protestant, Catholic, Jew* (1960), there was a "triple melting pot" working within the major religious communities—for example, Irish Catholics marrying Italian Catholics; German Jews marrying Russian Jews.[9]

But then, just when the media-academic complex had tooled up an entire industry based on the "unmeltable ethnics," as they were described by social critic Michael Novak,[10] they started to melt. The figures are dramatic. According to Robert C. Christopher in his 1989 *Crashing the Gates: The De-WASPing of America's Power*

Elite, half of all Italian Americans born since World War II married non-Catholics, mainly Protestants; some 40 percent of Jews marrying in the 1980s chose Gentile spouses, a phenomenon rare if not unknown only twenty years earlier.[11]

Christopher, a former *Newsweek* editor and a political liberal, naturally saw this development as an emerging cultural synthesis free (at last!) of any nasty ethnic connotations at all. But there is a simpler interpretation: the American nation was just swallowing, and then digesting—"WASPizing," to adapt Christopher's terminology—an unusually large and spicy immigrant meal.

Which brings us to one of the central points of this book:

- **This pattern of pauses for digestion has recurred throughout American history. Waves of immigration have been followed by lulls right back into Colonial times.**

After the Great Migration of 1629–41, there was practically no further immigration to New England for two hundred years.[12] Immigration into the rest of the Thirteen Colonies had distinct crests: in the 1720s, the early 1750s, and then again from the late 1760s until the outbreak of the American Revolution.[13] In between, usually because of European wars, the troughs were very deep.

For the story after the Revolution, look again at Charts 1 and 4 on pages 30 and 40–41. They show, after the turmoil of the Revolutionary War, the First Great Lull, remarkably similar to the one earlier this century. For nearly fifty years, there was practically no immigration at all. The United States grew rapidly through natural increase. But the white population remained about what it had been in the 1790 census: largely English, heavily British and overwhelmingly Protestant.

This was the nation about which de Crèvecoeur asked his celebrated question in *Letters from an American Farmer* (1782): "What then is the American, this new man?" Americans were indeed new—there were some other Europeans seasoning the stew. *But not that new.*

This also was the America described by Alexis de Tocqueville in *Democracy in America* (1835)—an irony, given that his name has now been adopted by an immigration economic think tank in

Washington, D.C. That de Tocqueville's analysis still has relevance is a tribute to his America's powers of assimilation and cultural transmission.

(De Tocqueville actually had a very low opinion of the immigrants he did see. He noted that in big cities they formed part of a "rabble more dangerous even than that of European towns . . . [they] carry our worst vices to the United States without any of those interests which might counteract their influence." He blamed them for recent riots in New York and Philadelphia. And he predicted that it would be through the big cities *"and the nature of their inhabitants"* [my italics] that the American Republic would perish.[14] Aaargh!)

After the First Great Lull, immigration crested about every fifteen or twenty years: in 1851–54, 1866–73, 1881–83, 1905–7, and 1921–24. In between it plunged, by as much as three quarters or more.

Just as important, the ethnic composition continuously changed. Earlier in the century, the largest element was Irish; in the middle, German; by the end, from southern and eastern Europe. After 1924, immigration was reduced to a trickle—but that trickle was from northern and western Europe. These variations in the magnitude and makeup of immigration were vital to the process of digestion.

And this pattern of pauses puts a different perspective on the immigration debate.

For example, immigration enthusiasts invariably try to brush aside all concerns about immigration: *"All these arguments have been heard before. They never came true."*

Of course, this is illogical. Just because a danger has been averted in the past does not mean it cannot happen in the future. Many passengers might have climbed aboard the lifeboat safely. One more may still capsize it.

But in fact these concerns, which have been indeed expressed by the most eminent Americans going right back to Colonial times, were perfectly reasonable. They were rendered moot only by changing circumstances.

Thus Benjamin Franklin worried about German immigration in 1751:

> Why should Pennsylvania, founded by the English, become a Colony of *Aliens,* who will shortly be so numerous as to Germanize us instead of our Anglifying them . . . ?[15]

Franklin was not proved wrong. Instead, German immigration was halted—in the short run, by the Seven Years War (1756–63); in the longer run, by the post-Revolution Great Lull.

Similarly, the post-Revolution Great Lull met the concerns of the Founding Fathers. Conversely, the nativist anti-Catholic Know Nothing insurrection, which had elected eight governors, over one hundred congressmen and thousands of local officials by 1855, was the reaction, harsh but human, of a Protestant nation that had forgotten immigration and faced apparently imminent inundation by Irish Catholics fleeing the 1845 potato famine.

Thereafter, Know Nothingism abruptly receded. Doubtless, this was in part due to the impending Civil War—Know Nothings, as we have seen, tended also to be ardent Abolitionists. But there was a second factor: *the supply of Irish Catholics turned out to be finite after all.*

First, Irish immigration stopped its exponential increase. Then it began a sharp decline. The Irish comprised up to a half of the 1851–54 wave. Then the Crimean War (1853–56) cut off immigration from the rest of Europe, but Irish were still only perhaps a fifth or less of this trough. The Know Nothings themselves, an alert and literate lot, were instantly aware that their key issue was suddenly dying on them.[16]

In this historical perspective, the public policies that excluded Asian immigration for nearly a hundred years also appear rather different. The California legislature's 1876 report on immigration complained that the Chinese

> have never adapted themselves to our habits, mode of dress, or our educational system. . . . Impregnable to all the influences of our Anglo-Saxon life, they remain the same stolid Asiatics that have floated on the rivers and slaved in the fields of China for thirty centuries of time.[17]

Now, maybe this argument had a dark, nativistic motive. But on its face it is a highly rational and very specific complaint about the difficulty of assimilating immigrants from what was then a premodern society.

In the interim, the Orient has modernized. Today, immigrants from the area are often viewed (perhaps naively) as the most, well, "Anglo-Saxon" of the current wave.

Historical perspective also discredits another conventional ploy in the immigration debate: *"How can X be against immigration when the nativists wanted to keep his own great-grandfather out?"* This, of course, is like arguing that a passenger already on board the lifeboat should refrain from pointing out that taking on more will cause it to capsize.

But let's assume, for the sake of argument, that X is Irish American. Disqualifying him from the debate overlooks the long and painful adjustment to America that the Irish, like every immigrant group, had to make. The Irish too came to the United States from what was still basically a premodern agricultural society. Throughout the nineteenth century, they displayed social pathologies strikingly similar to those of the contemporary American black ghetto: poverty, disease, violence, family breakdown, drug addiction (alcohol in those days) and, perhaps not surprisingly, virtually no intermarriage.

Slowly, over generations, America changed the Irish—and they changed themselves. Today, in terms of measures like income, education and political affiliation, Irish Americans are more or less indistinguishable from the mainstream, into which they have extensively intermarried. (Well . . . alcoholism is a little higher. But so are incomes.[18])

In his *Economics and Politics of Race: An International Perspective,* the Hoover Institution economist Thomas Sowell describes this as "historically . . . one of the great social transformations of a people."[19] In words that apply exactly to today's immigration enthusiasts, he writes:

> If the Irish were pariahs in the nineteenth century and fully accepted in the twentieth century, the moralistic approach sees only society's belated change to doing the right thing. It ignores the very possibility that the Irish who are accepted today may be very different from the nineteenth-century emigrants from Ireland whose personal behavior

> would still be wholly unacceptable to others today, including today's Irish Americans.[20]

In short: Irish Americans have earned the hard way their right to opinions about who and how many their country can absorb.

The Irish changed themselves with a great deal of encouragement from a notably stern clergy. But the Roman Catholic Church itself made an adjustment to America.

Indeed, the word *"Americanization"* was invented in the 1850s by a Vermont Yankee convert to Catholicism, Orestes A. Brownson, who argued in his *Brownson's Quarterly Review* that the nativists had a point: the Irish should assimilate to the American nation that had already been formed; the Church should not identify itself with Old World autocracy—as Pius IX, after the 1848 revolutions in Europe, was increasingly inclined to do.

Brownson provoked a ferocious controversy. But, today, his view can be seen to have prevailed.[21]

IS THE UNITED STATES STILL CAPABLE OF ABSORBING IMMIGRANTS?

Let's be clear about this: the American experience with immigration has been a triumphant success. It has so far transcended anything seen in Europe as to make the application of European lessons an exercise to be performed with care.

But there are very clear reasons why the American nation has been able to absorb and assimilate immigrants. In considering further immigration, its enthusiasts must ask themselves honestly: *do these reasons still apply?*

One reason America could assimilate immigrants, as we have seen, is that there were regular pauses for digestion. Another reason is that the American political elite *wanted the immigrants to assimilate.* And it did not hesitate to ensure that they did.

Over two hundred years of U.S. history, a number of tried-and-true, but undeniably tough, assimilation techniques had been perfected. But today, they have been substantially abandoned.

The economic culture of the United States has changed significantly—from classical liberalism to government-regulated welfare statism. Earlier immigrants were basically free to succeed or fail. And many failed: as we have seen, as many as 40 percent of the 1880–1920 immigrants went back home. But now, public policy interposes itself, with the usual debatable results.

"You can't blame the immigrants for our bad policies," immigration enthusiasts are quick to argue. Of course you can't. But if there's a thunderstorm when you've got a cold, you don't blame the rain. You just stay indoors. Or you go out and get pneumonia.

Some public subsidies to immigrants are direct, like welfare. Others are indirect, such as the wholly new idea that immigrant children should be taught in their own language. This effectively transfers part of the cost of immigration from the immigrant to the American taxpayer—and to the American schoolchild.

New York's public school system now offers courses in more than a hundred languages. It is hunting for teachers of Albanian, who will probably themselves be immigrants.

And it's not just the American economic culture that has changed. So has the political culture. Almost a century ago, the last Great Wave of immigrants were met with the unflinching demand that they "Americanize." Now they are told that they should retain and reinforce their diversity.

Ethnically fueled "multiculturalism" taught in the public schools, as described by Lawrence Auster and by the eminent liberal historian Arthur Schlesinger, Jr., in his bestseller *The Disuniting of America,*[22] inevitably raises the question: *Is there still an "American Idea"—and if so, what is it?*

Actually, the outlines of what might be described as the new American Anti-Idea are already clear. It's a sort of bureaucratically regulated racial spoils system, rather like Lebanon before its ethnic divisions finally erupted. Government power is used not to achieve economic efficiency, which traditional socialism has ceased to promise, but ethnic equity—justified in the name of extirpating "discrimination."

That's *private* discrimination, of course. Government-sponsored discrimination is not merely acceptable but mandatory, in the form of "affirmative action" quotas.

"Quotas were originally supposed to be remedial," says Professor Frederick R. Lynch of Claremont College, author of *Invisible Victims: White Males and the Crisis of Affirmative Action.* "Now they are being justified by affirmative action professionals as a way of 'managing diversity.' "[23] Indeed, an entire industry has grown up holding seminars and training sessions for corporations struggling to cope with racial "diversity."

That "diversity," needless to say, is being introduced into the United States essentially by current immigration policy.

As we have seen, American immigration policy is riddled with anomalies. But how about this one?

- **No matter how new, all immigrants from the right "protected classes"—black, Hispanic, Asian—are eligible for preferential hiring and promotion. They are counted toward government quota requirements that were allegedly imposed on employers to help native-born minority Americans.**

Hence the number of Africans and West Indians teaching at American colleges.

Symptomatic of the American anti-idea: the emergence of a strange anti-nation inside the United States—the so-called "Hispanics."

If you write about immigration and demography in America, you are more or less forced to use this term. But it is a classification that makes no sense. *It's not racial*—most "Hispanics" are mestizos (white-Amerindian mixtures) but there are significant numbers of whites and also of blacks. *It's not cultural*—"Hispanics" come from countries running the gamut from Europe to the Third World. Most absurd of all, *it's not even linguistic*—many "Hispanics" speak only English and, indeed, some are Indian-language speakers from Latin America.

Arguably against their wishes, "Hispanics" are being treated by U.S. government agencies as a homogeneous "protected class" essentially as a result of ethnic lobbying in Washington. They have been supplied with "leaders" financed in large part by the Ford Foundation. They are now much less encouraged to "Americanize" than anything seen in the previous Great Wave. Instead, they are being issued with a new, artificial "Hispanic" identity.

Most Americans don't realize how aggressive this phenomenon has become. Linda Chavez, former aide in the Carter and Reagan White Houses and now director of the Center for the New American Community at the Manhattan Institute for Policy Research, reports that the Washington, D.C., public school system attempted to place her son in "bilingual," i.e., Spanish-language, classes apparently solely on the basis of his first name, Pablo. His last name, that of Ms. Chavez's husband, is Gersten. In fact, he did not speak Spanish—and neither does Chavez herself: her family has been in New Mexico for generations. But there are forces in America working to undo all that.[24]

In effect, Spanish-speaking immigrants are still being encouraged to assimilate. But not to America.

Is the United States still capable of absorbing immigrants? Is it still trying? Consider these policies:

1. *Massive, heterogeneous immigration.*
2. *"Bilingualism"*—i.e., foreign language-ism—and
3. *"Multiculturalism"*—i.e., non-Americanism—in the education system.
4. *"Affirmative Action"*—i.e., government-mandated discrimination against white Americans.
5. *Systematic attack on the value of citizenship,* by making it easier for aliens to vote, receive government subsidies, etc.

Sounds much more like deconstructionism—the deconstruction of the American nation as it existed in 1965.

IMPERFECT DISUNION?

Given the one-way nature of the American immigration debate, you know what to expect when *The Wall Street Journal* headlines a front-page story *"Mosaic of Hope: Ethnic Identities Clash with Student Idealism at a California College."*

The college in question was Occidental in Los Angeles. *The Wall Street Journal* described it as a "prestigious private liberal arts college . . . Founded in 1887 to educate the white elite." Which, of course, used to be called the American elite.

Still, Occidental was apparently successful in achieving this reprehensible goal. One of its graduates, class of '57, was "bleeding-heart conservative" and immigration enthusiast, former Bush administration Secretary of Housing and Urban Development Jack Kemp.

Now Occidental College is aiming for a different elite. Under its president, John Brooks Slaughter, "who," *The Wall Street Journal* tells us, "is black," Occidental "is reaching out for an emerging America." In 1987, it

> "went multicultural," aggressively recruiting minority students and revamping its curriculum to give more emphasis to non-western cultures. Today, more than 40% of its 1,650 students are minority.

Let's not go into the details of what is going on at Occidental. Essentially, *The Wall Street Journal* hints discreetly, the students are dividing into warring camps.

Look, however, at what *The Wall Street Journal* typically described as "the bedrock fact" underlying the Occidental experiment: *"America's white majority is shrinking, both in relative size and importance."*

The truth, of course, is that America's white majority is *NOT* "shrinking." In fact, in absolute numbers, it is still growing. But it is being inundated, quite deliberately, as a matter of public policy following the 1965 Immigration Act.

And worth real contemplation are the final lines of the story. *The Wall Street Journal*'s starry-eyed hack, one Dennis Farney, is in a discussion class entitled "The American Dream." Let me quote this:

> The students, as diverse as their America is diverse, are gathered around a conference table. And their visitor [i.e., Farney] asks: suppose they were to grade the American civilization, grade it just as their professor grades them? How would they grade America?
>
> It is freshman Jona Goong, a Hawaiian of Chinese ancestry, who says it best.
>
> "If I were to grade America," she says, softly, "I would give it an incomplete."[25]

Really. Well, my twin brother and I did have to grade America, from a distance of three thousand miles, in the summer of 1967, when for various reasons we decided all was lost in England. We gave it an A+. And we still give it an A+ . . . what's left of it.

And—if only for my son Alexander's sake—I'd like it to stay that way.

12

IMMIGRATION HAS CONSEQUENCES: THE WAR AGAINST THE NATION-STATE

The United States shall guarantee to every State in this Union a Republican form of government, and shall protect each of them against invasion. . . .

—Constitution of the United States, Article IV, section 4

So a nation is the interlacing of ethnicity and culture. And a nation-state is its political expression. But all over the world in the twentieth century, nations and nation-states have been under intense attack. And to the attackers, immigration is a potential ally.

In this chapter, we'll look at two distinguished reactions to the nation-state phenomenon, which I think epitomize the two opposing poles of modern sentiment.

The first is Canadian: from Pierre Trudeau, prime minister of Canada almost continuously from 1968 to 1984, the architect of the modern Canadian state (. . . polity), and probably the greatest leader that Canada has produced this century. Which does *not* mean that what he did was sensible—just that he did it on an heroic scale.

To appreciate Trudeau's position, you have to understand that he was and is a very peculiar man. He is a Québecois, that is, a product of the French-speaking province (and emergent nation-state) of Quebec. But he is also a man of the left—much further left, indeed, than has been generally appreciated. As a leftist, his conscious ideology had no place for nationalism: the workers of the world were supposed to unite, dammit.

And there was a further factor. To be on the extreme left in French-speaking Quebec in the 1940s, when the province was totally dominated by the Roman Catholic Church and the authoritarian nationalist Union Nationale government of Maurice Duplessis, was a very uncomfortable experience. And it produced in Trudeau a special case of the neurosis that is widespread in the Western world today: an absolutely reflexive horror and fear of nationalist sentiment.

In Trudeau's case, he seems to this day to view nationalism as clerical fascism. And indeed Duplessis was suspiciously unenthusiastic about World War II.

All of which may puzzle Americans who remember Trudeau as a "Canadian Nationalist." The reason: "Canadian Nationalism," as developed in the 1960s, was always an artificial invention, the populist disguise for the anti-American and statist ambitions of various intellectuals and bureaucrats. On the real, ethnocultural, nationalist issues like language and immigration, Trudeau showed clearly that he believed government policies, not people, were what counted.

This is how he put it in 1962:

> The road to progress lies through international integration; nationalism will have to be abandoned as a rustic and clumsy tool . . .

He described his vision of a bilingual, bicultural Canada which would simultaneously be the political expression of both English and French Canadians as

> an example to all those new Asian and African states . . . who must discover how to govern their polyethnic populations with proper regard for justice and liberty. What better reason for cold-shouldering

> the lure of annexation to the U.S.? Canadian federalism is an experiment of major proportions; it could become a brilliant prototype for the molding of tomorrow's civilization.[1]

And in a speech before the U.S. Congress, implicitly appealing for help after Quebec had rejected his vision and elected a separatist government, Trudeau claimed that the breakup of Canada into its component nations would be

> [a] crime against the history of mankind. . . .[2]

An extraordinary claim given that it was an American president, Woodrow Wilson, who in effect invented the principle of self-determination and imposed it on the dubious European Great Powers at Versailles in 1919.

Note the quaint but telling streak of "Internationale"-style emotionalism and imagery running through Trudeau's comments. And, in particular, the antithesis Trudeau posits between "progress" and the "rustic" tool of nationalism. It's reminiscent of the passage in *The Communist Manifesto* where Marx and Engels take a moment off from bashing the beastly bourgeoisie to congratulate them for at least rescuing the proletariat from what they described, succinctly, as "rural idiocy."

And it's highly significant. Because it epitomizes a key assumption: that nationalism is *premodern*—that is, it is out of place in the rational, efficient, impersonal, secular society that began to emerge with the Industrial Revolution.

Political scientists call this epochal social change "modernization." By this standard, nationalism does look emotional, traditional, prescriptive. Surely with the spread of education and enlightenment, it will disappear?

IS THE NATION-STATE OUTDATED?

This assumption is extremely widespread. Here's an editorial from *The New York Times* (December 9, 1992) dealing with the disturbances in Germany caused by the collapse of Bonn's ludicrously liberal "refugee" policy and the subsequent immigrant influx, which reached the astonishing rate of 60,000 a month.

"Nobody," the *Times* editorialists wrote, "can reasonably fault Germany for trying to limit and regulate a huge influx of refugees."

Naturally, this means they *do* want to fault Germany for trying to limit and regulate a huge influx of refugees.

The *Times* went on:

> But Chancellor Helmut Kohl and the Bonn political establishment have regrettably taken the easy way out. They would do better to set a quota on immigrants and nurture a more pluralist society by adopting a formula for citizenship based on residence rather than blood ties.
>
> Equally distressing is Bonn's failure to revise an outdated naturalization law rooted in ethnicity. Under the existing system, a Turkish guest worker who has lived in Germany for 30 years and speaks German fluently is denied the citizenship automatically granted a Russian-speaking immigrant who can prove German ancestry.

What we have here is a total absence of any understanding of the nation as family, to which outsiders may be admitted indeed, but only under very special circumstances and with great care. And if there was any nation in the world where care should have been taken—for God's sake!—it was Germany. Instead, the "Bonn political establishment," in its eagerness to please foreign critics, has apparently succeeded in raising the ghost of Nazism.

But, more generally, note again the curious assumption that "naturalization law rooted in ethnicity" is somehow "outdated." In fact, exactly the reverse is true:

- **The nation-state, the sovereign political entity based on a particular ethnicity, is the product of modernization.**

What are now regarded as archetypal nation-states, like Germany and Italy, were actually united only in the nineteenth century. Most human historical experience has been in multiethnic states (. . . polities). But they have also been primitive—and tyrannies.

Multinational and multilingual states (. . . polities) organized on other principles, like the Hapsburg Empire, did not survive into the modern, democratic age.

And for good reason. The essential point is this:

- *Modern society is organized around the free flow of information.*

So modernization inevitably puts a premium on linguistic unity. It doesn't matter what language the people in the next village speak if you have no truck or trade with them. But if you do, it does.

- SPECIAL NOTE FOR ECONOMISTS: When you think about it, the emergence of the nation-state on the world scene is very much like the simultaneous emergence of the firm in developing capitalist economies. Both can be traced to lower transaction costs, efficiencies in the transmission of information and the superior economies of specialization.

A CANADIAN CASE STUDY

There's a very significant passage in the Canadian novel *Two Solitudes,* by Hugh MacLennan. MacLennan is a real party-line "Canadian Nationalist" and I'm sure would be highly annoyed by the use to which I put his work. But that's what happens to you when you write books. His title refers to the mutual isolation that prevailed between English and French in Canada, which MacLennan, writing in 1945, felt should be broken down. And in this passage he did achieve true artistic insight—which, Plato assures us in one of his Socratic dialogues, is unrelated to intelligence.

It's the fourth year of World War I, which Canada entered when Britain did, in 1914. This decision split the country, as always on ethnic lines: English Canadians for, French Canadians against.

An English-speaking girl is picking up her mail at a French-owned store in deepest rural Quebec. And she sees an envelope marked O.H.M.S.—(On His Majesty's Service). Instantly she knows what it is: notification that her husband has been killed at the front.

It was a day in early July when Janet Methuen stood in Polycarpe Drouin's store with a letter in her hand from His Majesty the King, via the Canadian Ministry of Defence. She read it through, and when she had finished she lifted her head and looked around the store, seeing nothing. She began to walk forward and bumped into the side of the Percheron model, her arms hanging at her sides, the letter in one hand and the envelope in the other.

Drouin came from behind the counter. His voice was soft and kind, his face wrinkled, his eyes friendly. "You are all right, Madame?"

Janet turned her head rigidly and saw his tap-like nose and the wrinkles about his eyes blur and then water into focus. She saw him look at the letter in her hand and immediately she lifted her chin. She was as pale as unbleached muslin.

"I get you a drink, maybe?" Drouin said.

She heard her own voice, like a scratchy phonograph in another room, "I'm quite all right, thank you." But she continued to stand without moving.

Drouin went to the kitchen behind the store and returned with a glass of water, spilling some of it in his hurry. When he offered it she gave him a frozen smile, "I'm quite all right, thank you," she repeated tonelessly.

Her mind kept repeating a phrase she had read some months before in a magazine story: "I mustn't let people see it . . . I mustn't let people see . . . I mustn't let . . ." The words jabbered in her mind like the speech of an idiot.

Drouin looked sideways at the only other person in the store, a farmer who had come in to buy some tar paper. Their eyes met and both men nodded. The farmer had also seen the long envelope with O.H.M.S. in one corner.

"Get a chair, Jacques," Drouin said in French. "The lady wants to sit down." But before the men could get one to her, Janet went to the door and went out. The silence in her wake was broken as the chair hit the floor. Drouin shook his head and went around the counter. "That's a terrible thing," he said.

"Her husband, maybe?"

"The old captain [Janet Methuen's father-in-law] says her husband is overseas."

The farmer scratched his head. "When I saw that letter this morning," Drouin went on, "I said to my wife, that's a bad thing, a letter

> like that. You never hear anything good from the government in Ottawa, I said."
>
> The farmer was still scratching his head. "And she didn't cry," he said. "Well, maybe she doesn't know how."
>
> Drouin bent forward over the counter in his usual jack-knife position. After a time, he said, "You can't tell about the English. But maybe the old captain will be hurt bad," he added, as though he had just thought of it.

To any WASP, of course, this girl's reaction is perfectly normal. What MacLennan is tapping into here is the fact that cultural attitudes toward things like bereavement differ profoundly and persistently, much more so than is often realized.

And these cultural differences result in incomprehension and sometimes in serious conflict. Which is why the nation-state, where everyone understands one another, is an efficient way of organizing human beings. In economists' jargon, they have lower transaction costs.

But there's a second point. MacLennan has the storekeeper say to his crony:

> "When I saw that letter this morning, I said to my wife, that's a bad thing, a letter like that. You never hear anything good from the government in Ottawa, I said."[3]

This is the genuine voice of premodern Quebec. And Quebec, really until the 1960s, was premodern. Goldwin Smith, the British writer who became Canada's de Tocqueville, compared it to a frozen mammoth preserved in the tundra. Louis Joseph Papineau, who led an unsuccessful rebellion against British rule, provided a classic description of this premodern way of life in the 1830s:

> Our people don't want English capital nor English people here,—they have no ambition beyond their present possessions and never want to go beyond the sound of their own Church bells.[4]

In premodern societies, frozen mammoths can slumber peacefully. Ethnic groups can coexist because they rarely have to deal with each other.

But in modern societies, held together from top to bottom by information flows, there are just too many points of contact. When people do start to hear something good from their government, in the form of services, or even to hear from it at all, it starts to matter what language it speaks to them in. And in fact one of the first signs that Quebec nationalism was getting assertive was a demand that federal government pension checks should be bilingual.

Ottawa's envelopes don't say O.H.M.S. anymore. And not only because English Canadian leftists are writing the Queen out of Canada's history just as Columbus has been written out of America's.

So if the nation-state is a product of modernization, there's also a corollary:

- *Modernization puts a premium on unity.*

Modern societies are held together by information flows. Anything that impedes these information flows renders them less efficient. In the first instance, that means linguistic unity. Ultimately, it means cultural and perhaps ethnic unity.

THE NATION-STATE'S ENEMY: THE NEW CLASS

So why is the nation-state in disrepute? One conventional explanation: *"Nationalism leads to wars."* Above all, of course, World War I, the disaster from which the civilized world is only just recovering.

But actually the religious wars of the sixteenth and early seventeenth centuries were just as devastating. And by the eighteenth century, these wars had indeed resulted in a reaction against religion, to which the nation-state was seen as an antidote. Similarly, in terms of sheer murderousness, nothing can touch the explicitly anti-nationalist ideology of Marxism.

The lesson of history is simply this: *human beings like war. They will always find an excuse for it.*

(My little son jumped, then wheeled to look at me, his face alight with joy, when he first heard firecrackers reverberating through the Manhattan canyons in the week before July Fourth. He was not yet two. But the frenzy to enlist at the outbreak of war in the Britain of 1914, in the North and South of 1861, was all there.)

The key to the contemporary campaign against the nation-state is sociological: the rise of what Irving Kristol has called "The New Class."[5] These are the professionals who run and benefit from the state (. . . polity) and its power to tax: the government bureaucracy; the educational establishment; the media elite, which interlocks with both; and all their various client constituencies, to whom they channel tax monies.

You all know these people. Probably your brother-in-law is one of them. Certainly your child's schoolteachers are. What's new in the twentieth century is that a common set of attitudes and ambitions has begun to unify all of them. This is a phenomenon at least as significant as the emergence of a class-conscious proletariat in the cities of the Industrial Revolution two centuries earlier.

The idea of the "New Class" has a long, respectable pedigree. Its emergence was predicted by the famous Austrian economist Joseph Schumpeter. He argued that, although this New Class was financially supported by capitalism, it would be alienated from it, because it would feel deprived of prestige and power. Hence it would be attracted to the government intervention justified by the doctrine of socialism. And, Schumpeter predicted, *the New Class would use its superior political organization to impose socialism regardless of the economic consequences,* just as the tapeworm doesn't care about the health of its host.

In the context of the present debate, the point is this:

- **The New Class dislikes the nation-state.**

The New Class dislikes the nation-state for exactly the same reason it dislikes the free market: *both are machines that run of themselves, with no need for New-Class-directed government intervention.*

Additionally, all self-respecting elites want to distinguish themselves from the peasants. If the peasants are innocently patriotic, the elite will favor a knowing internationalism.

The Australian sociologist Katherine Betts discovered this phenomenon in *Ideology and Immigration,* her study of the very similar Australian situation. Using polling data, Dr. Betts found that while nontraditional immigration was viewed with increasing hostility among ordinary Australians, the university-educated were sharply more likely to favor it. Favoring immigration, she concluded, was *"part of a cluster of values defining social status for Australian intellectuals."*[6]

And finally, the self-interest of this New Class *is* internationalism: cooperation with the New Classes of other countries above the heads of their populations.

This was brought home to me when I attended a European Council meeting, which is the name given to the meeting of political heads of the European Community (now "Union") countries. This one was in Strasbourg. The actual meetings are in private. Nevertheless some three thousand journalists were there, a great sea of them eating catered European Community lunches off china plates, complete with red and white wine—none of the Styrofoam cups of coffee and sticky Danish pastries that journalists have to settle for in the United States—and all discussing which restaurant they would favor with their expense accounts that night.

And there are *four* of these things a year. What a boondoggle! (Most of the time—I believe the next one was in Birmingham, England.) And how easy to rationalize with ringing Europhoric rhetoric!

The classic statement of New Class attitudes toward the nation-state came from Cokie Roberts, reporter for National Public Radio and ABC News, during the debate on term limits for congressmen. She argued that her father, former Democratic House Majority Leader Thomas Hale Boggs, Sr., was able to buck the prejudices of his Louisiana constituents and vote against segregated housing because of the seniority he had accumulated.

Roberts claimed "some experienced souls" were necessary in Congress to provide "institutional memory, explaining the importance of protecting congressional prerogatives . . ." She went on:

> To say that we want only non-professionals governing us is to show a basic disrespect for government, and though that sentiment may be popular, it is dangerous. *We have nothing binding us together as a nation—no common ethnicity, history, religion or even language—except the Constitution and the institutions it created.*[7] [Italics added!]

When Roberts says "nation," of course, she means "state" (or polity). And, when she says, incredibly, that Americans have no common ethnicity, history, religion or language, what she really means is frankly if naively made clear: more power for the political class, aka "the Constitution and the institutions it created."

Anything that further deconstructs the American nation—multiculturalism, bilingualism—will tend to bring about the situation Roberts hopefully describes. And the political class, driven by this view of its self-interest, will applaud.

From the point of view of members of the American New Class, immigration is manna from heaven. It gives them endless excuses to intervene in society. It enables them to distinguish themselves from the xenophobic masses. And, by introducing diverse populations, it strikes at the nation-state's Achilles' heel: the need for homogeneity.

Eventually, Roberts may even get her wish. Like the Prussian army, the American political class will *be* the nation (state . . . polity). Given enough diversity, only their exercise of raw authoritarian power can possibly hold the warring tribes together. By reneging on the Constitutionally enjoined duty to protect the states "against invasion," the American political class will have not only destroyed the nation but also betrayed its obligation to guarantee a "Republican form of government."

But not yet. At the end of the twentieth century, the central issue in American politics is what might be described as "The National Question"—

- **Is America still that interlacing of ethnicity and culture we call a nation—and can the American nation-state, the political expression of that nation, survive?**

AT THE OTHER POLE: FOR THE NATION-STATE

Remember that none of this is necessary. There is no economic necessity for this immigration. You have to make a positive political argument.

Pierre Trudeau, as we have seen, did have a positive political argument. It was wildly unrealistic, but it was an argument. He actually believed in the abolition of national sentiment. The American political class is not as articulate, although no less unreal.

But—and here we come to the other pole of modern sentiment—it's worth considering what the Russian novelist Aleksandr Solzhenitsyn said on the subject of nations in his Nobel Prize acceptance speech.

Solzhenitsyn, remember, actually grew up in the Soviet Union under an explicitly anti-national ideology. And he went to war to defend it. So to reach his present views, he traveled a long road. His language is religious, but it could just as easily be moral or scientistic:

> The disappearance of nations would impoverish us no less than if all peoples were made alike, with one character, one face. Nations are the wealth of mankind, they are its generalized personalities: the smallest of them has its own particular colors, and embodies a particular facet of God's design.[8]

13

DOING THE RIGHT THING? THE MORALITY OF IMMIGRATION

We know no spectacle so ridiculous as the British public in one of its periodical fits of morality.

—**LORD MACAULAY,**

on Thomas Moore's *Life of Byron* in the *Edinburgh Review,* June 1830

I don't know if you would call it the Greatest Show on Earth. But it's certainly one of the most remarkable spectacles in the United States.

Every sundown at Virginia Street in San Ysidro, over by Stewart's Bridge across the Tijuana River or at any of a number of other jumping-off points along the Chula Vista sector of the U.S.-Mexican border south of San Diego, you can see crowds of illegal immigrants gathering—or "staging," in the language of the U.S. Border Patrol—waiting for dark so they can cross.

They are already illegal because many of these staging points are well within U.S. territory. The Border Patrol has been compelled to fall back to a more defensible line. The routine is so well established that vendors regularly arrive to sell the illegals food and drink. It is so blatant that they will openly light fires to keep warm.

The Border Patrol knows to within seconds each evening when the rush will start. It is so predictable that it could be shown live on the nightly TV news—if the national networks in faraway New York City were interested. And up on the ridge, despite the dark, the Border Patrol officers watching through the powerful truck-mounted infrared scope swiveling on its twenty-foot camera tower can quite clearly see any illegal crossings within a five-mile range. They show up as ghostly white figures on a softly glowing screen.

Usually, the illegals start to trickle across in small groups of two or three, dodging through the brush of no-man's-land. Occasionally, however, a large group will simply charge isolated officers and overwhelm them. The Border Patrol calls this a "banzai." If objects are thrown at the officers, as they frequently are on the border, this is "getting rocked."

The Border Patrol knows, also, that most of the illegals will get through. There are just too many illegals and too few officers. In 1992, a total of 565,581 illegals were caught crossing this fourteen-mile sector of the border—an average of over 1,500 a night, nearly half of all the apprehensions along the twenty-five-hundred-mile U.S.-Mexican frontier. (By contrast, along the three-thousand-mile U.S.-Canadian frontier in 1992, there were just over 15,000 apprehensions.)

Just over a thousand officers are assigned to the San Diego sector. They reckon they catch about one illegal in three.

AMERICA—COLONY OF THE WORLD?

People respond to this spectacle on the border in very different ways. For example, *The New York Times*'s A. M. Rosenthal wrote another column about immigration in early 1993. Once again, he recounted the story of his illegal-alien father (see pages 112–13). He went on:

> Ever since then I have detested the word "alien." It should be saved for creatures that jump out of bellies in movies. Immigrant is a better word, historically proud.
>
> Decades later, prowling along a river with Texas Rangers to see

> them catch crossing Mexicans, I stopped and sat on the ground. I said that's enough—I am one of them, the wetbacks, and not them, the hunters.[1]

I, of course, was for years a legally resident alien. And it seems to me the United States had a perfect right to call me anything it wants.

There can be no doubt that many of Rosenthal's readers would have thrilled to this display of his exquisite sensibility. But, privately, I didn't.

As a matter of fact, it struck me as so self-indulgent as to disqualify him from attempting to influence the destiny of a nation. He reminded me of the captain of a supertanker, on the bridge and responsible for steering his ship through shoals, getting drunk on his own self-righteousness.

My own response to the spectacle on the border: mounting irritation with the immigration enthusiasts who insist dogmatically, gloatingly, that the illegal influx cannot be controlled. Quite obviously, it can—especially by the country that put a man on the moon. What is missing is not the way. It is the will.

The Border Patrol has fewer than four thousand officers. (Another thousand were promised in the 1990 Immigration Act, but the funds were never appropriated.) The service is so underfunded that it cannot field enough vehicles for the officers it does have. They have to chase the illegals on foot, trying to follow directions called to them over the radio by the infrared-scope operator. (And there's only one such scope.) They are so hemmed about with regulations that, for example, your young Border Patrol guide will calmly turn his jeep out of the immediate battle zone for a few minutes, onto the I-5 freeway, and immediately point out squads of illegals marching brazenly northward on the hard shoulder. The illegals know that arrest attempts have been forbidden there, supposedly for fear of accidents.

Incredibly, as late as 1991 there was not even a frontier fence in the San Diego sector, nor any lights. Illegals drove across the border in vehicles, several abreast. The U.S. government had to be literally shamed into action: Muriel Watson, a Border Patrol officer's widow, organized a monthly demonstration whereby enraged private citizens began driving to the border at night and simultaneously switching on their cars' headlights. After her fourth "Light Up the Border" demonstration, Watson was interviewed on Roger Hedgecock's top-rated radio talk show on San Diego's KSDO and achieved national fame.

Yet seeing the border also brings home how easy securing it could be. The new nineteen-mile fence from the coast—a clumsy metal barrier, you can see where the illegals dig under it daily like raccoons—ends in the Otay Mesa, a cruel-looking desert wall. This is terrain you could die in. Some illegals have. Only an estimated 200 to 250 miles of the U.S.-Mexican border are thought to be passable at all. The problem is far from infinite. (For further proposals, see pages 257–63).

Similarly, when the dogs start barking in the houses just below while you are watching through the infrared scope, you can actually see the ghostly illegals and their guides filing down the canyons suddenly hesitate and stop. Which provokes a simple question: Why doesn't the Border Patrol use dogs?

This shocks your young guide. "Have you ever seen a police dog in a crowd?" he says. He thinks the solution, reasonably enough, is to hire more Border Patrol officers.

Well, yes. But, thinking about his reaction, several questions occur. Such as: why is it acceptable to use police dogs on American citizens but not on foreign invaders? And: the dogs don't have to *eat* the illegals. They could be trained differently, to hold them—or just to track them.

But the real answer is something your guide has told you earlier. The illegals (or at least their professional smugglers) are acutely attuned to U.S. Border Patrol activities. They even time their crossings to coincide with the duty shifts of officers they regard as lazy.

To paraphrase the ads for the movie *Field of Dreams:* if these people hear dogs baying, they will not come.

Apparently, no one has worked this out. Which tells you how profound is the paralysis that has overcome that once-fabled Yankee ingenuity in the face of this most straightforward of technical problems.

It is a paralysis that stems from a reflexive, masochistic submission, at a deep psychological level, to the demands of others—a sure sign that the United States has become "A Colony of the World," to appropriate the title of the recent book on the phenomenon by former senator Eugene McCarthy, who frankly says that he now regrets co-sponsoring and voting for the Immigration Act in 1965.[2]

Mexican-American ingenuity may be in better shape. In late 1993, El Paso Border Patrol sector chief Silvestre Reyes organized "Operation Blockade," deploying as many of his agents as possible right on the border around the clock. The aim was to deter illegals from entering, rather than intercepting them after entry—the standard Border Patrol procedure, whether to economize on force or because only big apprehension numbers scare money out of Congress.

It worked. Apprehensions, a proxy for illegal border crossings, fell by three quarters or more. Crimes in which illegal immigrants specialize also fell—auto theft was down by half. To Hispanic critics, Reyes responded memorably:

> Are we supposed to be less American because we are Hispanic? I don't think so. I've fought for this country. I've committed my career to controlling its borders.[3]

THE ROSENTHAL REFLEX

So there I was, standing next to the infrared truck in the cold dark desert night. Some twenty miles to the north, the nightly fireworks of San Diego's SeaWorld amusement park were fading in the sky. I was momentarily distracted, brooding on this awesome spectacle of a great nation morally incapable of defending itself against the most elemental invasion.

The scope operator was keeping up a steady running commentary. Flurries of phantom illegals were flitting through the darkness below us. With his help, his colleagues were catching group after group, marching them off with their hands, clearly visible, held high above their heads. But, increasingly, ever more were getting through and escaping to the north.

"One went into the bushes to your left," I suddenly heard him say. *"Looks like he's got a child with him, he's dragging it by the hand."*

To my utter amazement, I was overwhelmed by pure Rosenthalian reflex. Tears filled my eyes. The image seared into my mind. To this day, I genuinely can't say whether I really saw it on the infrared screen or not.

Of course, what I had instantly seen was my own little boy, Alexander.

Followed, perhaps, by some seeping sense of my own gathering middle age, the loss of the ruthlessness of youth—there is a reason one Civil War cavalry general used to argue that teenaged boys made the best troopers. Maybe I'm ready for a job on *The New York Times.*

At that point on the border the Tijuana River, through which that father must have dragged his child, is filled with raw sewage (Mexican sewage, although it then flows through U.S. territory).

And the entire no-man's-land is infested with bandits preying on the illegals. When we had arrived at the celebrated Smuggler's Canyon after nightfall, my guide had flatly refused to go up into it on the grounds that it was now too dangerous. (The novelist Joseph Wambaugh wrote a powerful 1984 true-crime bestseller, *Lines and Shadows,* about a San Diego Police Department undercover squad's heroic but ultimately vain effort to control this nightly carnage in the late 1970s. And traffic then was a fraction of what it is today.)

My young guide, in general remarkably cheerful about the Border Patrol's thankless task, said it was the illegals' children that he found the most distressing, too. Particularly when the Border Patrol got there too late and found that the bandits had already managed to steal them.

Steal them? I said stupidly.

"They sell them to child-prostitution rings."

BEING CRUEL TO BE KIND

The 1986 Immigration Reform and Control Act did not stop illegal immigration, wrote *Wall Street Journal* editor Robert L. Bartley in his contribution to the *National Review* symposium on my cover story,

> *"nor will any measures that the American conscience will allow."*[4]

I don't believe this. I find that ordinary Americans are always much more tough-minded than editorial writers and public officials. This is true for a wide range of issues, from crime to welfare to immigration. Possibly it's because ordinary people have to live with the consequences of self-indulgence dressed up as compassionate policy—unlike the political elite.

But just look at this spectacle on the border. It's a scandal. It's been going on, night after night, for years. And, during all that time, the elite custodians of "the American conscience" have paid no attention, except fleetingly, when illegal immigrants actually land by accident on New York's beaches.

Border enforcement is another question in the Great American Immigration Debate that must be refocused. The question should not be: *"How can we be cruel enough to enforce the law on the border?"* The question should really be: *"How can we be cruel enough not to enforce it?"*

In other words:

- *The real affront to the American conscience is the political elite's moral weakness that lures 2 to 3 million foreigners to put themselves through this torment every year.*

The reason that father was dragging his child through the Tijuana River sewage is that he knew there was a good chance he would not be caught. And that if he were caught, he would be set free within hours to try again. And that if he made it into the United States, he and his child (and eventually quite probably many of their relatives) would be lavishly rewarded.

"Good fences make good neighbors," Robert Frost reports a

New England friend saying, in his poem "Mending Wall." In this case, a good border fence might have kept a neighbor from moral hazard.

Any parent confronted with a two-year-old at bedtime is familiar with the human truth: *"There are times when you have to be cruel to be kind."* Only the editors of national newspapers can afford to sit on the ground and ignore it.

The Wall Street Journal's Bob Bartley, of course, resolves this moral problem, quite consistently, by moving in the opposite direction: a proposed Constitutional amendment, *There shall be open borders*—abandon border enforcement altogether. And, for the economic, social and national reasons outlined in this book, I think this is wrong.

But, in any case, given the inconceivably larger influx that would result, open immigration would not end desperate scenes on the border (although it would dramatically increase desperate scenes *north* of the border, as the immigrants overran America).

Public health concerns alone would dictate continued controls. Which the immigrants will not respect. Why should they?

For example, at the moment, a significant proportion of the illegals that the Border Patrol catches every night turn out to be the relatives of those amnestied under IRCA. These relatives will soon be eligible to be sponsored by their family members for legal entry (after which they will be able to sponsor their own close relatives, but that's another matter). However, they refuse to wait at all.

And their attitude is entirely rational . . . if ominously selfish and amoral. American policy has sent a very clear message: *it does not pay to obey U.S. law.*

IMMIGRATION AND QUESTIONS OF MORALITY

American intellectuals approach the issue of immigration in a highly moralistic way. And their morality works in only one direction. For example, the huge academic industry has produced *not one* serious philosophical treatment of this topic that is other than pro-immigration.[5]

The illegal-immigration scandal on the border, of course, is only part of the problem. These intellectuals seem to view all of immigration policy as an opportunity for public displays of exquisite sensibility. The immigration debate provides them with the equivalent of a revivalist meeting. They get to fall on the floor and speak in tongues.

It definitely slows things down. At other people's expense.

For example, after my *National Review* cover story came out, I found myself invited to the University of Cincinnati Law School to debate immigration. I love this sort of thing. As a provincial from a small country, I am fascinated by the way in which America really is a federal society. The different urban centers of commerce, culture and politics are genuinely independent from—and, indeed, positively indifferent to—each other.

Plus, of course, you could never on your own think up all the weird questions people ask.

The weird question I remember these American law students asking on this occasion went directly to the morality of immigration:

> QUESTION: *Isn't immigration a civil right?*
>
> [ANSWER: *No! Are you serious?*]

Isn't immigration a *what*? Well, I should have anticipated it, I suppose. Current U.S. policy, as we have seen, does indeed treat legal immigration as a sort of bastard civil right, extended to relatives of the arbitrarily selected group of foreigners who happen to have shouldered through the door first since the 1965 Immigration Act.

But that was not what the students meant. They meant that all foreigners just have a right, a civil right, to emigrate to the United States. (In fact, I suspect that, like many Americans, the students didn't realize foreigners have an independent existence at all. They just viewed them as an exotic type of American minority. Like Hollywood's Maurice Chevalier or Charles Laughton.)

And on this level, needless to say, the proposition is hopelessly incoherent, logically and morally. How can foreigners have civil rights when they are not members of the *civitas*? And why *these* foreigners—at the expense of the infinite number of other foreigners?

Just as we saw on page xvi with *Time* magazine's funny view of what constitutes a "democratic" immigration policy, these students' invocation of the concept of "civil rights" was just another example of the degeneration of an idea as it diffuses through time and space. They were like Russian serfs, continuing to doff their caps at the mention of the title "Czar" nearly two millennia, two thousand miles and an unimaginable cultural distance from the world of the Roman aristocratic clan called "Caesar," from whom the term had originally derived.

I don't think I shook their simple faith.

QUESTION: *Aren't we morally obliged to accept immigrants?*

[ANSWER: *Even if we are, that's just the start of the problem.*]

If immigration to the United States is not a civil right, then maybe it's an overriding moral right? This notion is particularly popular among the men and women who staff the major American religious organizations.

(The laity is notably less enthusiastic. A 1992 Gallup Poll found that self-reported Christians, Catholics and Protestants alike were not only heavily opposed to current mass immigration—but were actually *more* opposed than those respondents who professed no religion.[6])

Curiously, morality seems to have reversed itself completely since the 1960s. In 1967, 1968, and 1972 the United Nations passed resolutions condemning the developed nations for seducing away the educated of the Third World—the so-called "brain drain."

Some splendid scripture gets quoted to support immigration. Leviticus 19:33–34 has resonance for Jews in particular:

> *If a stranger sojourn with thee in your land, ye shall not vex him. But the stranger that dwelleth with you shall be unto you as one born among you, and thou shalt love him as thyself; for ye were strangers in the land of Egypt.*

It's a curious passage, because elsewhere in the Old Testament the Children of Israel are instructed to be very careful indeed about those alien influences. For example, many Americans might see more relevance to their country's current plight in the dire warning of Deuteronomy 28:43–44:

> *The stranger that is within thee shall get up above thee very high; and thou shalt come down very low. He shall lend to thee, and thou shalt not lend to him; he shall be the head and thou shalt be the tail.*

Mainline Christian denominations often cite a New Testament text to justify immigration: Matthew 25:31–46—the Last Judgment. Christ describes a time when "the Son of Man" will divide the nations, and condemn one group to hell, saying—

> *For I was an hungred, and ye gave me no meat; I was thirsty, and ye gave me no drink. I was a stranger, and ye took me not in; naked, and ye clothed me not; sick, and in prison, and ye visited me not.*

Naturally, the condemned nations get upset:

> *Then shall they also answer him, saying, 'Lord, when saw we thee an hungred, or athirst, or a stranger, or naked, or sick, or in prison, and did not minister unto thee?'*
>
> *Then shall he answer them, saying, Verily I say unto you, inasmuch as ye did it not to one of the least of these, ye did it not to me.*

This text is interpreted surprisingly literally by liberal theologians, who usually view fundamentalism with disdain. They suggest that any "stranger" prevented from entering the United States may be, in effect, well, Jesus.

The problem, however, is this: *there are rather a lot of Jesuses out there.* (See pages 49–54.) No conceivable U.S. immigration policy can "minister" to all of them.

Once again, the sensibility is exquisite. But it is not a practical guide to action.

Let's look at the practicalities. Suppose that the United States does have an obligation to "minister" to the poor of the world. Then, obviously, it must do so *effectively.*

How could the United States "minister" effectively? There are two possibilities, depending upon your understanding of the way the world works.

> Either: *1. Americans are sitting on a pile of wealth. They should simply share it.*
>
> Or: *2. Americans have created a system that produces wealth. They can only share wealth to the extent that sharing it does not impair the system.*

From an economist's standpoint, there is simply no argument about which of these possibilities is right. Quite obviously, wealth is not a matter of resources: it is a matter of resourcefulness.

Some countries with large populations and great natural riches, like Brazil—or Mexico—are poor. Other countries with few resources and small populations, like Switzerland, are rich. And countries with no resources but fairly large, hardworking and ingenious populations, like Japan, can become very rich indeed.

In other words, the United States is not a pile of wealth but a fragile system—a lifeboat. And lifeboats can get overcrowded and sink.

On the other hand, lifeboats can tow large numbers of survivors along in their wake. In fact, this is usually what happens in shipwrecks.

The lifeline everyone can hang on to, in this case, is trade. By buying and importing straw hats (or whatever), the wealth generated by the American system can penetrate the remotest fastnesses of China (or wherever).

But it is not at all necessary for Chinese peasants to come in person to America in order for the American system to "minister" to them effectively.

In fact, it may be easier if they don't.

It's worth remembering that in the last century, the same religious moralists who now support immigration provided much of the motivating force behind imperialism. The partition of the world by the Western powers was quite often in response to missionaries' demands that Something Be Done about slavery, starvation and assorted degradations beyond the frontiers of civilization. The great poet of the British Empire, Rudyard Kipling, was not being at all ironic when he wrote his famous lines applauding the U.S. seizure of the Philippines:

Take up the White Man's burden,
Send forth the best ye breed—
Go, bind your sons to exile
To serve your captives' need.

A hundred years later, the White Person's Burden is apparently that the same "captives" be brought here. It amounts to an inverted imperialism. It confirms the United States as a colony of the world.

QUESTION: *What about the American tradition of accepting refugees?*

[ANSWER: *What tradition?*]

It's just another manufactured immigration myth. The truth is that almost the first federal legislation affecting immigration, the Alien and Sedition Acts of 1798, was largely motivated by fear of refugees from the French Revolution. Subsequently, some immigrants arriving in America were fleeing disruption at home (although that can be exaggerated—contrary to the general impression, for example, relatively few Germans came to the United States as a direct result of the collapse of the democratic revolutions of 1848[7]). But there was no explicit recognition of refugees as such until select groups began to be admitted in the years following World War II. The United States did not acquire a comprehensive refugee policy until the Refugee Act of 1980. And, as we have seen, that was promptly captured and debauched by special interest groups.

QUESTION: *But didn't the United States cause all these refugees because of its foreign policy?—look at El Salvador/Nicaragua/Vietnam.*

[ANSWER: *Does that mean you want to accept 5 million white South Africans?*]

People who make this argument seem to mean only those foreign policy controversies where they disagree with the United States and want to punish it. Thus, resisting communism was always pretty controversial with a small but vocal group of Americans. Forcing the whites to give up power in South Africa was not.

Nevertheless, it cannot be denied that U.S. policy played a key role in breaking the white South African government's will. And the country might easily become another Lebanon.

Well—where's the welcome mat?

The reality is this: the United States is the only global superpower. It is the central pillar of world order. This means there is practically nothing for which U.S. action, or inaction, cannot be blamed. And there will always be Americans ready to do the blaming.

And to accept it. Which is why, *twenty years after Saigon fell,* the United States is still admitting Vietnamese claiming to be children of American servicemen. In 1992 alone, a total of 17,253 arrived under the AmerAsian Homecoming Act. Only 4,261 were the alleged children themselves—the rest were their immediate relatives, typical of the way "family reunification" tends to take over all categories. But of those 4,261, over a third (37 percent) were born *more than nine months after the last U.S. troops left Vietnam.* They were obvious frauds . . . but the U.S. government admitted them anyway. In fact, as directed by the 1990 immigration legislation, because of their "American" fathers, they were deemed to be instant U.S. citizens.[8]

QUESTION: *Isn't opposition to immigration just racism?*

[ANSWER: *Reread Chapter 8, pages 173–75.*]

NAVIGATING THE SEA OF PAIN

"The world is a comedy to those that think, a tragedy to those that feel," said the eighteenth-century English writer Horace Walpole.

A good line. But really it should be the other way around. To those that feel, causing the United States to admit a few more immigrants (well—a lot more immigrants) generates a warm, self-congratulatory, comforting glow. To those that think, however, more immigration is quite plainly not a solution, even for the potential immigrants themselves. Tragedy is unavoidable. So, no glow.

In fact, there is no solution to the problem of human pain. It is an infinite sea. And to the extent that we might alleviate pain in one area, by admitting some immigrants, we can exacerbate it in another, by excluding other immigrants or by threatening the communities of the native-born.

How can we navigate on this sea of pain? In December 1968, the pioneer ecologist Garrett Hardin published a famous essay in *Science* magazine about another such distressing moral chaos, "The Tragedy of the Commons." In this essay, Hardin noted that where land is held in common, as sometimes in feudal European villages, or when the public range was open, as in the American West, it is inevitably overgrazed and eroded.

Why? Hardin acknowledged that it was in the interest of all the herders *collectively* to be prudent in the numbers of animals they put out to pasture. But, he pointed out, it was against the interest of any herder *individually.* This was because the individual herder had no means of ensuring that the benefits of his restraint would not be guzzled up by his neighbors' beasts. So, for each herder, competitive irresponsibility was the rational strategy.

Hardin's insight has been greeted with cheers (somewhat to his irritation) by a whole school of free-market economists. They have used it to explain so-called "market failure"—those awkward situations where free markets don't seem to work. The cause of the tragedy of the commons, the economists argue, is *inadequately specified property rights.* (It's a classic metamarket issue, to use the terminology of Chapter 8.) If the commons were divided up between private owners, they say, those owners would have an incentive to look after the land.

And this is exactly what happened in eighteenth-century Britain. The commons were "enclosed" by private landlords. And agricultural productivity was revolutionized.

Why had the previous generation of economists tended to overlook the crucial function of property rights? Perhaps because, particularly after the disaster of the Depression, the whole institution of private property seemed somehow embarrassing—just as restricting immigration makes respectable people feel vaguely ill at ease, quite wrongly, today.

Quips rule the intellectual world. And the dominant quip about private property was made by the French nineteenth-century socialist Pierre-Joseph Proudhon: *"Property is theft."*

But Proudhon also said something else that really does deserve to be remembered: *"If all the world is my brother, then I have no brother."*[9] This is a succinct statement of the impossibility of rational and meaningful moral action if our responsibilities are viewed as limitless—the condition that Garrett Hardin calls "promiscuous altruism."

The only way to navigate in the sea of human pain is to make distinctions. The moral market will fail unless some equivalent of property lines is specified. Our rights and duties have to be put in some sort of priority.

And there is an ordering principle in the modern world: once again, it is our old friend the nation-state.

Viewed in the context of the American nation-state, it is immediately obvious that, for example, the plight of poor American blacks must be considered before that of landless laborers in Latin America. American blacks are part of the U.S. national community.

Equally, the numbers and type of immigration must be subordinated to the integrity of the American nation-state—the lifeboat that is towing the economy of the entire world.

The value of community is not a particularly conservative idea. Recently, a group of liberal academics led by George Washington University sociologist Amitai Etzioni founded the "Communitarian Network," designed in part to recapture family issues from the religious right.[10] It has not addressed immigration . . . yet.

Philosophers and theologians might be shocked by the idea that we are not monsters if we favor our own nation-state above the great mass of humanity. But normal people make a very similar moral distinction effortlessly.

For example, my little son, Alexander, is a New York City baby. Directly after he was born, he was visited by a remarkable procession of New York career women, all bearing gifts. He accepted this as his due. But I found it fascinating.

New York is a very tough city, particularly for women. And they have the additional affliction of having to deal with the Manhattan male, by all accounts a distressing species. Yet, whatever the difficulties and disappointments in their own lives, these young women responded to Alexander with unenvious, unalloyed delight. Their generosity was something I would not have expected to find in myself in their circumstances. It was one of the rare occasions that improve your view of human nature.

Nevertheless, women combine this genuine feeling for all children with a special love of their own. They see no contradiction in doing so. And they are right. Only philosophers and theologians sit around thinking up imaginary circumstances in which a woman would have to choose between all children, or other children, and her children.

The same is true for the nation-state. Like the family, it is one of those happy inventions through which human beings are enabled to experience the world. It is a foundation upon which a more general approach to the world might perhaps be built. But it is not something for which a more general approach to the world can be substituted.

Respect for the nation-state, perhaps, is the ultimate family value.

TURNABOUT IS FAIR PLAY, ISN'T IT?

While we're on this subject of the morality of immigration, let's ask a question of our own:

- **If immigration is such a moral imperative, why don't the Mexicans/Chinese/Indians/Koreans/Japanese** (fill in any of the other recent top-ten suppliers of immigrants to the United States) **allow it?**

Don't say: "These countries already have enough people." The United States already has more than all of them except mainland China and India.

And don't say: "They're too poor." As we have seen, the whole economic theory of immigration, as developed by immigration enthusiasts, is that immigration does not displace workers: it complements them. Well, it should work both ways.

Moreover, most of these countries are lacking in the very skills that Americans have in abundance—both technical and entrepreneurial. Finally, it's precisely in these low-income countries that the returns to these skills are relatively the highest. That's why George Borjas argues that Third World immigration to the United States is "negatively selected," with the unskilled having more incentive to come. (See page 144, Chapter 7.) And it's why there are thousands of young Americans in the former Communist countries of Eastern Europe, running small businesses and helping it develop—between 30,000 and 50,000 in the Czech Republic alone, according to some estimates.[11]

But there is no equivalent young American community in China—although its economy has recently been growing at a sustained real rate of 10 percent a year, the fastest recorded growth rate in history and enough to make a lot of millionaires.

For comparison, note that there are about 28,500 Americans living in Hong Kong (population: 6 million).[12] If you project a similar ratio for all of China (population: 1.2 billion), that suggests a possible total of 5.7 million American expatriates.

Well, why not? After all, there are 1.6 million U.S. residents of Chinese origin.

This is why not: if you phone the embassy of the People's Republic of China in Washington, D.C., and ask about immigrating, you get this answer:

> CHINESE EMBASSY OFFICIAL [*laughs*]: "China does not accept any immigrants. We have a large enough population. A foreigner can visit on a tourist visa that can be extended for up to six months. Then you must leave. To apply for a temporary work permit, you must first have an official letter of invitation from a company authorized by the Chinese government."

In 1992, mainland China was the sixth largest contributor of immigrants to the United States—sending 38,907, about 3 percent of the total.

Americans get laughed at a lot when they ask about emigrating to the countries whose citizens are immigrating here. Or worse:

> MEXICO (*number one 1992 immigrant contributor, with 91,332—plus 122,470 legalized under IRCA*): "Unless you are hired by a Mexican company that obtains a temporary work permit, or are a retiree older than sixty-five who can prove financial self-sufficiency, you must get a six-month tourist visa *and apply in person to the Ministry of the Interior in Mexico City.* If your visa expires before the process is completed, you must get a new visa and begin again."

Not surprisingly, there are only about 25,000 legal immigrants to Mexico each year. Mexico also devotes a lot of energy to hunting down illegal immigrants, mainly from Central America. They are deported—80,000 in the first six months of 1990 alone—without right of appeal. Foreign residents are bureaucratically discouraged from becoming Mexican citizens. But guess what? Natives of Spain and other Latin American countries get special treatment.[13]

> SOUTH KOREA *(immigrants to the United States in 1992: 19,359):* "Korea does not accept immigrants."

> PHILIPPINES *(immigrants to the United States in 1992: 61,022):* You need to be married to a Filipino or have capital to invest. Otherwise: "Put your request in writing and mail it to the Immigration Department in Manila."

> TAIWAN *(immigrants to the United States in 1992: 16,344):* "Wow! I can't answer that question. Let me transfer you to my supervisor." You need Taiwanese relatives by blood or marriage, or investment capital.

> JAMAICA *(immigrants to the United States in 1992: 18,915):* "You cannot simply immigrate to Jamaica. You can only enter Jamaica as a tourist [*for a maximum of six months*] or as a worker. To obtain a work permit, you must first have a job offer. Either the company or you must fill out the necessary documentation for a work permit. After working in Jamaica for more than five years, you can then apply for permanent residency status—but you must submit numerous personal records proving your financial stability and good char-

acter. Such records include an annual report of total income, bank statements and an estimate of the value of all the property you own in Jamaica and overseas and your police record. It is quite a process."

EGYPT *(immigrants to the United States in 1992: 3,576):* "Egypt is not an immigrant country. We do not permit immigrants. While work permits exist, when the specific assignment is completed, the individual must leave the country."

And my personal favorite:

INDIA *(immigrants to the United States in 1992: 36,755): First official:* "Are you of Indian origin?" [*Told no.*] "Submit your question in writing to the embassy." [*Hangs up.*] *Second official:* "Are you of Indian origin?" [*Asked if important.*] "Yes." [*Transfers call.*] *Third official:* "Since you are not of Indian origin, while it is not impossible for you to immigrate to India, it is a very difficult, very complex, and very, very long process. Among other things, it will require obtaining clearances from both the Ministry of Foreign Affairs and the Ministry of Home Affairs."

Note that these Indian officials are asking not about *citizenship,* but about *origin.* For those unaccustomed to recognizing such things, this is racial discrimination. It is even more stringent than the 1921 Quota Act—an outright "brown-India policy."

The world is laughing at America.

This hypocrisy on the part of the major emigrant countries may be only a theoretical issue for most Americans—as yet. However, it's perfectly possible that the American children of immigrants from these countries might one day want to take their skills back to their ancestral homelands. The liberation of Eastern Europe has already attracted some third-generation Americans to take a look. And tens of thousands of Brazilians of Japanese origin have returned to Japan.

Currently, however, this hypocrisy most hurts the other, poorer, Third World countries. For example, in 1983, Nigeria (immigrants to the United States in 1993: 4,327) expelled up to *2 million* illegal immigrants who had come from Ghana, Niger and its other neighbors. In 1985, it expelled another 700,000.

The United States, however, is the flower that the rest of the world is struggling to pluck. Should it not at least ensure that its native-born citizens are treated equally in exchange?

GIVING IMMIGRATION CRITICS A GOOD NAME

Critics of current U.S. immigration policy worry about what to call themselves. They think their inability to get a public hearing is partly because they don't, quite literally, have a good name.

Being "anti-immigration" just doesn't sound very good. (Besides being inaccurate: most critics merely want reform.) Too much like being "anti-immigrant." Negative. Nasty. Possibly—aargh!—nativist. No decent TV news director wants anything to do with *that.*

As an immigrant, I have a modest proposal for these critics of immigration.

As we have seen, any general moral obligation to minister to strangers is met, and more than matched, by the specific and even stronger moral obligation to protect our own family.

And on the political level, the equivalent of the family is the nation-state—every one of them, in Aleksandr Solzhenitsyn's words quoted on page 233, a particular facet of God's design.

So I suggest that the critics of immigration adopt a name that has a long and honorable role in American history.

They should call themselves—"Patriots."

PART THREE

Shipwreck and Salvage

14

WHAT, THEN, IS TO BE DONE?

. . . The tradition of British medical science is entirely opposed to any emphasis on [treatment]. British medical specialists are usually quite content to trace the symptoms and define the cause. It is the French, by contrast, who begin by describing the treatment and discuss the diagnosis later, if at all. We feel bound to adhere in this to the British method, which may not help the patient but which is unquestionably more scientific.

—**C. NORTHCOTE PARKINSON,**
"Injelititis, or, Palsied Paralysis," *Parkinson's Law* (1958)

Just over one hundred years ago, at a Chicago meeting of the American Historical Society in 1893, a young historian called Frederick Jackson Turner read a paper on "The Significance of the Frontier in American History." The argument he set forth was to dominate Americans' thinking about themselves for more than a generation.

Turner began by noting that the Bureau of the Census had just announced that there was no longer a continuous line of free, unsettled land visible on the U.S. map. The American "frontier" had closed.

For the first time since the Puritans came down the gangplank with a watchful eye cocked on the distant tree line, America was no longer bounded by a clear point beyond which civilization ceased. There was no longer a distinct region where Americans could always go to claim land of their own, to escape from authority, to begin their lives anew.

Closing along with the frontier, said Turner, was "the first period of American history." He argued that the frontier had shaped the American character—its informality, equality, self-reliance. And he worried about what would happen without the social "safety valve" that the frontier had represented.

A century later, the second period of American history may be closing too. It may be time to face the fact that the United States can no longer be an "immigrant country."

IMMIGRATION POLICY IN A DECOLONIZED AMERICA

For Americans even to think about their immigration policy, given the political climate that has prevailed since the 1960s, involves a sort of psychological liberation movement. In Eugene McCarthy's terms, America would have to stop being a colony of the world. The implications are shocking, even frightening: that Americans, without feeling guilty, can and should seize control of their country's destiny.

If they did, what would a decolonized American immigration policy look like?

Remember that the United States has been on an immigration binge since 1965. The hangover will be terrible; the temptation to take another drink overwhelming. But the alternative is dissolution. To recover, the patient needs a relentless, driving will. And he must accept extreme measures, such as total abstinence, which have become tragically necessary because of thirty years of irresponsible policy.

The first step is absolutely clear:

- **The 1965 Immigration Act, and its amplifications in 1986 and 1990, has been a disaster and must be repealed.**

And a future, American, immigration policy must be shaped by these four principles:

- *The United States must regain control of its borders—over both illegal and legal immigration.*
- *Immigration must be treated as a luxury for the United States, not as a necessity.*
- *The costs of any immigration should fall on the immigrant, not on native-born Americans.*
- *Any immigration must meet a fundamental test: What does it mean for "The National Question"? Will it help or hurt the ability of the United States to survive as a nation-state—the political expression of that interlacing of ethnicity and culture that now constitutes the American nation?*

Ideally, working out the details of a future, American immigration policy deserves at least as much intellectual energy as immigration enthusiasts have poured into thinking up rationalizations for the current chaos. But here are some quick suggestions:

ILLEGAL IMMIGRATION: END IT

First line of defense: the border

The Border Patrol should be increased from its present four thousand—under the circumstances, a Border Patrol the size of the Los Angeles Police Department (about eight thousand) seems hardly unreasonable. The border, especially the crucial one hundred miles where 90 percent of apprehensions occur, should be sealed (at long last) with a fence, a ditch and whatever other contrivances that old Yankee ingenuity finds appropriate. Consideration should be given to jailing repeat offenders, perhaps in special prisons, for at least as long as is necessary to disrupt the economic patterns that have currently developed around lax border enforcement.

Second line of defense: inside the United States

The Immigration and Naturalization Service's Investigations Division, its main enforcement unit in the United States, should be increased as urgently as the Border Patrol. Presently, it has a mere

1,650 employees—and there are at least 4 million illegals here. A second Operation Wetback, the much-reviled anti-illegals drive of 1954, will be necessary. This will require coordinated effort by all levels of government, including federal agencies like the Internal Revenue Service and the Department of Housing and Urban Development, which currently decline to cooperate with immigration-law enforcement. Americans may eventually have to carry identification cards, like many Europeans—and legal U.S. resident aliens, whose official status is affirmed by the famous "green card," now actually blue. (Perhaps the Clinton administration's proposed universal health-care card could serve.) Libertarians will dislike this, but it is hardly more an encroachment on personal freedom than the income tax. The economic basis of the illegal-immigrant presence in the United States must be systematically attacked. This attack must go beyond tactics like employer sanctions and the ending of direct and indirect subsidies from the American taxpayer to reach strategic points, like the ability of illegals to remit money to their countries of origin without proof of legal residence. Blocking financial flows in this way proved useful in the drug war. Other drug war expedients suggested by Huber Hanes, a former Border Patrol officer who has been circulating a proposed Border Line and Boundary bill: fining illegals, who typically carry large amounts of cash, and deputizing local police to enforce federal immigration law, which—puzzling to non-lawyers—they currently cannot do.

State and local governments that refuse to cooperate must be punished. (Just imagine what would happen if they were practicing segregation.) Deportation procedures, for both legal and illegal aliens, should be streamlined, and criminal aliens automatically deported.

There must under no circumstances be another amnesty.

Both on the border and inside the United States, the national effort against illegal immigration must be constantly reinforced by legislation. U.S. immigration law has already been significantly weakened by activist judges. But there is nothing sacred about a wrongheaded judicial ruling. The answer is to pass another law. When Americans do seize control of their immigration policy again, it will inevitably take the form of an epic clash between the legislative and judicial branches.

And the moral pressure will be intense.

A common argument will be that employed in mid-1993 by Representative José Serrano (D.-New York), the Puerto Rican–born chairman of the Congressional Hispanic Caucus, while denouncing an anti-illegal-immigrant amendment to the Clinton administration's national service plan: *"I resent having to prove I'm a citizen . . ."*[1]

To this, the American answer must be: *tough.* Life is unfair, as another Democrat—President John F. Kennedy—once memorably noted. Representative Serrano has, presumably, ample means to prove his identity. I will be happy to do the same (I don't mind now, actually) when there are 2 to 3 million illegal Englishmen crossing the border every year.

Could any American politician be so callous?

Well, do they want to keep their country?

LEGAL IMMIGRATION: CUT IT BACK —OR CUT IT OFF?

Quality

Current policy should be reversed: skilled immigration must be favored before family reunification. To put it another way, the United States could do without that portion of the current influx that is below the average American's educational achievement.

The immigrant influx could be further reharmonized with U.S. labor-market conditions by requiring more potential immigrants to have offers of employment. Since an immigrant's country of origin turns out to be an excellent predictor of likely success or failure in the United States, the admissions policy might take account of this reality. (Isn't honesty the best policy? To end abuse of their asylum process, in 1987 the British frankly banned a whole list of specified "troublesome" nationalities from approaching immigration officials while in transit—including Somalis, Iranians and Libyans.[2]) A further possibility: Ben Wattenberg's idea of an English-language requirement for immigrants.

No immigration should be permitted from countries that do not allow reciprocal emigration from the United States.

Quantity

America needs another time-out from immigration. It needs another pause for digestion, to match the Great Lulls of 1790–1840 and 1925–65.

This means a *drastic cutback of legal immigration.* From the current 1 million a year to perhaps 400,000, the target suggested by the Rockefeller Commission on Population Growth and the American Future in 1972. Or 350,000, as proposed by Reverend Theodore Hesburgh's Select Commission on Immigration and Refugee Policy in 1981. Or 300,000, as proposed by FAIR in 1992—which the organization describes as a "moratorium" because it would mean zero net immigration, since up to some 300,000 people are estimated to leave the United States each year.

Or, maybe, even less. There is a case for *an immediate temporary cutoff of all immigration*—say three to five years. Thereafter it might be advisable to adopt the more flexible Australian and Canadian approach. These countries have no specific immigrant total written into law, and can vary the total accepted yearly according to their labor-market conditions (and to public opinion—ultimately the only legitimate arbiter). Returning the INS to the Labor Department from the Justice Department, as proposed by Vernon M. Briggs, Jr., in his *Mass Immigration and the National Interest,*[3] might reduce the current legalistic–civil rights bias. When you have a hammer, as Justice Department lawyers do, everything looks like a nail.

Whatever the total, however, cutting back immigration certainly means *radical reform of the "family-reunification" policy.* Currently, the United States is the only industrialized country that allows the automatic immigration of "non-nuclear" extended-family members. Had immigration been restricted just to the "nuclear" family members of American citizens—parents, spouses and dependent children—only about 250,000 immigrants would have entered in 1992. (And even this flow would diminish in time, because many of these sponsoring American citizens are actually themselves recent immigrants.)

But an automatic quarter million immigrants a year, before any skilled immigration at all, is still a lot. In the end, the fact must be faced: *even close family reunification is not sacred.* The restrictionist legislation in the 1920s, for example, made no provision for it. (And, of course, families can be reunited in two ways—the immigrant can always leave.)

This is a distressing prospect. I know. Maggy and I benefited personally from the generous American policy on family reunification. She is a Canadian, and I was a resident alien in the United States when I married her. Then, because of our marriage, she herself was admitted as a resident alien.

But this was a legal right—hardly a moral right. It was a privilege granted by American policy. And the truth is that our lives would not have been destroyed if Maggy had not been permitted to immigrate. I would probably be writing a book on Canadian immigration policy right now.

Cutting back on immigration also means *cutting back on "refugees," "asylees" and the various other special categories* that have been slipped through Congress by interest-group lobbying. Probably all these categories should be abolished entirely. Any individual member of one of them, of course, could apply to immigrate in the usual way.

COSTS MUST FALL ON THE IMMIGRANTS

Anything that artificially distorts the demand for immigrants, notably financial transfers by the government, must be reviewed critically. *Payments to illegal immigrants must be eliminated.* This includes the transfer implicit in free public education, which means another clash with the judges: the Supreme Court's split-decision *Plyler v. Doe* ruling (1982) forcing school systems to accept the children of illegals. And it means a principled stand against all forms of government-imposed "bilingualism."

No immigrant should count as a member of a "protected class" for the purposes of U.S. affirmative action programs. Instead, Americans should be asking themselves: *if the "protected classes" are so oppressed in the United States that they must be rescued by this unprecedented government intervention, how can it be right to allow any more members of the "protected classes" to immigrate into this oppression?*

IMMIGRATION AND THE NATIONAL QUESTION

On page 232, I raised what I described as *The National Question:*

- **Is America still that interlacing of ethnicity and culture that we call a nation? Can the United States survive as a nation-state, the political expression of that nation?**

To begin at the most sensitive point:

The American nation of 1965, nearly 90 percent white, was explicitly promised that the new immigration policy would not shift the country's racial balance. But it did.

Race is destiny in American politics. Its importance has only been intensified by the supposedly color-blind civil rights legislation of the 1960s—which paradoxically has turned out to mean elaborate race-conscious affirmative action programs. Any change in the racial balance must obviously be fraught with consequences for the survival and success of the American nation.

It is simply common sense that Americans have a legitimate interest in their country's racial balance. It is common sense that they have a right to insist that their government stop shifting it. Indeed, it seems to me that they have a right to insist that it be shifted back.

This does not necessarily mean an absolute ban on any group. *"Numbers are of the essence,"* in the words of Enoch Powell, the prophetic critic of Britain's disastrous postimperial immigration policy. In small numbers, all kinds of immigrants can arrive in America and be assimilated. Culture is a substitute for ethnicity. But numbers so high that they shift the American demographic balance make this impossible.

One right that Americans certainly have is the right to insist that immigrants, whatever their race, become Americans. The full force of public policy should be placed behind another "Americanization" campaign, modeled on that during the last Great Wave of Immigration. All diversion of public funds to promote "diversity," "multiculturalism" and foreign-language retention must be struck down as subversive of this American ideal. Hyphenated identities must remain a private matter, as throughout most of American history. An English-language requirement for potential immigrants would make Americanization easier. The English-language requirement for citizenship should be enforced and the various recent exceptions, such as for spouses and the elderly, abolished—they were symbolic gestures anyway, and now the symbols are needed elsewhere. There must be a concerted legislative attack on bilingual manifestations, beginning with the U.S. Department of Education's promotion of "bilingual" education. (The Quebec government's defense of French through restrictions on English should be studied with care.) A Constitutional amendment making English the official language of the United States could be a decisive step.

The Census Bureau's category of "Hispanic" should be abolished. It should be replaced with a national-origin or racial classification where appropriate.

Judging immigration in the context of the National Question sounds grim. But actually it could relax the tension. For example, it focuses attention on the demographic impact of immigration. Admitting elderly parents (leaving aside the issue of whether they are likely to become a public charge) would obviously not have a long-term demographic impact.

In the context of the National Question, the ultimate issue is not whether foreigners show up in the United States but when they are admitted to the national community and obtain full political rights and privileges. In an era of mass movement, the fact that the children of even illegal immigrants are automatically U.S. citizens is plainly outdated. It must be ended, by amending the Constitution if necessary. It may also be time to consider lengthening the five-year waiting period before immigrants can naturalize—perhaps to ten years, as in Italy and Germany, or even to fourteen years, as it was in the United States from 1798 to 1801.

"Nationalize, then naturalize" was one of the Know Nothings' slogans. But today American citizenship is being acquired in much the same spirit as a driver's license. This is why you regularly read of "American citizens" being involved in peculiar political intrigues in foreign countries—of which becoming prime minister of Greece

(Andreas Papandreou) and running for the presidency of Serbia (Milan Panic) are among the most respectable.

And, in turn, this makes immigration control difficult. Public policy is currently unable to discriminate between a new immigrant citizen's arranged marriage back in the old country and a tenth-generation American's foreign spouse. It probably should.

Again, discouraging foreign residents' access to the political community may seem rather grim. But actually it could relax the tension. Many foreign residents in the United States are perfectly happy with their half-and-half status. (For example, the British. They are notoriously laggardly about naturalizing, largely because they don't feel foreign in the first place.) Recently, there have been cases of famous foreign-born wives only reluctantly agreeing to naturalize because estate-tax law has been changed to discriminate savagely, and foolishly, against resident noncitizens.

It may be time for the United States to consider moving to a conception of itself more like that of Switzerland: tolerating a fairly large foreign presence that comes and goes, but rarely if ever naturalizes. It may be time to consider reviving a version of the *bracero* program, the agricultural guest-workers program that operated from the 1940s to the 1960s, allowing foreign workers to move in and out of the country in a controlled way, without permanently altering its demography and politics. (Many immigration critics dislike "guest-worker" programs because the "guests" tend to become permanent and deepen the "channels" followed by illegal immigrants. But it is hard to see how this could be worse than the current massive combination of illegal immigration and "citizen children." And it may be a transitional solution, allowing the U.S. immigration era to close without unnecessary hardship.)

This new conception may be a shock to American sensibilities. Many Americans, like my students at the University of Cincinnati Law School, are under the charming impression that foreigners don't really exist. But they also tend to think that, if foreigners really do exist, they ought to become Americans as quickly as possible.

However, the fact is that we—foreigners—are, in some sense, all Americans now, just as Jefferson said everyone had two countries, his own and France, in the eighteenth century. That is why we are here, just as the entire world flocked to Imperial Rome. The trick the Americans face now is to be an empire in fact, while remaining a democratic republic in spirit. Avoiding the Romans' mistake of diluting their citizenship into insignificance may be the key.

SHIPWRECK AND SALVAGE

What do I really think will happen?

In politics as elsewhere, if you ask a stupid question, you get a stupid answer—or at any rate a terse answer. And asking people if they want their communities to be overwhelmed by weird aliens with dubious habits is a stupid question. The answer is inevitable.

Until now in America, chance circumstances and shifts in public policy have always combined to change this question before that inevitable answer became too embarrassing. But the greater the number of immigrants, and the greater their difference from the American mainstream, the louder and ruder the answer will be.

The political elite may choose not to hear. Others, however, will.

I think . . . *that immigration restriction is inevitable in America.* It will be resisted hysterically. It will be sabotaged in every possible way. It will probably require repeated legislation. But that will only intensify the ultimate nationalist eruption.

And no political issue, once it reaches the surface, has more elemental power than immigration. It could quite easily destroy the present political-party system, as it helped to do in the years before the Civil War.

Precisely because of the bitterness of the battle, and because of the need to find any sheltering compromise, the ultimate restriction will probably be as crude as anything seen in the 1920s. To avoid the embarrassing question *"Who?"* politicians may find it simpler to answer the question *"How Many?"* with *"None."* Immigration could be ended entirely.

This would be tragic for the United States. But it would not be, in the full sense, a tragedy. Immigration is a luxury, not a necessity.

But I also suspect that the immigration cutoff will be too late. *Diversity,* the buzzword of the 1990s, will prove *divisive*—the now-forgotten buzzword of the 1970s. The contradictions of a society as deeply divided as the United States must now inexorably become, as a result of the post-1965 influx, will lead to conflict, repression and, perhaps, ultimately to a threat thought extinct in American politics for more than a hundred years: secession.

Deep into the twenty-first century, throughout the lifetime of my little son, American patriots will be fighting to salvage as much as possible from the shipwreck of their great republic. It will be a big wreck, and there will be a lot to salvage. But the struggle must be contrasted sadly with the task of completing the "Great Society" upon which Americans were encouraged to think they were embarking in 1965.

And the politicians and pundits who allowed this to happen truly deserve, and will certainly receive—in the words of the epigraph heading Chapter 5—the curses of those who come after.

15

CONCLUSION: THE BOWELS OF CHRIST?

I beseech you, in the bowels of Christ, think it possible you may be mistaken.

—**OLIVER CROMWELL,**
leader of the anti-Royalist parliamentary forces in the English Civil War, in a letter to the General Assembly of the Church of Scotland, August 3, 1650

About a year after my *National Review* immigration cover story was published, I found myself on the rostrum at one of the magazine's periodic conferences. This one was in La Jolla, California. A session on immigration was about to start. On my left was the Japanese American lawyer and commentator Lance Izumi, formerly speechwriter to California governor George Deukmejian and Reagan administration attorney general Ed Meese, now a fellow at San Francisco's Pacific Research Institute for Public Policy.

As the audience was assembling, Lance turned to me and began talking about the World War I passage from Hugh MacLennan's novel *Two Solitudes,* which I had cited in an article in *Social Contract* magazine, and which is reproduced here on pages 227–28.

"Of course," he said of the WASP girl's reaction to the

news of her husband's death, which had so confounded her French neighbors, "that's exactly how the Japanese would respond."

Then he got up and delivered an incisive critique of illegal immigration. He pointed out that it upsets even his liberal Democratic father, who feels that, after all, the Izumis were obeying the law when they came to America.

"East is East, and West is West, and never the twain shall meet," said Kipling. But, as I have said, my impression is that most Americans respect and indeed like the East Asian immigrants. Their ethnic "message," as Thomas Sowell calls it, may be different. But it apparently has some deep compatibilities.

It's happened before. Chinese arrived in the South directly after the Civil War, working at first as laborers. But they seem to have graduated quickly to shopkeeping and, in the era of segregation, to a sort of honorary white status. Indeed, to an actual white status: unreinforced by immigration, the Chinese communities concentrated in areas like Louisiana's Natchitoches Parish and Texas's Robertson County intermarried and, by 1980, had essentially vanished from the Census returns.[1]

Lance Izumi himself happens to think that there are limits to the absorptive capacity of U.S. society. "It just takes time to turn foreigners into little Americans," he says. "It just would be easier if we were dealing with smaller numbers—legal or illegal."

Could the possibly-easier assimilation of East Asians mean that immigration may not be quite the problem for the United States that the raw numbers suggest? That the Pincers on page 63 may not grip quite so hard after all?

Similarly, anyone looking at the debate preceding the Great Restriction of the 1920s may be troubled by the sheer extremes of pessimism expressed about the Eastern and Southern European influx. I have managed to talk myself out of this, largely because I think the cut-off actually helped assimilation. But the immigrants did, basically, assimilate.

I'm sure I'm right. There are some areas I'm watching—and reasons I'm not optimistic.

SOME LIBRA LAMENTATIONS

Asian immigrants might assimilate easily

As we have seen, some (but not all) Asian immigrant groups rapidly become economically successful. They even vote more like the American majority than do other ethnic minorities.

BUT . . . there are ominous signs that some Asians feel alienated from America's majority society despite their success.

Ronald Takaki opens his book *A Different Mirror: A History of Multicultural America* by relating the following shocking trauma:

> I had flown from San Francisco to Norfolk and was riding in a taxi to my hotel to attend a conference on multiculturalism. Hundreds of educators from across the country were meeting to discuss the need for greater cultural diversity in the curriculum. My driver and I chatted . . . the rearview mirror reflected a white man in his forties. "How long have you been in this country?" he asked. "All my life," I replied, wincing. "I was born in the United States." With a strong southern drawl, he remarked: "I was wondering because your English is excellent!" Then, as I had done many times before, I explained: "My grandfather came here from Japan in the 1880s. My family has been here, in America, for over a hundred years." He glanced at me in the mirror. Somehow I did not look "American" to him; my eyes and complexion looked foreign.
>
> Suddenly, we both became uncomfortably conscious of a racial divide separating us. An awkward silence turned my gaze from the mirror to the passing landscape, the shore where the English and the Powhatan Indians first encountered each other . . .

Takaki says that he entered his hotel "carrying a vivid reminder of why I was attending this conference."[2]

But *why* was Takaki attending the conference? On any reasonable scale, his complaint is trivial to the point of paranoia. He, after all, is the famous author and tenured professor from the University of California at Berkeley. The white Southerner is, perfectly politely, driving the cab.

To the extent that there is any content to Takaki's complaint, it is because he is Asian in a predominantly white society. And there is no cure for that except radically increasing the numbers of minorities and breaking down white America's sense of identity—

Ohhh! So *that's* why he was attending a conference on multiculturalism!

Hispanics might assimilate easily

There are some bright spots in the Hispanic picture. The notion that they are in fact assimilating faster than the conventional wisdom has been extensively explored in the work of Linda Chavez and political scientist Peter Skerry.[3] For example, Chavez argues that although the gap between Hispanic and white education, earnings and poverty levels appears not to be closing, it's partly a statistical mirage resulting from the recent immigrant influx. She finds that U.S.-born Mexican Americans, after adjustment for factors like experience, earn close to the non-Hispanic average.

Chavez believes most third-generation Hispanics speak only English. And, in a little-reported development that appears to have astonished everyone, Protestant evangelicals are making Hispanic converts, as they are throughout Latin America. Peter Skerry reports that about 10 percent of Mexican Americans in Los Angeles and San Antonio are Protestants. This proportion has doubled since 1960. Conversion might be viewed as a proxy for Americanization . . . although these congregations are usually Spanish-speaking and unpluralistically anti-Catholic.

BUT . . . "it's not something that can't be wrecked with the wrong policies," Chavez says of Hispanic assimilation. Ironically, it is Puerto Ricans who show the clearest signs of developing into a permanent underclass, despite (or because of) being entitled to government benefits as American citizens.

And the grip of the Hispanic professional politicians on their community is clearly tightening. Skerry shows that in the old-fashioned, community-based politics of San Antonio, Hispanics have behaved like traditional American ethnics on the road to integration. In the modern, media-dominated politics of Los Angeles, Hispanics have been welded into a distinct, race-conscious minority group.

So in California at least, the conditions encouraging earlier waves of Hispanic immigrants to assimilate may already have changed. One recent survey of second-generation Mexican Americans in California schools showed that while more than 85 percent claimed to speak English "well" or "very well," about the same proportion spoke Spanish about as well. *And more than half (55 percent) said they preferred to speak Spanish.* No other immigrant group showed this degree of retention of their parental language—and this preference for it.[4]

Allowing further massive Hispanic immigration may be one of the wrong policies that will wreck the assimilation of those already here. "Many Mexican Americans are involved in a process they call reverse assimilation—going back to their roots," *The San Diego Union-Tribune* reported in 1993. And it quoted a local Mexican American to illustrate the dynamic:

> I'm reverting to my original culture. I'm doing that along with many, many people because there are so many of us in the United States.
>
> My radio and television are always tuned to Spanish. I surround myself with Spanish-speaking people. I deal daily with bilingual people. [Other Americans] should face it—this is not going away. We're here to stay.[5]

A hundred years ago, self-appointed French Canadian spokesmen were making equally arrogant noises about their apparently imminent takeover of New England. But the Great Restriction, particularly work-permit regulatory changes in 1930, changed all that. Without the reinforcement of continuing immigration, the French Canadian enclaves assimilated. Thus today, for example, as much as 30 percent of the population of New Hampshire is of French Canadian origin. But French is spoken virtually nowhere.[6]

Intermarriage

The ultimate symptom of assimilation is intermarriage. And fragmentary evidence suggests that the latest immigrants may not be as unmeltable, even initially, as was the 1890–1920 wave. Over half of all Japanese Americans reportedly marry non-Japanese. The intermarriage rate for some other Asians is also high. Mexican Americans are more difficult to track, but estimates of their intermarriage rate in California range between a third and a half. In San Antonio, the rate is lower, but it is still comparable to that of European ethnics of two generations ago. And far above that of American-born blacks.[7]

Intermarriage would make the claws of the Pincers on page 63 somewhat fuzzier. The respective groups' genetic contribution to the American population, so to speak, would be the same. But the combination would be quite different. And the pressure from the Pincers would, perhaps, be dissipated.

BUT . . . there is some evidence that, while more Hispanics are intermarrying, the proportion of all Hispanic marriages has fallen, swamped by the sheer growth of the Hispanic population.[8] And intermarriage, like assimilation, can work two ways. Padraic Pearse had an English father, but he was still a Gaelic revivalist and a leader of the 1916 Easter Rising *putsch* against Ireland's union with Britain. For that matter, Raoul Lowery Contreras, the *El Hispaño* columnist I quoted on page 106 attacking George Will, Tom Metzger and myself, is part Anglo. Intermarriage cannot guarantee social harmony. That can be done only by an American majority that is confident and strong.

Lions may lie down with lambs

It's logically possible—that is, literally imaginable but practically inconceivable—that no known political laws apply to America. The unparalleled racial and ethnic diversity divisiveness introduced by the 1965 Immigration Act might simply harmonize smoothly. The lion might lie down with the lamb. Ben Wattenberg's Universal Nation might actually materialize, like the Heavenly Host in a Christmas pageant. Pigs—as the old saying has it—might fly.

BUT . . . even if a Universal Nation did materialize—what was wrong with America as it existed in 1965? As it exists—with all the changes inflicted to date by the 1965 Immigration Act—today?

Why does it have to be changed?

WHAT IF?

I've said that when you write on a topic like immigration, you enter into a conversation with America. After my critics and I had fought our round in the *National Review* symposium on my cover story, a subscriber wrote in this letter:

> *Readers who find themselves bogged down in the pros and cons of* [Third World] *immigration can simplify the issue by asking the same question airplane pilots and sailors pose before setting off in threatening weather, "What if?"*
>
> *What if Julian Simon, Ben Wattenberg and Bob Bartley are wrong? Are we prepared for any or all of the possible consequences: public assistance programs watered down or driven out completely, our environment overwhelmed, massive poverty, a shrinking percentage of our population in good jobs, a splintered society in which ethnic strife is as common as a rainy day, leading to that time in the next century when the U.S. goes totalitarian because the nation is no longer governable as a republic with four huge ethnic minorities (one of which is white)? . . .*
>
> *Now, what if Peter Brimelow and George Borjas are wrong? Can we handle a labor shortage and a reduction in the spread of fast food restaurants? We can solve the labor problem by going to our southern border and whispering, "we can use a few workers." As for the restaurants, here's a vote for more home cooked meals.*
>
> —Tev Laudeman, Louisville, Ky.

Tom Paine summed up his conservative rival pamphleteer Edmund Burke's *Reflections on the Revolution in France,* with its famous lament for the executed Queen Marie Antoinette, in one brilliant line: *"He pities the plumage, but forgets the dying bird."*

The American political elite has been in love, blindly, with the new immigrant plumage. It has not yet noticed that the bird—the American nation—might die.

Why take the risk?

Acknowledgments

As an author, I hate writing acknowledgments. Partly because you don't get paid for them—but mostly because it forces me to face the magnitude of my debts. And I always leave someone out, further adding to my post-publication depression.

An amazingly large number of individuals and institutions helped me to prepare this book. Many of their names are found in the text and notes, albeit in ways that typically give no indication of the extent of their helpfulness, although it was sometimes extraordinary. I am grateful to everyone who appears there, even when hostile. A special hello to Professor Julian Simon, a guaranteed intellectual stimulant albeit in directions of which he would not always approve, and to his ever-affable ally, Stephen Moore of Ed Crane's Cato (*O sancta simplicitas!*) Institute in Washington, D.C.

In particular, I want to thank my employers, Malcolm S. Forbes, Jr., and James W. Michaels, respectively proprietor and editor of *Forbes* magazine, for their heroic toleration of this project, the more so because it could be construed to contradict the magazine's trenchantly expressed point of view. My exposure to *Forbes*'s sledgehammer literary style has been most instructive. I am also grateful to other friends at *Forbes,* especially my frequent co-writer, Leslie Spencer (Mrs. James Huffman).

Similarly, I want to thank William F. Buckley and John O'Sullivan, respectively proprietor and editor of *National Review* magazine, for nurturing my 1992 cover story on immigration and its subsequent mutation into the present work. And I am also grateful to other friends at *National Review,* especially research director Dorothy McCartney and her efficient staff, librarians John J. Virtes, Russell Jenkins and Frederick W. Campano; managing editor Linda Bridges; senior editor Richard Brookhiser; economics analyst Edwin S. Rubenstein.

Without the constant help and counsel of my friend and indefatigable researcher, Joseph E. Fallon, this book could never have been written. I want here to thank him most sincerely and also to express the hope that the completed work approaches what he might wish. (Thanks also to all those whom Joe has been indefatigable with!)

In like vein, I am deeply grateful to the remarkable Dr. John H. Tanton of Petoskey, Michigan, a practicing ophthalmic surgeon who is also a founder of the Federation for Immigration Reform, of U.S. English and more recently of English Language Advocates, and editor and publisher of *The Social Contract*—truly a citizen who has taken up arms for his country. And to his staff at U.S. Foundation, Dorothy Koury, Niki Calloway, and Peggy Raddatz.

Immigration is a dangerously intricate subject, one reason why debate on the topic has been so crabbed. Several friends read some or all of the manuscript in order to interdict any obvious factual and conceptual errors. A partial list: Professor George J. Borjas of the University of California, San Diego; George High and Rosemary Jenks of the Center for Immigration Studies; Stephen J. Markman, formerly assistant attorney general of the United States for Legal Policy; Dr. Michael Walker, director of the Fraser Institute, Vancouver, British Columbia, Canada. This does not at all mean they agree with my conclusions—sometimes emphatically not. It does mean, however, that any attempt to refute me on purely technical grounds is likely to prove more difficult than optimists may think. This is a warning.

At the risk of boring our wives, I must say that only twins understand what it is to have a twin—my brother and fellow immigrant, John Brimelow.

Thanks also to: Gerda Bikales; David F. Durham, Monique Miller and other friends at Carrying Capacity Network; Richard Estrada; Harry Evans, Jonathan Karp at Random House; Tim W. Ferguson; Scip Garling, James Dorcy and other friends at the Federation for American Immigration Reform; Robert Goldborough of Americans for Immigration Control; Henry Graff; John Grimwade; Ernest van den Haag; Garrett Hardin; Harvey H. Hukari; Ed Jagels; Jesse Laguna; Edward Levy; Donald Mann of Negative Population Growth; Philippe Mao; Jack Martin of the Center for Immigration Studies; Merrill Matthews, Jeanette Nordstrom at the National Center for Policy Analysis; Father Richard J. Neuhaus; Mark Nowack at Population-Environment Balance; James Piereson; James Plascyk; Paul Craig Roberts; Llewellyn Rockwell, Jeffrey Tucker at the von Mises Institute; Ben Seeley, now of Border Solution Task Force; Daniel Stoffman; Andrew Stuttaford; Palmer Stacey, John Vinson of the American Immigration Control Foundation; John B. Trevor; John W. Wall; Andrew Wylie, Sarah Chalfant at Wylie, Aitken & Stone . . . and to some very long-suffering officials with American and foreign governments.

Finally, my son, Alexander, to whom this book is dedicated, for his motivational cries of "Go Work!" whenever I looked like bathing or otherwise irritating him; and my beloved wife, Maggy—my inspiration and my reward.

APPENDIX 1

Immigration to the United States by Region: 1820–1967

Years	*Total Immigration*	*Europe*	*Canada*	*Latin America and Caribbean*	*Asia*([1])	*Africa*
1820	8,385	7,690	209	178	6	1
1821–30	143,439	98,797	2,277	9,287	30	16
1831–40	599,125	495,681	13,624	19,800	55	54
1841–50	1,713,251	1,597,442	41,723	20,746	141	55
1851–60	2,598,214	2,452,577	59,309	15,411	41,538	210
1861–70	2,314,824	2,065,141	153,878	12,729	64,759	312
1871–80	2,812,191	2,271,925	383,640	20,404	124,160	358
1881–90	5,246,613	4,735,484	393,304	33,663	69,942	857
1891–1900	3,687,564	3,555,352	3,311	35,661	74,862	350
1901–10	8,795,386	8,056,040	179,226	182,662	323,543	7,368
1911–20	5,735,811	4,321,887	742,185	401,486	247,236	8,443
1921–30	4,107,209	2,463,194	924,515	592,170	112,059	6,286
1931–40	528,431	347,566	108,527	51,485	16,595	1,750
1941–50	1,035,039	621,147	171,718	153,810	37,028	7,367
1951–60	2,515,479	1,325,729	377,952	559,281	158,249	14,092
1961–67	2,135,324	866,732	226,619	791,857	218,865	20,193
Total	43,976,285	35,282,384	3,782,017	2,900,630	1,489,068	67,712
Percent of Total		80.2%	8.6%	6.6%	3.4%	0.2%
		88.8%				

(The remaining 1 percent is divided among two categories—"not specified" and "Oceania." Immigrants in both categories were virtually all of European origin from Europe, Australia or New Zealand.

Thus during these 147 years, Europeans constituted almost 90 percent of all immigrants.)

[1] Asia includes the Pacific islands, but excludes Australia and New Zealand.

Source: "Immigrants Admitted by Country or Region of Birth" for fiscal years 1950–93, and *Statistical Yearbook of the Immigration and Naturalization Service, 1992,* Immigration and Naturalization Service, U.S. Department of Justice.

APPENDIX 1 (B)

Immigration to the United States by Region: 1968–1993

Years	*Total Immigration*	*Europe*	*Canada*	*Latin America and Caribbean*	*Asia*([1])	*Africa*
1968	454,448	137,754	27,662	222,164	59,775	5,078
1969	358,579	118,028	18,582	137,645	76,439	5,876
1970	373,326	116,039	13,804	137,200	95,796	8,115
1971–80	4,493,314	800,368	169,939	1,811,801	1,605,855	80,779
1981–90	7,338,062	761,550	156,938	3,457,829	2,759,298	176,893
1991	1,827,167	146,671	13,504	1,277,642	345,922	33,542
1992	973,977	153,260	15,205	423,647	346,766	24,707
1993	904,292	158,254	17,156	338,082	359,577	27,783
Total	16,723,165	2,391,924	432,790	7,806,010	5,649,428	362,773
Percent of Total		14.3%	2.6%	46.7%	33.8%	2.2%
		16.9% (Europe and Canada)				

(The remaining 0.4 percent principally refers to immigration from "Oceania." This category covers Australia, New Zealand and the islands of the Pacific Ocean. Approximately 50 percent came from Australia and New Zealand.)

While 17 percent of all immigrants between 1967 and 1993 came from Europe and Canada, this does not mean they were European immigrants. Unlike the period 1820 to 1967, Africans, Asians and Latin Americans are now able to immigrate to Europe and Canada and then reimmigrate to the United States under the quota for European countries and Canada.

[1] Asia includes the Pacific islands, but excludes Australia and New Zealand.

Source: "Immigrants Admitted by Country or Region of Birth" for fiscal years 1950–93, and the *Statistical Yearbook of the Immigration and Naturalization Service, 1992,* Immigration and Naturalization Service, U.S. Department of Justice.

APPENDIX 2

Top 15 Countries of Immigration to United States: 1989–1993

Total Immigration 6,332,843
Non-IRCA 3,649,489
IRCA 2,683,354

Rank	*Country*	*Number of Total*	*% of Total*	*Number of Non-IRCA*	*% of Non-IRCA*	*Number of IRCA*	*% of IRCA*
1	Mexico	2,370,770	37.4	376,219	10.3	1,994,551	74.3
2	Philippines	308,865	4.9	282,400	7.7	26,465	1.0
3	Vietnam	279,187	4.4	278,853	7.6	334	0.01
4	El Salvador	238,411	3.8	85,646	2.3	152,765	5.7
5	China (mainland)	201,597	3.2	192,221	5.3	9,376	0.3
6	Dominican Republic	197,712	3.1	173,589	4.8	24,123	0.9
7	U.S.S.R.	195,817	3.1	195,356	5.4	461	0.02
8	India	183,782	2.9	163,011	4.5	20,771	0.8
9	Korea	130,426	2.1	120,326	3.3	10,100	0.4
10	Jamaica	109,520	1.7	92,633	2.5	16,887	0.6
11	Poland	108,187	1.7	92,121	2.5	16,066	0.6
12	Haiti	102,605	1.6	45,905	1.3	56,700	2.1
13	Guatemala	99,270	1.6	35,725	1.0	63,545	2.4
14	Iran	93,863	1.5	80,713	2.2	13,150	0.5
15	U.K.	82,658	1.3	77,879	2.1	4,779	0.2
Total		4,702,670	74.3%	2,292,597	62.8%	2,410,073	89.8 %

During the past five years, the INS has reported as "immigrants" large numbers of illegal aliens as they obtained amnesty under the provisions of the 1986 Immigration Reform and Control Act (IRCA). These provisions applied only to illegal immigrants who could show they had been in the United States before January 1, 1982. This special type of "immigration" is now thought to have ended (until the next amnesty). Here the resulting statistical distortion has been disentangled.

Source: "Immigrants Admitted by Country of Birth and Major Category of Admission," Fiscal Years 1989, 1990, 1991, 1992 and 1993, Demographic Statistics Branch, Statistics Division, Immigration and Naturalization Department.

APPENDIX 3

Immigrant Welfare Participation Rates in 1990, by National Origin Group (%)

Country of Birth	All Immigrants	Pre-1980 Arrivals
Europe:		
Austria	4.3	4.5
Czechoslovakia	4.9	4.9
France	4.8	5.9
Germany	4.1	4.2
Greece	5.5	5.6
Hungary	5.1	5.1
Italy	5.4	5.6
Poland	5.7	5.9
Portugal	7.1	7.6
U.S.S.R.	16.3	10.1
United Kingdom	3.7	4.1
Yugoslavia	5.3	5.7
Asia:		
Cambodia	48.8	24.4
China	10.4	11.1
India	3.4	4.2
Iran	7.5	4.1
Japan	2.3	3.7
Korea	8.1	8.6
Laos	46.3	34.1
Lebanon	7.3	8.8
Philippines	9.8	10.5
Taiwan	3.3	4.2
Vietnam	25.8	15.9
North and South America:		
Argentina	4.8	5.7
Canada	4.8	5.1
Colombia	7.5	8.9
Cuba	16.0	15.3
Dominican Republic	27.9	29.9
Ecuador	11.9	13.8
El Salvador	7.3	10.2

Country of Birth	*All Immigrants*	*Pre-1980 Arrivals*
Guatemala	8.7	11.4
Haiti	9.1	9.7
Jamaica	7.5	8.7
Mexico	11.3	12.8
Nicaragua	7.8	11.8
Panama	9.0	8.7
Peru	5.9	7.8
Africa:		
Egypt	5.5	6.7
Ethiopia	5.9	3.0
Nigeria	3.2	3.3
South Africa	1.6	1.6
Australia	3.7	3.8

All immigrants 9.1
U.S. native-born 7.4

Source: George Borjas's tabulations from the 1990 Public Use Sample of the U.S. Census. The statistics are calculated in the subsample of households where the household head is at least eighteen years of age and does not reside in group quarters.

Appendix 4

In the course of writing this book, I have come across quite a number of anti-immigration groups ("Patriot" groups, as I like to call them) and others of related interest. Some, such as FAIR and AICF on the national level, are well established. Others, especially at the local level, are in the state of chronic uproar that characterizes emerging political movements. For that reason, I must emphasize that their appearance here does not necessarily imply that I endorse them, or even that they will still exist when this book is in readers' hands. Nevertheless, since professional politicians in democracies are followers not leaders, it is upon groups like this that the future of the American nation will depend.

National Organizations Concerned with Immigration

American Immigration Control Foundation
P.O. Box 525
Monterey, Virginia 24465
Telephone (703) 468-2022
FAX (703) 468-2024

(*The Path to National Suicide:*
An Essay on Immigration and Multiculturalism
by Lawrence Auster is available from AICF:
Price $3.00 for 1 copy.
$2.00 for 2 to 9 copies.
$1.00 for 10 or more copies.)

Carrying Capacity Network
2000 P Street N.W.
Suite 240
Washington, D.C. 20036
Telephone (202) 296-4548
FAX (202) 296-4609

Federation for American Immigration Reform
1666 Connecticut Avenue N.W.
Suite 400
Washington, D.C. 20009
Telephone (202) 328-7004
FAX (202) 387-3447

Negative Population Growth, Inc.
210 The Plaza

P.O. Box 1206
Teaneck, New Jersey 07666-1206
Telephone (201) 837-3555
FAX (201) 837-0288

Population-Environment Balance
2000 P Street N.W.
Suite 210
Washington, D.C. 20036
Telephone (202) 955-5700
FAX (202) 955-6161

Regional Organizations Concerned with Immigration

Border Solution Task Force
7292 Miramar Road
San Diego, California 92121
Telephone (619) 549-1285
FAX (619) 549-1287

California Coalition for Immigration Reform
P.O. Box 2744-117
Huntington Beach, California 92649
Telephone (714) 846-9682
FAX—same as telephone

Voice of Citizens Together
13601 Ventura Boulevard
Suite 163
Sherman Oaks, California 91423
Telephone (818) 501-2061
FAX (818) 501-0359

Appendix 5

The Harberger Triangle and the Immigration Surplus

On page 160, I said that George Borjas's use of the Harberger Triangle, the technique by which he estimates that overall economic gains from immigration accruing to native-born Americans are minimal, was too horrible to leave lying around in the main part of this book where it might terrify the unwary. But hardened readers can contemplate it here:

See what I mean? But economists really do think like this all the time. They can't help it.

In effect, the Harberger Triangle offers us a simplified model of the economy. It consists of capital (the vertical axis, C) and labor (the horizontal axis, L). Technology—what I describe on pages 164–68 as the [???] factor—is considered to be fixed. So the line A-MP_L represents the additional, or "marginal," output that would be achieved for each additional worker employed, assuming that their skills are equal.

Chart 16

IMMIGRATION AND ECONOMIC GROWTH: THE HARBERGER TRIANGLE

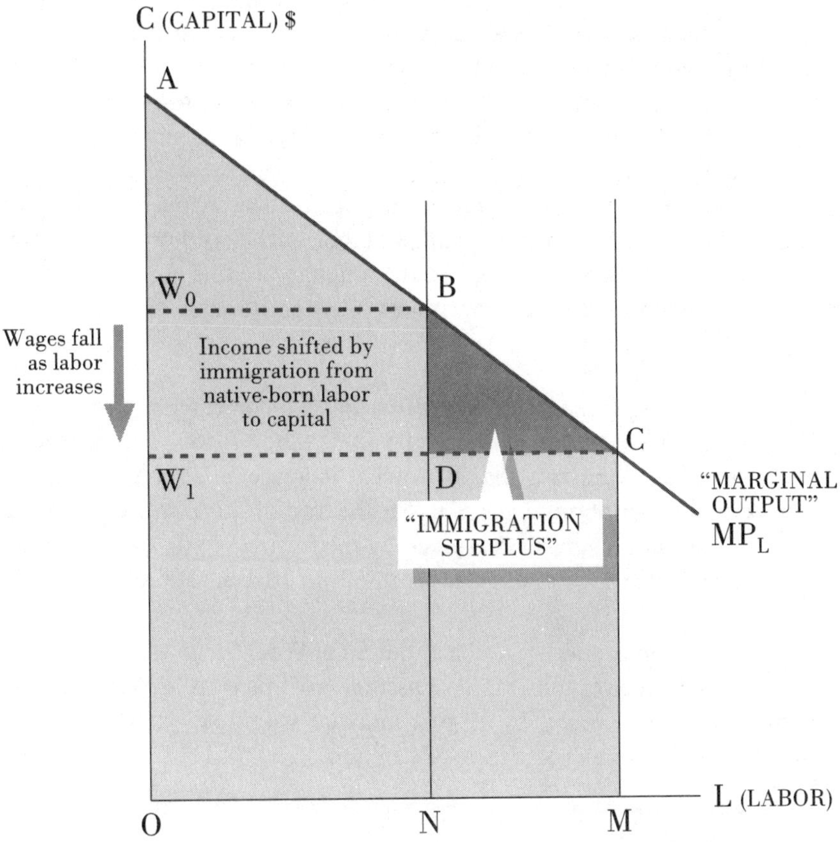

Suppose the supply of native-born labor in the United States is the vertical line that goes through N. It intersects the "marginal output" line, A-MP_L, at B. So the output of the American economy is the quadrilateral ABNO. And the price of that labor, reading across to the C axis, is \$$w_0$.

Then a lot of immigrants arrive. This changes the supply of labor. The whole labor supply line shifts to the right, from N to M. It now intersects the "marginal output" line at C. So the output of the American economy is now the quadrilateral ACMO. It's larger than the pre-immigration quadrilateral, because it has gained the addition on its right edge, BCMN. So the American economy's total output has increased.

Most of that increased output goes to the immigrants. In the language of this chart, they get the quadrilateral DCMN, which is the new market-clearing wage (w_1) multiplied by their number, which is the difference between N and M.

But some of the increased output does go to natives. In the language of this chart, it's the triangle BCD—the area above the new wage level and below the "marginal output" line. This is what Borjas calls the "immigration surplus." It's small.

And it only exists if immigration drives down wages. If immigration did not drive down wages, that would imply a horizontal "marginal output" line, an infinite demand for labor—and immigrants would get all of the increased output. As it is, the "immigration surplus" represents the profits that owners of capital get to keep because the increase in labor supply means they can pay lower wages.

Well, how big is the "immigration surplus"? This obviously depends on statistical relationships between capital, labor output and prices that must be established through research. In the language of this chart, they show up as the angles of the respective lines. George Borjas works it out like this:

> Labor gets about 70 percent of national income. Immigrants make up just less than a tenth of the U.S. labor force. The consensus among economists is that 10 percent increase in labor supply drives wages down about 3 percent. So the size of the triangle BCD, the "immigration surplus," is given by the formula ½ (0.7 × 0.1 × 0.03) which = 0.001, or about one-tenth of one percent of GNP.

In a $6 trillion economy, that's about $6 billion.

Even if you get very liberal, and assume a 10 percent increase in labor would drive down wages by 10 percent, that would still work out at an "immigration surplus" of a mere $21 billion.

But although the "immigration surplus" is small, immigrants still have a substantial economic impact. By increasing competition for jobs, they in effect cause a substantial redistribution of income from native-born workers to native-born owners of capital. In the language of the chart, native-born workers lose the rectangle w_0BDw_1. Native-born owners of capital gain it, plus the "immigration surplus." Borjas calculates that at current values this redistribution amounts to about $120 billion—or about 2.0 percent of GNP.

Of course, it has to be emphasized: THIS IS AN EXTREMELY SIMPLE CALCULATION. It requires a number of heroic assumptions.

And there are circumstances in which the immigration surplus could be larger. For example, there might be what economists call "external effects," a sort of synergy resulting from increased scale, even though technology has not changed. However, there's no evidence this actually occurs. For example, the U.S. economy is not plagued by unexpected, unexplained growth. Rather the reverse.

More importantly, a more skilled immigrant inflow might work better in the U.S. economy than does the current, relatively unskilled, immigrant population. George Borjas has calculated that if *all the immigrant workforce currently in the United States* was skilled, the immigration surplus might be as much $54 billion, just less than a percentage point of GNP.

Of course, an extra $54 billion or so would be nice to have. But in return for electing a whole new people, it's a pathetically small sum.

And, in any case, it's an option that is no longer open—short of deporting the unskilled results of the post-1965 immigration binge.

NOTE TO ECONOMISTS: Don't like these numbers? Well, go work out your own.

It's about time you did.

[Source: "The Economic Benefits from Immigration," George J. Borjas, forthcoming.]

Notes

PREFACE

1. "Sometimes the Door Slams Shut," *Time,* Special Issue, Fall 1993, 33.

CHAPTER 1

1. Peter Brimelow, "Time to Rethink Immigration?" *National Review,* June 22, 1992.
2. Interview with Bureau of the Census spokesman; unofficial preliminary estimate as of April 1993.
3. *Los Angeles Times,* January 6, 1992.
4. Judith T. Fullerton and Company, *Access to Prenatal Care for Hispanic Women of San Diego County.* Latina/Latino Research Program, California Policy Seminar (Berkeley: Regents of the University of California, 1993).
5. Daniel James, *Illegal Immigration—An Unfolding Crisis* (Lanham, Md.: University Press of America, 1991); interview.
6. Senate Committee on Government Affairs, Permanent Subcommittee on Investigations, *Investigation of the INS Criminal Alien Program,* minority staff statement, November 10, 1993.

7. Bureau of the Census, *Population Profile of the U.S.: 1993,* prepared by the Bureau of the Census (Washington, D.C., 1993), 32–33; "Assessment of Potential Impact of Undocumented Persons on Health Reform: Report by National Health Foundation to Presidential Task Force on Health Reform," *New York Times,* May 3, 1993.
8. See, for example, Peter Brimelow, "American Perestroika?" *Forbes,* May 14, 1990.
9. Spokesman interview. Center for Education Statistics, Department of Education, Washington D.C.
10. Orange County Grand Jury, Human Services Committee, *Impact of Immigration on the County of Orange,* Report of July 16 (Santa Ana, Calif., 1993), 5.
11. Bureau of the Census, *Census of Population and Housing: The Foreign-Born Population in the U.S.,* prepared by the Bureau of the Census (Washington, D.C., 1990), CP-3-1.
12. Virginia Postrel, editorial, *Reason,* May–October 1993.
13. Robert L. Bartley, letter to the editor, *National Review,* February 1, 1993.
14. Tyler Anbinder, *Nativism and Slavery: The Northern Know Nothings and the Politics of the 1850's* (New York: Oxford University Press, 1992), 34–43, 120–21, 111–13, 27–29, 99–101, 106, 274. Henry J. Gardner is quoted in William G. Bean, "Party Transformation in Massachusetts with Special Reference to the Antecedents of Republicanism" (Ph.D. diss., Harvard University, 1922), 264.
15. Bernard A. Weisberger, "A Nation of Immigrants," *American Heritage,* February–March 1994, 75.
16. Julian L. Simon, *The Economic Consequences of Immigration* (Cambridge, Mass.: Basil Blackwell, 1989), 45–46.
17. Stephan Thernstrom, ed., *Harvard Encyclopedia of American Ethnic Groups* (Cambridge, Mass.: Belknap Press, Harvard University Press, 1980), 529–30.
18. Wayne Lutton interview. See also Lutton, *The Myth of Open Borders: The American Tradition of Immigration Control* (Monterey, Va.: American Immigration Control Foundation, 1988).
19. Daniel Seligman, *A Question of Intelligence: The IQ Debate in America* (New York: 1992), 128–30; Mark Snyderman and R. J. Herrnstein, "Intelligence Tests and the Immigration Act of 1924," *American Psychologist,* September 1983, 986–95.
20. Thomas Paine, *Common Sense, The Rights of Man, and Other Essential Writings of Thomas Paine,* ed. Sydney Hook (New York: Meridian, 1984), 50, 39.
21. Thernstrom, *Harvard Encyclopedia of American Ethnic Groups,* 323, 479.
22. Jack Miles, "Blacks vs. Browns," *Atlantic Monthly,* October 1992, 41–68.
23. Don Feder, *Washington Times,* June 15, 1993.

CHAPTER 2

1. George J. Borjas, *Friends or Strangers: The Impact of Immigrants on the U.S. Economy* (New York: Basic Books, 1990), 5.
2. INS spokesman interview.
3. Ronald Reagan quoted in Wayne Lutton and Palmer Stacey, *The Immigration Timebomb* (Monterey, Va.: American Immigration Control Foundation, 1985), vii.

4. Ira Mehlman, "The New Jet Set," *National Review,* March 15, 1993.
5. Center for Immigration Studies, "Immigration-Related Statistics, 1993." Backgrounder no. 4–93, June 1993.
6. Simon, *The Economic Consequences of Immigration,* 338.
7. *1992 INS Yearbook,* Statistical Yearbook of the INS (Washington, D.C.: U.S. Government Printing Office), 11, 21.
8. George Washington quoted in Matthew Spalding, "From Pluribus to Unum: Immigration and the Founding Fathers," *Policy Review*, Winter 1994, 40.
9. Thernstrom, *Harvard Encyclopedia of American Ethnic Groups,* 489.
10. Ibid., 503.
11. Jeffrey S. Passel and Barry Edmonston, *Immigration and Race in the United States: The 20th and 21st Centuries* (Washington, D.C.: Urban Institute, 1992), 2–3.
12. Campbell Gibson, "The Contribution of Immigration to the Growth and Ethnic Diversity of the American Population," *Proceedings of the American Philosophical Society* 136, no. 2 (1992), 165.
13. Passel and Edmonston, *Immigration and Race: The 20th and 21st Centuries,* 8; Thernstrom, *Harvard Encyclopedia of American Ethnic Groups,* 6.
14. David Hackett Fischer, *Albion's Seed: Four British Folkways in America* (New York: Oxford University Press, 1989), 17.
15. Gibson, "The Contribution of Immigration," 173.
16. Passel and Edmonston, *Immigration and Race: The 20th and 21st Centuries,* 6, fig. 10.
17. Michael S. Teitelbaum, "The Population Threat," *Foreign Affairs,* Winter 1992–93, 64.
18. David A. Coleman, "The World on the Move? International Migration in 1992" (paper given at the European Population Conference, Geneva, March 23–26, 1993); and interview.
19. United Nations Population Fund, *The State of World Population 1993* (New York: UN Population Fund, 1993), 2.
20. Ibid., 7.
21. Ibid., 12.
22. See George J. Borjas, "The Economics of Immigration: A Survey," *Journal of Economic Literature,* December 1994.

CHAPTER 3

1. Patrick Burns, letter to the editor, *National Review,* August 3, 1993.
2. Philip Hart quoted in Lawrence Auster, *The Path to National Suicide: An Essay on Immigration and Multiculturalism* (Monterey, Va.: American Immigration Control Foundation, 1990), 14.
3. Lyndon B. Johnson quoted in *Congressional Quarterly Almanac:* 1965 (Washington, D.C.: Congressional Quarterly Service, 1965), 479.
4. See, for example, poll by Tarrance Associates, October 1983, cited in *Wall Street Journal,* "Feelings About Foreigners," May 23, 1993.
5. Jeffrey S. Passel and Barry Edmonston, *Immigration and Race: Recent Trends in Immigration to the U.S.* (Washington, D.C.: Urban Institute, 1992), table 8.
6. Ibid., 17.

7. Ibid.
8. William H. Frey interview (Ann Arbor: University of Michigan Population Studies Center), and William H. Frey, "The New White Flight," *American Demographics* (April 1994). Frey's work is also discussed in a two-part series by Jonathan Tilove and Joe Hallinan, "U.S. Melting Pot Starts to Brew a Bitter Taste" and "Whites Flee Immigrants for 'Whiter' States," Newhouse News Service; see, for example, *Sunday Oregonian,* August 8, 1993, and *Ann Arbor News,* August 22, 1993.
9. B. Meredith Burke, "An Environmental Impact Statement for Immigration," *Wall Street Journal,* April 1, 1993.

CHAPTER 4

1. Passel and Edmonston, *Immigration and Race: Recent Trends,* table 3.
2. Ibid., 17.
3. Lawrence Auster, *The Path to National Suicide: An Essay on Immigration and Multiculturalism* (Monterey, Va.: AICF, 1990), 10–26.
4. Cynthia Gorney, "Sirhan," *Washington Post,* August 20, 1979.
5. *Scope* (Center for Immigration Studies; Summer 1993), 15.
6. Rosemary Jenks, Center for Immigration Studies, interview.
7. Department of State official, interview.
8. INS official, interview.
9. Jerry Tinker, telephone interview by Joseph E. Fallon, September 10 and October 13, 1993.
10. U.S. Department of Commerce News, Economics & Statistics Administration, Bureau of the Census, CB91-215. "Census Bureau Releases 1990 Count on Specific Racial Groups," released June 12, 1991.
11. Auster, *The Path to National Suicide,* 14.
12. George J. Borjas, *Friends or Strangers: The Impact of Immigrants on the U.S. Economy* (New York: Basic Books, 1990), 7–25.
13. Robert B. Reich, review of *Friends or Strangers,* by Borjas, *Washington Monthly,* quoted on paperback edition cover, 1991.
14. INS official quoted by Pete Carey and Steve Johnson, "Special Interests Shaped Reform of 1990 Legal Immigration Law," in, e.g., *Riverside Press Enterprise,* July 16, 1993.
15. Ben J. Wattenberg, *The First Universal Nation: Leading Indicators and Ideas About the Surge of America in the 1990s* (New York: Free Press, 1991), 72–75, 12.
16. Bureau of the Census, *Census of Population and Housing,* CP-3-1.
17. Ronald Reagan quoted in *Congressional Quarterly Almanac: 1980* (Washington, D.C.: Congressional Quarterly Service, 1980), 13B.
18. Passel and Edmonston, *Immigration and Race: The 20th and 21st Centuries,* 8, figures 15 and 16.

CHAPTER 5

1. *Newsweek,* August 9, 1993; *Los Angeles Times,* September 20, 1993; *Orlando Sentinel,* July 27, 1993; *New York Times,* October 18, 1993.

2. Michele A. Heller, "Too Many Immigrants?" *Hispanic Magazine,* April 1994, 27.
3. "Public Opinion and Demographic Report," *American Enterprise,* January–February 1994, 97.
4. Deborah Sontag, "Calls to Restrict Immigration Come from Many Quarters," *New York Times,* December 13, 1992.
5. "Man Rapes and Robs Two Women in Chelsea," *New York Times,* May 27, 1993; "Two Women in Rape Nightmare," *New York Post,* May 27, 1993.
6. Dean Rusk and Sam Ervin quoted by Auster, *The Path to National Suicide,* 21, 17.
7. Michael Kinsley, TRB, *New Republic,* December 28, 1992.
8. Emmanuel Celler quoted in *Congressional Quarterly Almanac: 1965* (Washington, D.C.: Congressional Quarterly Service, 1965), 472, 470.
9. Joseph Sobran, "The Natives Are Restless," *National Review,* February 22, 1985, 25.
10. Raoul Lowery Contreras, "Racists Wish to Turn America as It Had Evolved in 1965 [*sic*]," (Sacramento) *El Hispaño,* August 11, 1993.
11. Norman Podhoretz, *Making It* (New York: Random House, 1967), 3–27.
12. Paul Gigot, *Wall Street Journal,* December 13, 1991.
13. Borjas, *Friends or Strangers,* 158.
14. Donald R. Morris, *The Washing of the Spears: A History of the Rise of the Zulu Nation Under Chaka and Its Fall in the Zulu War of 1879* (New York: Simon and Schuster, 1965), 47–121.
15. Simon, *The Economic Consequences of Immigration,* xxix.
16. Julian L. Simon, interview by James Cook, *Forbes,* April 2, 1990.
17. Julian L. Simon, *The Ultimate Resource* (Princeton, N.J.: Princeton University Press, 1981), 9.
18. Julian L. Simon, *Good Mood: The New Psychology of Overcoming Depression* (La Salle, Ill.: Open Court, 1993), 5, 212.
19. Walt Harrington, "The Heretic Becomes Respectable," *Washington Post Magazine,* August 18, 1985.
20. Michael J. Mandel, "Does America Need More 'Huddled Masses'? Yes," *Business Week,* March 12, 1990.
21. Borjas, *Friends or Strangers,* viii.
22. A. M. Rosenthal, "A Haitian Father," *New York Times,* December 3, 1991.
23. INS spokesman interview.
24. Ira Mehlman.

CHAPTER 6

1. Deborah Sontag, *New York Times,* December 13, 1992.
2. Earl Raab, *Jewish Bulletin,* July 23, 1993, 17.
3. Earl Raab, *Jewish Bulletin,* February 19, 1993, 23.
4. Podhoretz, *Making It,* 186–87.
5. Kevin P. Phillips, *The Emerging Republican Majority* (New Rochelle, N.Y.: Arlington House, 1969), 254.

6. Margaret L. Usdansky, "Minority Boom in Texas, California," *USA Today,* April 22, 1994.
7. Rosemary Jenks, ed., Center for Immigration Studies, "Argentina," in *Immigration and Nationality Policies of Leading Migration Nations* (Washington, D.C.: Center for Immigration Studies, 1992), 5.
8. See, for example, Hermann Kinder and Werner Hilgemann, eds., *The Anchor Atlas of World History,* trans. Ernest A. Menze (Garden City, N.Y.: Anchor Press, Doubleday, 1974), 1:117.
9. Colin McEvedy and Richard Jones, *Atlas of World Population History* (Harmondsworth, U.K.: Penguin Books, 1978), 19–39; Geoffrey Barraclough and Norman Stone, *The Times Atlas of World History,* 3d ed. (London: Times Books, 1989), 98–99.

CHAPTER 7

1. Julian Simon, *National Review,* February 1, 1993, 27–29.
2. Thomas Sowell, *The Economics and Politics of Race: An International Perspective* (New York: Quill, 1983), 90–92; *Ethnic America: A History* (New York: Basic Books, 1981), 98–99.
3. Simon, *The Economic Consequences of Immigration,* 337.
4. See, for example, *Wall Street Journal,* July 3, 1990.
5. Simon, *The Economic Consequences of Immigration,* 342.
6. Center for Immigration Studies spokesman.
7. Borjas, *Friends or Strangers,* 219.
8. Unless otherwise indicated, data in Chapter 7 and Chapter 8 are drawn from the work of George J. Borjas (Professor of Economics, University of California, San Diego, Research Associate, National Bureau of Economic Research). Principal sources are "The Economics of Immigration," *Journal of Economic Literature,* December 1994; "Immigration Research in the 1980s: A Turbulent Decade," in *Research Frontiers in Industrial Relations and Human Resources,* ed. D. Lewin, O. Mitchell, P. Sherer (Industrial Relations and Research Association, 1992); "Immigration and Ethnicity," *NBER Reporter,* National Bureau of Economic Research, Fall 1993; "The Economic Benefits from Immigration," forthcoming; "Assimilation and Changes in Cohort Quality Revisited: What Happened to Immigrant Skills in the 1980s," *Journal of Labor Economics,* forthcoming; "Ethnic Capital and Intergenerational Mobility," *Quarterly Journal of Economics,* February 1992.

   See also George Borjas, Richard B. Freeman, eds., *Immigration and the Work Force: Economic Consequences for the United States and Source Areas* (Chicago: University of Chicago Press, 1992); George Borjas, *Friends or Strangers: The Impact of Immigration on the U.S. Economy* (New York: Basic Books, 1990).

   Borjas's conclusions are widely echoed in the literature on the recent migration: for example, Michael Baker and Dwayne Benjamin, "The Performance of Immigrants in the Canadian Labor Market," *Journal of Labor Economics,* forthcoming; Deborah A. Cobb-Clark, "Immigrant Selectivity and Wages: The Evidence for Women," *American Economic Review,* September 1983; Rachel M. Friedberg, "The Labor Market Assimilation of Immigrants in the

United States: The Role of Age at Arrival," Brown University, 1992; Robert J. LaLonde and Robert H. Topel, "The Assimilation of Immigrants in the U.S. Labor Market," in *Immigration and the Work Force,* ed. G. Borjas and R. Freeman, above.

9. Stephen Moore, *Insight,* November 22, 1993.
10. Spokesman, Office of Educational Research and Improvement, Education Information Branch, Department of Education, interview.
11. House Committee on Ways and Means, Subcommittee on Human Resources, *Immigrants and Welfare: New Myths, New Realities,* report prepared by Michael Fix and Jeffrey S. Passel, Urban Institute, Washington, D.C., presented November 15, 1993.
12. House Committee on Ways and Means, Subcommittee on Human Resources, *Patterns of Public Assistance Receipt Among Immigrants: Results from the 1990 and 1980 Censuses,* report prepared by Frank D. Bean et al. Population Research Center, University of Texas at Austin, presented November 15, 1993.
13. 1992 Statistical Yearbook of the INS (Washington, D.C.: U.S. Government Printing Office), table 66, 162.
14. Anbinder, *Nativism and Slavery,* 108.
15. Wayne Lutton, *The Myth of Open Borders: The American Tradition of Immigration Control* (Monterey, Va.: American Immigration Control Foundation, 1988), 4, 11.
16. Thernstrom, *Harvard Encyclopedia of American Ethnic Groups,* 491.
17. "The Immigration and Control Act: A Report on the Legalized Alien Population"; John Bjerke, Project Director (INS: U.S. Government Printing Office, 1992).
18. House Committee on Ways and Means, Subcommittee on Human Resources, testimony by Mark J. Lefcowitz, Department of Human Development, Fairfax County, Va., November 15, 1993.
19. IRS spokesman, interview by Roy Beck, in *Social Contract,* March 11, 1994.
20. Phyllis A. Bermingham quoted in Roy Beck, "The Ordeal of Immigration in Wisconsin," *Atlantic Monthly,* April 1994.
21. Simon, *The Economic Consequences of Immigration,* 128.
22. Donald Huddle, "The Net National Costs of Immigration in 1993," (Washington, D.C.: Carrying Capacity Network), issued July 20, 1993, update issued June 27, 1994. Subsequent Huddle studies published by Carrying Capacity Network include "The Net Costs of Immigration to California" (November 4, 1993); "The Net Costs of Immigration to Texas" (March 2, 1994).
23. Interview with New York City Board of Education spokesman.
24. Department of State official, interview by author.
25. John C. Goodman and Aldona Robbins, *The Immigration Solution* (Dallas, Tex.: National Center for Policy Analysis, 1992).
26. Sanford C. Bernstein and Company, Municipal Research, *The State of California* (New York: Sanford C. Bernstein and Company, 1991), 4, 7.
27. George J. Borjas, *National Review,* December 13, 1993, 42–43.

CHAPTER 8

1. Richard A. Easterlin, "Immigration: Economic and Social Characteristics," in *Harvard Encyclopedia of American Ethnic Groups,* ed. Thernstrom, 485.
2. Edwin S. Rubenstein, economic consultant, New York, citing Economic Report of the President 1994, interview.
3. Peter Brimelow and Leslie Spencer, "You Can't Get There from Here," *Forbes,* July 6, 1992.
4. Claudia Goldin, *The Political Economy of Immigration Restriction in the United States, 1890 to 1921,* National Bureau of Economic Research, Working Paper no. 4345 (Cambridge, Mass., 1993).
5. Edwin S. Rubenstein, economic consultant, New York City, interview; data from McKinsey.
6. Larry Neal and Paul Uselding, "Immigration, a Neglected Source of American Economic Growth: 1790 to 1912," *Oxford Economic Papers* (March 1972).
7. Economic Council of Canada, *New Faces in the Crowd: Economic and Social Impacts of Immigration* (Ottawa: Economic Council of Canada, 1991).
8. Neville R. Norman and Kathryn F. Meikle, *The Economic Effects of Immigration on Australia* (Melbourne: Committee for Economic Development of Australia, 1985).
9. Virginia D. Abernethy, *Population Politics: The Choices That Shape Our Future* (New York: Insight Books, 1993), 197–211; Richard A. Easterlin, Michael L. Wachter, and Susan M. Wachter, "Demographic Influences on Economic Stability: The United States Experience," *Proceedings of the American Philosophical Society* (1978).
10. Neal and Uselding, "Immigration, a Neglected Source of American Economic Growth: 1790 to 1912," *Oxford Economic Papers,* March 1972.
11. Michael S. Teitelbaum and Jay M. Walker, *The Fear of Population Decline* (Orlando, Fla.: Academic Press, 1985).
12. Simon Smith Kuznets, *Modern Economic Growth: Rate, Structure and Spread* (New Haven, Conn.: Yale University Press, 1966).
13. Simon, *The Economic Consequences of Immigration,* 252.
14. Julian L. Simon quoted in *Forbes,* April 2, 1990.
15. Jared Taylor, *Shadows of the Rising Sun* (New York: William Morrow, 1983), 172.
16. Ronald Takaki, *A Different Mirror: A History of Multicultural America* (Boston: Little, Brown, 1993), 154.
17. James Paul Allen and Eugene James Turner, *We the People: An Atlas of America's Ethnic Diversity* (New York: Macmillan, 1988), 147.
18. Frederick Douglass, *My Bondage and My Freedom* (1885; reprint, New York: Dover Publications, 1969), 454.
19. Booker T. Washington quoted in John Tanton, "Cast Down Your Bucket Where You Are," *Social Contract,* occasional paper 92-12, 1992.
20. Cited in Simon, *The Economic Consequences of Immigration,* 228–29.
21. Ibid., 249, 347.
22. Borjas, "The Economics of Immigration," 48.
23. Andrew Hacker, *Two Nations: Black and White, Separate, Hostile, Unequal* (New York: Charles Scribner's Sons, 1992), 132.
24. Milton Friedman, interview by Peter Brimelow, *Forbes,* December 12, 1988.

CHAPTER 9

1. Fischer, *Albion's Seed,* 787, 834, 874.
2. Interviews with Office of Territorial and International Affairs, Department of the Interior, Washington, D.C., and for the offices of American Samoa, Federated States of Micronesia, Commonwealth of Northern Mariana Islands, and the Republic of the Marshall Islands.
3. Ted Robert Gurr, ed., *Violence in America,* vol. 2, *The History of Crime,* 3d ed. (Beverly Hills, Calif.: Sage Publications, 1989).
4. Ted Robert Gurr, "Drowning in a Crime Wave," *New York Times,* April 13, 1989.
5. George Borjas, interview.
6. Federal prison figures from Senate Committee on Government Affairs, Permanent Subcommittee on Investigations, *Investigation of the INS Criminal Alien Program.*
7. Los Angeles County, Countywide Criminal Justice Coordination Committee, Ad Hoc Subcommittee on Criminal Aliens, *Impact of Repeat Arrests of Deportable Criminal Aliens in Los Angeles County,* Final Report, July 15 (Los Angeles, 1992).
8. House Committee on the Judiciary, Subcommittee on Immigration, Refugees, and International Law, testimony by Judge David O. Carter, November 1, 1989.
9. Statement of Kathleen M. Hawk, Director, Federal Bureau of Prisons to House Judiciary Committee Subcommittee on International Law, Immigration and Refugees, February 23, 1994 (one percent confined for "other drug offenses").
10. California State Department of Corrections, Center for Immigration Studies, interviews.
11. Jared Taylor, *Paved with Good Intentions: The Failure of Race Relations in Contemporary America* (New York: Carroll and Graf, 1992), 37.
12. Robert I. Friedman, "Brighton Beach Goodfellas," *Vanity Fair,* January 1993.
13. *New York Times,* April 5, 1994.
14. Sowell, *Ethnic America,* 29.
15. Thernstrom, *The Harvard Encyclopedia of American Ethnic Groups,* 491.
16. Carol Innerst, *Washington Times,* March 21, 1993; August 19, 1994.
17. *New York Times,* May 4, 1987.
18. Spokesman for the Centers for Disease Control, Atlanta, quoted in the *Detroit News,* April 11, 1992.
19. *American Medical News,* March 23–30, 1992; *San Diego Union,* August 31, 1986; *American Family Physician,* March 1992.
20. U.S. Institute of Medicine spokesman quoted in John Maurice, (London) *New Scientist;* as reprint, *World Press Review,* February 1994.
21. *Forbes,* July 6, 1992.
22. Wattenberg, *The First Universal Nation,* 73.
23. Leon F. Bouvier, *50 Million Californians?* (Washington, D.C.: Center for Immigration Studies, 1991).

CHAPTER 10

1. Quoted in Lutton, *The Myth of Open Borders;* Carlos E. Cortés, "Mexicans," in *Harvard Encyclopedia of American Ethnic Groups,* ed. Thernstrom, 701.
2. See, for example, K. L. Billingsley, "Seizing the Southwest for a New Nation Called Aztlan," *Washington Times,* October 24, 1993.
3. Fernando Romero, "Mexico's Influence Growing in U.S.," *San Diego Union-Tribune,* August 22, 1993.
4. All figures from *New York Times,* November 5, 1992.
5. Gerald F. Seib, "A Black Thing: Quiet Discontent Over the System," *Wall Street Journal,* May 11, 1994.
6. Anbinder, *Nativism and Slavery,* 106.

CHAPTER 11

1. Daniel Patrick Moynihan, *Pandaemonium: Ethnicity in International Politics* (New York: Oxford University Press, 1993), 1.
2. Philip Gleason, "American Identity and Americanization," in *Harvard Encyclopedia of American Ethnic Groups,* ed. Thernstrom, 44.
3. Jesse Chickering quoted in Harold J. Abramson, "Assimilation and Pluralism," in ibid., 152.
4. Allen and Turner, *We the People,* 207.
5. Anbinder, *Nativism and Slavery,* 111.
6. John Jay, "The Federalist," no. 2, in *The Federalist Papers,* by Alexander Hamilton, James Madison, and John Jay, ed. Clinton Rossiter (1787–88; reprint, New York: Mentor, 1961), 38.
7. Theodore Roosevelt quoted in Edmund Morris, *The Rise of Theodore Roosevelt* (1979; reprint, New York: Ballantine Books, 1980), 462–65, 477.
8. Calvin Coolidge quoted in Borjas, *Friends or Strangers,* 29.
9. Will Herberg, *Protestant, Catholic, Jew: An Essay in American Religious Sociology,* rev. ed. (Garden City, N.Y.: Anchor Books, Doubleday, 1960).
10. Michael Novak, *The Rise of the Unmeltable Ethnics* (New York: Macmillan, 1972).
11. Robert C. Christopher, *Crashing the Gates: The De-WASPing of America's Power Elite* (New York: Touchstone, Simon and Schuster, 1989), 53–54.
12. Fischer, *Albion's Seed,* 17.
13. Thernstrom, *Harvard Encyclopedia of American Ethnic Groups,* 322.
14. Alexis de Tocqueville, ed. J. P. Mayer, *Democracy in America,* 2 vols. (1835 and 1840; reprint, New York: Anchor Books, Doubleday, 1969), 278, footnote.
15. Benjamin Franklin quoted in Thernstrom, *Harvard Encyclopedia of American Ethnic Groups,* 657.
16. Anbinder, *Nativism and Slavery,* ix, 275.
17. Report of the California legislature quoted in Borjas, *Friends or Strangers,* 27.
18. Sowell, *Ethnic America,* 42.
19. Sowell, *The Economics and Politics of Race,* 71.
20. Sowell, *Ethnic America,* 296.
21. Thernstrom, *Harvard Encyclopedia of American Ethnic Groups,* 37–38.

22. Arthur Schlesinger, Jr., *The Disuniting of America* (New York: W. W. Norton, 1992).
23. Frederick R. Lynch, *Invisible Victims: White Males and the Crisis of Affirmative Action* (New York: Praeger, 1991).
24. Linda Chavez, interview.
25. Dennis Farney, "Mosaic of Hope: Ethnic Identities Clash with Student Idealism at a California College," *Wall Street Journal,* December 2, 1992.

CHAPTER 12

1. Pierre Elliott Trudeau, "New Treason of the Intellectuals," in *Federalism and the French Canadians* (Toronto: Macmillan of Canada, 1968), 179.
2. Pierre Elliott Trudeau quoted in Richard Gwyn, *The Northern Magus: Pierre Trudeau and Canadians* (1980; reprint, Markham, Ontario: Paperjacks, 1981), 246.
3. Hugh MacLennan, *Two Solitudes* (Toronto: Laurentian Library, Macmillan, 1972), 410–12.
4. Louis Joseph Papineau in *Colombo's Canadian Quotations* (Edmonton, Canada: Hurtig, 1974), 462.
5. Irving Kristol, *Two Cheers for Capitalism* (New York: Basic Books, 1978), 26–31.
6. Katherine Betts, *Ideology and Immigration* (Melbourne: Melbourne University Press, 1988), 52.
7. Cokie Roberts, "Good Old-Fashioned Public Servants," *Washington Post,* October 28, 1992.
8. Aleksandr Solzhenitsyn, *"One Word of Truth" . . . The Nobel Speech on Literature, 1970* (London: The Bodley Head, 1972), 15–16.

CHAPTER 13

1. A. M. Rosenthal, "Aliens: Let Them Work," *New York Times,* February 9, 1993.
2. Eugene McCarthy, *A Colony of the World: The United States Today* (New York: Hippocrene Books, 1992).
3. Silvestre Reyes quoted in Daniel James, "El Paso Shows How to Defend the Line," *Human Events,* February 11, 1994, 10–11.
4. Bartley, *National Review,* February 1, 1993.
5. John Lachs, Professor of Philosophy, Vanderbilt University, Nashville, Tennessee, interview.
6. Roy Beck, "Religions and the Environment: Commitment High Until U.S. Population Raised," *Social Contract*, Winter 1992–93, 87.
7. Thernstrom, *Harvard Encyclopedia of American Ethnic Groups,* 410.
8. Rosemary Jenks, Center for Immigration Studies; INS Press Office, interviews.
9. Pierre-Joseph Proudhon quoted in Garrett Hardin, *Living Within Limits: Ecology, Economics and Population Taboos* (New York: Oxford University Press, 1993), 235.
10. Barbara Vobejda, *Washington Post,* November 4, 1993.
11. "Editorial Notebook," *New York Times,* September 7, 1993.

12. Hong Kong government official in New York, interview.
13. Center for Immigration Studies, "Mexico," in *Immigration and Nationality Policies of Leading Migration Nations,* 8.

CHAPTER 14

1. José Serrano, in Ralph Z. Hallow, "Immigration Reformers Fearful of '2% Solution,' " *Washington Times,* July 29, 1993.
2. Rosemary Jenks, Center for Immigration Studies, "United Kingdom," in *Immigration and Nationality Policies of Leading Migration Nations,* 2.
3. Vernon M. Briggs, Jr., *Mass Immigration and the National Interest* (Armonk, N.Y.: M. E. Sharpe, 1992), 80–83.

CHAPTER 15

1. Allen and Turner, *We the People,* 178–79.
2. Takaki, *A Different Mirror,* 1–2.
3. Linda Chavez, *Out of the Barrio: Toward a New Politics of Hispanic Assimilation* (New York: Basic Books, 1991); Peter Skerry, *Mexican Americans: The Ambivalent Minority* (New York: Free Press, 1993).
4. Alejandro Portes and Ruben G. Rumbaut, "The Educational Progress of Children of Immigrants," *Annals of the American Academy of Political and Social Sciences* (December 1993).
5. *San Diego Union-Tribune,* August 22, 1993.
6. Scott Reid, *Lament for a Notion: The Life and Death of Canada's Bilingualism* (Vancouver, Canada: Arsenal Pulp Press, 1993), 49, 119–22.
7. Lance Izumi, interview with Chavez, *Out of the Barrio,* 139–40; Skerry, *Mexican Americans,* 68.
8. Census CPR–P20, No. 468, March 1992, Table F, Bureau of the Census, "Census Bureau Releases 1990 Census Counts on Hispanic Population Groups," CB91–216, Table 1, Race and Hispanic Origin for the U.S., June 12, 1994.

Index

Page numbers in *italics* refer to charts, tables, and maps.

ABOUT THE AUTHOR

PETER BRIMELOW says he has succeeded in becoming an alien in three countries. A senior editor of *Forbes* and *National Review,* he was born in England in 1947, was educated at Sussex and Stanford universities, and has worked for *Maclean's* and the *Financial Post* in Canada and for *Fortune* and *Barron's* in the United States. His writings have appeared in *The Wall Street Journal, Harper's, The New York Times,* and the London *Times,* for which he was a columnist. A U.S. citizen, he is married and has one son.

ABOUT THE TYPE

This book was set in Times Roman, designed by Stanley Morrison specifically for *The Times* of London. The typeface was introduced in the newspaper in 1932. Times Roman has had its greatest success in the United States as a book and commercial typeface, rather than one used in newspapers.